ICELAND

RECENT ECONOMIC AND POLITICAL DEVELOPMENTS HANDBOOK

VOLUME 1

SRATEGIC INFORMATION AND DEVELOPMENTS

International Business Publications, USA
Washington DC, USA - Iceland

ICELAND

RECENT ECONOMIC AND POLITICAL DEVELOPMENTS HANDBOOK

VOLUME 1 SRATEGIC INFORMATION AND DEVELOPMENTS

UPDATED ANNUALLY

We express our sincere appreciation to all government agencies and international organizations which provided information and other materials for this handbook

Cover Design: **International Business Publications, USA**

2018 International Business Publications, USA
ISBN 1-4330-6363-8

For additional analytical, business and investment opportunities information, please contact Global Investment & Business Center, USA at (703) 370-8082. Fax: (703) 370-8083. E-mail: ibpusa3@gmail.com Global Business and Investment Info Databank - www.ibpus.com

Printed in the USA

ICELAND

RECENT ECONOMIC AND POLITICAL DEVELOPMENTS HANDBOOK

VOLUME 1

SRATEGIC INFORMATION AND DEVELOPMENTS

TABLE OF CONTENTS

STRATEGIC AND DEVELOPMENT PROFILES

STRATEGIC PROFILE

Capital and largest city	Reykjavík 64°08′N 21°56′W
Official language and national language	Icelandic
Ethnic groups (2017)	• 91% Icelandic • 4% Polish • 5% other
Religion	Church of Iceland
Demonym	Icelandic
Government	Unitary parliamentary republic
• President	Guðni Th. Jóhannesson
• Prime Minister	Katrín Jakobsdóttir
• President of Parliament	Steingrímur J. Sigfússon (acting)
• President of Supreme Court	Þorgeir Örlygsson
Legislature	Althing
Formation	
• Settlement	9th century
• Commonwealth	930–1262
• Union with Norway	1262–1814
• Danish monarchy	1380–1944
• Constitution	5 January 1874
• Kingdom	1 December 1918
• Republic	17 June 1944
Area	
• Total	102,775km^2 (39,682 sq mi) (106th)
• Water (%)	2.7
Population	
• 1 March 2018 estimate	350,710 (172nd)
• Density	3.2/km^2 (8.3/sq mi) (233rd)
GDP (PPP)	2018 estimate
• Total	$18 billion (142nd)
• Per capita	$54,288 (16th)
GDP (nominal)	2018 estimate
• Total	$25 billion
• Per capita	$83,750 (3rd)
Gini	24.00 low · 2nd
HDI	▲ 0.921 very high · 9th
Currency	Icelandic króna (ISK)
Time zone	WET (UTC+0)
Date format	dd/mm/yyyy

Drives on the	right
Calling code	+354
Patron saint	Saint Thorlak
ISO 3166 code	IS
Internet TLD	.is

Iceland also called the **Republic of Iceland**, is a Nordic island country between the North Atlantic and the Arctic Ocean. It has a population of 329,100 and an area of 103,000 km^2 (40,000 sq mi), making it the most sparsely populated country in Europe. The capital and largest city is Reykjavík. Reykjavík and the surrounding areas in the southwest of the country are home to over two-thirds of the population. Iceland is volcanically and geologically active. The interior consists of a plateau characterised by sand and lava fields, mountains and glaciers, while many glacial rivers flow to the sea through the lowlands. Iceland is warmed by the Gulf Stream and has a temperate climate, despite a high latitude just outside the Arctic Circle. Its high latitude and marine influence still keeps summers chilly, with most of the archipelago having a tundra climate.

According to *Landnámabók*, the settlement of Iceland began in the year 874 when the Norwegian chieftain Ingólfr Arnarson became the first permanent settler on the island. In the following centuries, mainly Norwegians and to a smaller extent other Scandinavians settled Iceland, bringing with them thralls of Gaelic origin. From 1262 to 1814, Iceland was ruled by Norway and afterwards by Denmark. Until the 20th century, the country relied largely on fishing and agriculture. Iceland became independent in 1918 and a republic in 1944. Industrialisation of the fisheries and Marshall Plan aid following World War II brought prosperity and Iceland became one of the wealthiest and most developed nations in the world. In 1994, it became a part of the European Economic Area, which supported diversification into economic and financial services.

Iceland has a market economy with relatively low taxes compared to other OECD countries. It maintains a Nordic social welfare system that provides universal health care and tertiary education for its citizens. Iceland ranks highly in economic, political and social stability and equality. In 2013, it was ranked as the 13th most-developed country in the world by the United Nations' Human Development Index. Iceland runs almost completely on renewable energy. Affected by the ongoing worldwide financial crisis, the nation's entire banking system systemically failed in October 2008, leading to a severe depression, substantial political unrest, the Icesave dispute, and the institution of capital controls. Many bankers were jailed and the economy has made a significant recovery, in large part due to a surge in tourism.

Icelandic culture is founded upon the nation's Scandinavian heritage. Most Icelanders are descendants of Germanic and Gaelic (Celtic) settlers. Icelandic, a North Germanic language, is descended from Old Norse and is closely related to Faroese and West Norwegian dialects. The country's cultural heritage includes traditional Icelandic cuisine, Icelandic literature and medieval sagas. Iceland has the smallest population of any NATO member and is the only one with no standing army, its lightly armed coast guard being in charge of defence

Background:	Settled by Norwegian and Celtic (Scottish and Irish) immigrants during the late 9th and 10th centuries A.D., Iceland boasts the world's oldest functioning legislative assembly, the Althing, established in 930. Independent for over 300 years, Iceland was subsequently ruled by Norway and Denmark. Fallout from the Askja volcano of 1875 devastated the Icelandic economy and caused widespread famine. Over the next quarter century, 20% of the island's population emigrated, mostly to Canada and the US. Limited home rule from Denmark was granted in 1874 and complete independence attained in 1944. Literacy, longevity, income, and social cohesion are first-rate by world standards.

GEOGRAPHY

Location:	Northern Europe, island between the Greenland Sea and the North Atlantic Ocean, northwest of the UK
Geographic coordinates:	65 00 N, 18 00 W
Map references:	Arctic Region
Area:	total: 103,000 sq km land: 100,250 sq km water: 2,750 sq km
Area - comparative:	slightly smaller than Kentucky
Land boundaries:	0 km
Coastline:	4,988 km
Maritime claims:	continental shelf: 200 NM or to the edge of the continental margin exclusive economic zone: 200 NM territorial sea: 12 NM
Climate:	temperate; moderated by North Atlantic Current; mild, windy winters; damp, cool summers
Terrain:	mostly plateau interspersed with mountain peaks, icefields; coast deeply indented by bays and fiords
Elevation extremes:	lowest point: Atlantic Ocean 0 m highest point: Hvannadalshnukur 2,119 m

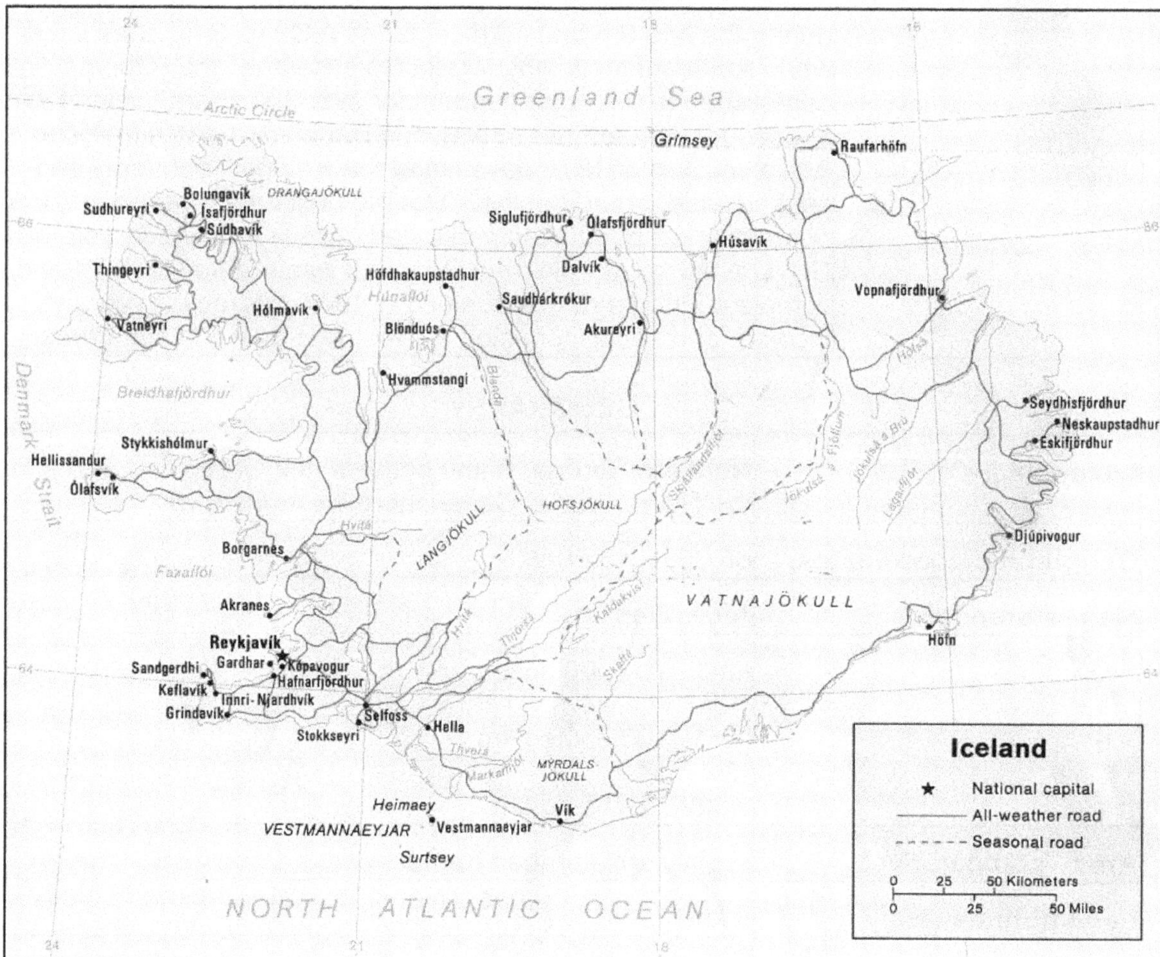

Base 504778 (546541) 10-81

Natural resources:	fish, hydropower, geothermal power, diatomite
Land use:	arable land: 0% permanent crops: 0% permanent pastures: 23% forests and woodland: 1% other: 76% (1993 est.)
Irrigated land:	NA sq km
Natural hazards:	earthquakes and volcanic activity
Environment - current issues:	water pollution from fertilizer runoff; inadequate wastewater treatment
Environment - international agreements:	party to: Air Pollution, Biodiversity, Climate Change, Desertification, Endangered Species, Environmental Modification, Hazardous Wastes, Law of the Sea, Marine

	Dumping, Nuclear Test Ban, Ozone Layer Protection, Ship Pollution, Wetlands signed, but not ratified: Air Pollution-Persistent Organic Pollutants, Marine Life Conservation
Geography - note:	strategic location between Greenland and Europe; westernmost European country; Reykjavik is the northernmost national capital in the world; more land covered by glaciers than in all of continental Europe

PEOPLE

Population:	277,906 (July 2001 est.)
Age structure:	0-14 years: 23.18% (male 33,238; female 31,191) 15-64 years: 65.01% (male 91,095; female 89,583) 65 years and over: 11.81% (male 14,681; female 18,118) (est.)
Population growth rate:	0.54% (est.)
Birth rate:	14.62 births/1,000 population (est.)
Death rate:	6.89 deaths/1,000 population (est.)
Net migration rate:	-2.28 migrant(s)/1,000 population (est.)
Sex ratio:	at birth: 1.08 male(s)/female under 15 years: 1.07 male(s)/female 15-64 years: 1.02 male(s)/female 65 years and over: 0.81 male(s)/female total population: 1 male(s)/female (est.)
Infant mortality rate:	3.56 deaths/1,000 live births (est.)
Life expectancy at birth:	total population: 79.52 years male: 77.31 years female: 81.92 years (est.)
Total fertility rate:	2.01 children born/woman (est.)
HIV/AIDS - adult prevalence rate:	0.14% (est.)
HIV/AIDS - people living with HIV/AIDS:	200 (est.)
HIV/AIDS - deaths:	less than 100 (est.)
Nationality:	noun: Icelander(s)

	adjective: Icelandic
Ethnic groups:	homogeneous mixture of descendants of Norse and Celts
Religions:	Evangelical Lutheran 93%, other Protestant and Roman Catholic, none (1997)
Languages:	Icelandic
Literacy:	definition: age 15 and over can read and write total population: 99.9% (1997 est.) male: NA% female: NA%

GOVERNMENT

Country name:

conventional long form: Republic of Iceland
conventional short form: Iceland
local long form: Lydveldid Island
local short form: Island

etymology: Floki VILGERDARSON, an early explorer of the island (9th century), applied the name "Land of Ice" after spotting a fjord full of drift ice to the north and spending a bitter winter on the island; he eventually settled on the island, however, after he saw how it greened up in the summer and that it was, in fact, habitable

Government type:

parliamentary republic

Capital:

name: Reykjavik
geographic coordinates: 64 09 N, 21 57 W
time difference: UTC 0 (5 hours ahead of Washington, DC, during Standard Time)

Administrative divisions:

8 regions; Austurland, Hofudhborgarsvaedhi, Nordhurland Eystra, Nordhurland Vestra, Sudhurland, Sudhurnes, Vestfirdhir, Vesturland

Independence:

1 December 1918 (became a sovereign state under the Danish Crown); 17 June 1944 (from Denmark; birthday of Jon SIGURDSSON, leader of Iceland's 19th Century independence movement)

National holiday:

Independence Day, 17 June (1944)

Constitution:

history: several previous; latest ratified 16 June 1944, effective 17 June 1944 (at independence)

amendments: proposed by the Althingi; passage requires approval by the Althingi and by the next elected Althingi, and confirmation by the president of the republic; proposed amendments to Article 62 of the constitution – that the Evangelical Lutheran Church shall be the state church of Iceland – also require passage by referendum; amended many times, last in 2013 (2016)

Legal system:

civil law system influenced by the Danish model

International law organization participation:

has not submitted an ICJ jurisdiction declaration; accepts ICCt jurisdiction

Citizenship:

citizenship by birth: no
citizenship by descent only: at least one parent must be a citizen of Iceland
dual citizenship recognized: yes
residency requirement for naturalization: 3 to 7 years

Suffrage:

18 years of age; universal

Executive branch:

chief of state: President Gudni Thorlacius JOHANNESSON (since 1 August 2016)
head of government: Prime Minister Katrin JAKOBSDOTTIR (since 30 November 2017)

cabinet: Cabinet appointed by the prime minister

elections/appointments: president directly elected by simple majority popular vote for a 4-year term (no term limits); election last held on 25 June 2016 (next to be held in June 2020); following legislative elections, the leader of the majority party or majority coalition becomes prime minister

election results: Gudni Thorlacius JOHANNESSON elected president; percent of vote - Gudni Thorlacius JOHANNESSON (IP) 39.1%, Halla TOMASDOTTIR (independent) 27.9%, Andri Snaer MAGNASON (independent) 14.3%, David ODDSSON (IP) 13.7%, Sturla JONSSON (Sturla Jonsson) 3.5%, invalid 1.5%

Legislative branch:

description: unicameral Althingi or Parliament (63 seats; members directly elected in multi-seat constituencies by proportional representation vote to serve 4-year terms)

elections: last held on 28 October 2016 (next to be held on 28 October 2017)

election results: percent of vote by party - IP 25.2%, LGM 16.9%, SDA 12.1%, CP 10.9%, PP 10.7%, Pirate Party 9.2%, People's Party 6.9%, Reform Party 6.7%. other 1.5%; seats by party - IP 16, LGM 11, SDA 7, CP 7, PP 8, Pirate Party 6, Reform Party 4, People's Party 4

Judicial branch:

highest court(s): Supreme Court or Haestirettur (consists of 9 judges)

judge selection and term of office: judges proposed by Ministry of Interior selection committee and appointed by the president; judges appointed for an indefinite period

subordinate courts: 8 district courts; Labor Court

Political parties and leaders:

Bright Future (Bjort framtid) or BF [Biort OLAFSDOTTIR]
Centrist Party (Midflokkurinn) or CP [Sigmundur David GUNNLAUGSSON]
Independence Party (Sjalfstaedisflokkurinn) or IP [Bjarni BENEDIKTSSON]
Left-Green Movement (Vinstrihreyfingin-graent frambod) or LGM [Katrin JAKOBSDOTTIR]
People's Party (Flokkur Folksins) [Inga SAELAND]
Pirate Party (Piratar) [Birgitta JONSDOTTIR]
Progressive Party (Framsoknarflokkurinn) or PP [Sigurdur Ingi JOHANNSSON]
Reform (Vidreisn) [Thorgerdur Katrin GUNNARSDOTTIR]
Social Democratic Alliance (Samfylkingin) or SDA [Logi Mar EINARSSON]

International organization participation:

Arctic Council, Australia Group, BIS, CBSS, CD, CE, EAPC, EBRD, EFTA, FAO, FATF, IAEA, IBRD, ICAO, ICC (national committees), ICCt, ICRM, IDA, IFAD, IFC, IFRCS, IHO, ILO, IMF, IMO, IMSO, Interpol, IOC, IOM, IPU, ISO, ITSO, ITU, ITUC (NGOs), MIGA, NATO, NC, NEA, NIB, NSG, OAS (observer), OECD, OPCW,

OSCE, PCA, Schengen Convention, UN, UNCTAD, UNESCO, UPU, WCO, WHO, WIPO, WMO, WTO

Diplomatic representation in the US:

chief of mission: Ambassador Geir Hilmar HAARDE (since 23 February 2015)
chancery: House of Sweden, 2900 K Street NW
telephone: [1] (202) 265-6653
FAX: [1] (202) 265-6656
consulate(s) general: New York

Diplomatic representation from the US:
chief of mission: Ambassador (vacant); Charge d'Affaires Jill ESPOSITO (since 20 January 2017)
embassy: Laufasvegur 21, 101 Reykjavik
mailing address: US Department of State, 5640 Reykjavik Place, Washington, D.C. 20521-5640
telephone: [354] 595-22-00
FAX: [354] 562-9118

Flag description:

blue with a red cross outlined in white extending to the edges of the flag; the vertical part of the cross is shifted to the hoist side in the style of the Dannebrog (Danish flag); the colors represent three of the elements that make up the island: red is for the island's volcanic fires, white recalls the snow and ice fields of the island, and blue is for the surrounding ocean

National symbol(s):

gyrfalcon; national colors: blue, white, red

National anthem:

name: "Lofsongur" (Song of Praise)
lyrics/music: Matthias JOCHUMSSON/Sveinbjorn SVEINBJORNSSON
note: adopted 1944; also known as "O, Gud vors lands" (O, God of Our Land), the anthem was originally written and performed in 1874

ECONOMY

Iceland's Scandinavian-type social-market economy combines a capitalist structure and free-market principles with an extensive welfare system. Prior to the 2008 crisis, Iceland had achieved high growth, low unemployment, and a remarkably even distribution of income. The economy depends heavily on the fishing industry, which provides 40% of export earnings, more than 12% of GDP, and employs 7% of the work force. It remains sensitive to declining fish stocks as well as to fluctuations in world prices for its main exports: fish and fish products, aluminum, and ferrosilicon. Iceland's economy has been diversifying into manufacturing and service industries in the last decade, particularly within the fields of software production, biotechnology, and tourism. Abundant geothermal and hydropower sources have attracted substantial foreign investment in the aluminum sector and boosted economic growth, although the financial crisis has put several investment projects on hold. Much of Iceland's economic growth in recent years came as the result of a boom in domestic demand following the rapid expansion of the country's financial sector. Domestic banks expanded aggressively in foreign markets, and consumers and businesses borrowed heavily in foreign currencies, following the privatization of the banking sector in the early 2000s.

Worsening global financial conditions throughout 2008 resulted in a sharp depreciation of the krona vis-a-vis other major currencies. The foreign exposure of Icelandic banks, whose loans and other assets totaled more than 10 times the country's GDP, became unsustainable. Iceland's three largest banks collapsed in late 2008. The country secured over $10 billion in loans from the IMF and other countries to stabilize its currency and financial sector, and to back government guarantees for foreign deposits in Icelandic banks. GDP fell 6.8% in 2009, and unemployment peaked at 9.4% in February 2009. GDP fell 3.4% in 2010. Since the collapse of Iceland's financial sector, government economic priorities have included: stabilizing the krona, reducing Iceland's high budget deficit, containing inflation, restructuring the financial sector, and diversifying the economy. Three new banks were established to take over the domestic assets of the collapsed banks. Two of them have foreign majority ownership, while the State holds a majority of the shares of the third. British and Dutch authorities have pressed claims totaling over $5 billion against Iceland to compensate their citizens for losses suffered on deposits held in the failed Icelandic bank, Landsbanki Islands. Iceland agreed to new terms with the UK and the Netherlands to compensate British and Dutch depositors, but the agreement must first be approved by the Icelandic President. Iceland began accession negotiations with the EU in July 2010; however, public support has dropped substantially because of concern about losing control over fishing resources and in reaction to measures taken by Brussels during the ongoing Eurozone crisis.

GDP (purchasing power parity):
$11.82 billion (est.)
country comparison to the world: 145
$12.24 billion (est.)
$13.15 billion (est.)
note: data are in 2010 US dollars

GDP (official exchange rate):
$12.59 billion (est.)

GDP - real growth rate:
-3.5% (est.)
country comparison to the world: 210
-6.9% (est.)
1.4% (est.)

GDP - per capita (PPP):
$38,300 (est.)
country comparison to the world: 25
$39,900 (est.)

$43,200 (est.)
note: data are in 2010 US dollars

GDP - composition by sector:
agriculture: 5.5%
industry: 24.7%
services: 69.9% (est.)

Labor force:
178,800 (2010)
country comparison to the world: 174

Labor force - by occupation:
agriculture: 4.8%
industry: 22.2%
services: 73% (2008)

Unemployment rate:
8.3% (est.)
country comparison to the world: 93
8.6% (est.)

Household income or consumption by percentage share:
lowest 10%: NA%
highest 10%: NA%

Distribution of family income - Gini index:
28
country comparison to the world: 122
25

Investment (gross fixed):
12.4% of GDP (est.)
country comparison to the world: 144

Budget:
revenues: $4.81 billion
expenditures: $5.673 billion (est.)

Public debt:
123.8% of GDP (est.)
country comparison to the world: 6
113.9% of GDP (est.)

Inflation rate (consumer prices):
5.5% (est.)
country comparison to the world: 147
12% (est.)

Central bank discount rate:

14.55%
country comparison to the world: 8
22% (31 December 2008)

Commercial bank prime lending rate:
18.99%
country comparison to the world: 21
19.29% (31 December 2007)

Stock of narrow money:
$4.413 billion
country comparison to the world: 96
$4.438 billion (31 December 2009 est.)

Stock of broad money:
$19.97 billion
country comparison to the world: 83
$24.28 billion (31 December 2009 est.)

Stock of domestic credit:
$46.03 billion
country comparison to the world: 65
$54.65 billion (31 December 2009 est.)

Market value of publicly traded shares:
$1.128 billion
country comparison to the world: 78
$5.557 billion (31 December 2008)
$40.56 billion (31 December 2007)

Agriculture - products:
potatoes, green vegetables; mutton, chicken, pork, beef, dairy products; fish

Industries:
fish processing; aluminum smelting, ferrosilicon production; geothermal power, hydropower, tourism

Industrial production growth rate:
-1% (est.)
country comparison to the world: 157

Electricity - production:
16.84 billion kWh (est.)
country comparison to the world: 73

Electricity - consumption:
16.48 billion kWh (est.)
country comparison to the world: 74

Electricity - exports:

0 kWh (est.)

Electricity - imports:
0 kWh (est.)

Oil - production:
0 bbl/day (est.)
country comparison to the world: 186

Oil - consumption:
18,900 bbl/day (est.)
country comparison to the world: 127

Oil - exports:
1,915 bbl/day (est.)
country comparison to the world: 114

Oil - imports:
16,390 bbl/day (est.)
country comparison to the world: 122

Oil - proved reserves:
0 bbl (1 January 2010 est.)
country comparison to the world: 144

Natural gas - production:
0 cu m (est.)
country comparison to the world: 140

Natural gas - consumption:
0 cu m (est.)
country comparison to the world: 184

Natural gas - exports:
0 cu m (est.)
country comparison to the world: 112

Natural gas - imports:
0 cu m (est.)
country comparison to the world: 199

Natural gas - proved reserves:
0 cu m (1 January 2010 est.)
country comparison to the world: 147

Current account balance:
$-42 million (est.)
country comparison to the world: 69
$-440 million (est.)

Exports:
$4.619 billion (est.)
country comparison to the world: 110
$4.05 billion (est.)

Exports - commodities:
fish and fish products 40%, aluminum, animal products, ferrosilicon, diatomite

Exports - partners:
Netherlands 30.7%, UK 12.7%, Germany 11.2%, Norway 5.8%, Spain 4.8% (2009)

Imports:
$3.677 billion (est.)
country comparison to the world: 131
$3.318 billion (est.)

Imports - commodities:
machinery and equipment, petroleum products, foodstuffs, textiles

Imports - partners:
Norway 13%, Netherlands 8.6%, Germany 8.3%, Sweden 8%, Denmark 7.3%, US 6.9%, China 5%, UK 4.5%, Brazil 4.1% (2009)

Reserves of foreign exchange and gold:
$4.206 billion (31 December 2010 est.)
country comparison to the world: 74
$3.883 billion (31 December 2009 est.)

Debt - external:
$3.073 billion
country comparison to the world: 125

Stock of direct foreign investment - at home:
$NA (31 December 2010)
$9.2 billion (31 December 2008)

Stock of direct foreign investment - abroad:
$8.8 billion

Exchange rates:
Icelandic kronur (ISK) per US dollar -
130.1 (2015 est.)
116.77 (2014 est.)
116.77 (2013 est.)
125.08 (2012 est.)
115.95 (2011 est.)

ENERGY

Electricity - production:
17.43 billion kWh (2012 est.)

country comparison to the world: 78

Electricity - consumption:
16.94 billion kWh (2012 est.)
country comparison to the world: 75

Electricity - exports:
0 kWh (2013 est.)
country comparison to the world: 151

Electricity - imports:
0 kWh (2013 est.)
country comparison to the world: 161

Electricity - installed generating capacity:
2.658 million kW (2012 est.)
country comparison to the world: 97

Electricity - from fossil fuels:
4.3% of total installed capacity
country comparison to the world: 205

Electricity - from nuclear fuels:
0% of total installed capacity (
country comparison to the world: 110

Electricity - from hydroelectric plants:
70.6% of total installed capacity (2012 est.)
country comparison to the world: 22

Electricity - from other renewable sources:
25.1% of total installed capacity
country comparison to the world: 8

Crude oil - production:
0 bbl/day (2014 est.)
country comparison to the world: 149

Crude oil - exports:
0 bbl/day (2013 est.)
country comparison to the world: 139

Crude oil - imports:
0 bbl/day (2013 est.)
country comparison to the world: 206

Crude oil - proved reserves:
0 bbl (1 January 2015 est.)
country comparison to the world: 148

Refined petroleum products - production:
0 bbl/day (2013 est.)
country comparison to the world: 196

Refined petroleum products - consumption:
16,310 bbl/day (2014 est.)
country comparison to the world: 138

Refined petroleum products - exports:
1,831 bbl/day (2013 est.)
country comparison to the world: 107

Refined petroleum products - imports:
15,040 bbl/day (2013 est.)
country comparison to the world: 125

Natural gas - production:
0 cu m (2014 est.)
country comparison to the world: 203

Natural gas - consumption:
0 cu m (2014 est.)
country comparison to the world: 156

Natural gas - exports:
0 cu m (2014 est.)
country comparison to the world: 117
Natural gas - imports:
0 cu m (2014 est.)
country comparison to the world: 210

Natural gas - proved reserves:
0 cu m (1 January 2014 est.)
country comparison to the world: 152

Carbon dioxide emissions from consumption of energy:
3.505 million Mt (2012 est.)
country comparison to the world: 137

COMMUNICATIONS

TRANSPORTATION

Railways:	0 km
Highways:	total: 12,691 km paved: 3,262 km unpaved: 9,429 km (1999)
Waterways:	none

Ports and harbors:	Akureyri, Hornafjordur, Isafjordhur, Keflavik, Raufarhofn, Reykjavik, Seydhisfjordhur, Straumsvik, Vestmannaeyjar
Merchant marine:	total: 2 ships (1,000 GRT or over) totaling 3,435 GRT/4,538 DWT ships by type: chemical tanker 1, petroleum tanker 1 (2000 est.)
Airports:	87 (2000 est.)
Airports - with paved runways:	total: 12 over 3,047 m: 1 1,524 to 2,437 m: 4 914 to 1,523 m: 7 (2000 est.)
Airports - with unpaved runways:	total: 75 1,524 to 2,437 m: 3 914 to 1,523 m: 20 under 914 m: 52 (2000 est.)

MILITARY

Military branches:	no regular armed forces; Police, Coast Guard; note - Iceland's defense is provided by the US-manned Icelandic Defense Force (IDF) headquartered at Keflavik
Military manpower - availability:	males age 15-49: 71,241 (est.)
Military manpower - fit for military service:	males age 15-49: 62,704 (est.)
Military expenditures - dollar figure:	$0
Military - note:	defense is provided by the US-manned Icelandic Defense Force (IDF) headquartered at Keflavik

TRANSNATIONAL ISSUES

Disputes - international:	Iceland, the UK, and Ireland dispute Denmark's claim that the Faroe Islands' continental shelf extends beyond 200 nm; the European Free Trade Association Surveillance Authority filed a suit against Iceland, claiming the country violated the European Economic Area agreement in failing to pay minimum compensation to Icesave depositors **Refugees and internally displaced persons:** **stateless persons:** 119 (2014)

IMPORTANT INFORMATION FOR UNDERSTANDING ICELAND

PROFILE

Geography
Area: 103,000 sq. km. (39,600 sq. mi.); about the size of Virginia or slightly larger than Ireland.
Cities: *Capital*--Reykjavik (pop. 118,898). *Other towns*--Kopavogur (30,779), Hafnarfjordur (26,099), Akureyri (17,754), Reykjanesbaer (13,971), Gardabaer (10,909).
Terrain: Rugged.
Climate: Maritime temperate.
Highest elevation: Hvannadalshnjukur at Vatnajokull Glacier, at 2,110 meters (6,923 ft.).

People
Nationality: *Noun*--Icelander(s). *Adjective*--Icelandic.
Population (January 1, 2011): 318,452.
Annual population growth rate (2010): 0.26%.
Ethnic group: Relatively homogenous mixture of descendants of Norwegians and Celts.
Religion: Evangelical Lutheran, 84.4%.
Language: Icelandic.
Education: Compulsory up to age 16. *Attendance*--99%. *Literacy*--99.9%.
Health: *Infant mortality rate* (2010)--2.2/1,000. *Life expectancy* (2010)--men 79.5 years, women 83.5 years.
Work force 178,600 (2008): *Commerce*--32.2%; *manufacturing*--9.7%; *fishing/fish processing*--4.1%; *construction*--9.8%; *transport and communications*--6.4%; *agriculture*--2.5%; *government, education, and health*--28.8%. Unemployment (January 2011): 8.5%.

Government
Type: Parliamentary republic.
Independence: 1918 (became "sovereign state" under Danish Crown); 1944 (establishment of republic);
Constitution: June 17, 1944.
Branches: *Executive*--president (head of state), prime minister (head of government), cabinet (10 ministers including the Prime Minister). *Legislative*--63-member unicameral parliament (Althingi). *Judicial*--Supreme Court, district courts, special courts.
Subdivisions: 26 administrative districts and 77 municipalities.
Major political parties: Social Democratic Alliance (SDA), Left-Green Party (LGP), Independence Party (IP), Progressive Party (PP), and The Movement.
Suffrage: Universal 18 years and above.
National holiday: June 17, anniversary of the establishment of the republic.

Economy
Natural resources: Marine products, hydroelectric and geothermal power.
Agriculture: *Products*--fish, potatoes, turnips, carrots, tomatoes, cucumbers, cereal grains, livestock, milk, and other dairy products.
Industry: *Types*--aluminum smelting, fishing and fish processing technology, ferro-silicon alloy production, hydro and geothermal power, tourism, information technology.

Trade: *Exports of goods* (2010)--$4.8 billion: marine products 39.3%; industrial products 55.47%; agricultural products 1.5%; and miscellaneous 3.73%. *Partners* (2010)--EEA 83.5% (Netherlands 34%, Germany 13.9%, U.K. 10%, Spain 4.8%, Norway 4.2%); U.S. 4.5% ($218.6 million). *Imports* (2009)--$3.8 billion: industrial supplies 32.8%; capital goods, parts, accessories 22.8%; consumer goods 14.6%; fuels and lubricants 13.05%; food and beverages 9.7%; transport equipment 6.8%. *Partners* (2010)--EEA 61% (Germany 7.5%, Norway 9.0%, Netherlands 8.5%, Denmark 7%, Sweden 5.2%, U.K. 5.09%); U.S. 8.04% ($306 million); China 6.0%; Japan 2.4%.

GEOGRAPHY

Iceland is a volcanic island in the North Atlantic Ocean east of Greenland and immediately south of the Arctic Circle. It lies about 4,200 kilometers (2,600 mi.) from New York and 830 kilometers (520 mi.) from Scotland. About 79% of Iceland's land area, which is of recent volcanic origin, consists of glaciers, lakes, a mountainous lava desert (highest elevation 2,000 meters--6,590 ft.--above sea level), and other wasteland. About 28% of the land is used for grazing, and 1% is cultivated. The inhabited areas are on the coast, particularly in the southwest where about 60% of the population lives. Because of the Gulf Stream's moderating influence, the climate is characterized by damp, cool summers and relatively mild but windy winters. In Reykjavik, the average temperature is 11°C (52°F) in July and -1°C (30°F) in January.

PEOPLE

Most Icelanders are descendants of Norwegian settlers and Celts from the British Isles, and the population is remarkably homogeneous. According to Icelandic Government statistics, 94% of the nation's inhabitants live in urban areas (localities with populations greater than 200) and about 63% live in the Reykjavik metropolitan area. Of the Nordic languages, the Icelandic language is closest to the Old Norse language and has remained relatively unchanged since the 12th century. The Icelandic alphabet contains letters not found in modern English. For example, Þ is transliterated as "th", and ð is transliterated as "d". About 84% of the population belongs to the state church, the Evangelical Lutheran Church, or other Lutheran Churches. However, Iceland has complete religious freedom, and about 20 other religious congregations are present.

Most Icelandic surnames are based on patronymy, or the adoption of the father's first given name. For example, Magnus and Anna, children of a man named Petur, would hold the surname Petursson and Petursdottir, respectively. Magnus' children, in turn, would inherit the surname Magnusson or Magnusdottir, while Anna's children would claim their father's first given name as their surname. Women normally maintain their original surnames after marriage. This system of surnames is required by law, except for the descendants of those who had acquired family names before 1913. Most Icelanders, while reserved by nature, rarely call each other by their surnames, and even phone directories are based on first names. Because of its small size and relative homogeneity, Iceland holds all the characteristics of a very close-knit society.

Cultural Achievements

The Sagas, almost all written between 1180 and 1300 A.D., remain Iceland's best-known literary accomplishment, and they have no surviving counterpart anywhere in the Nordic world. Based on Norwegian and Icelandic histories and genealogies, the Sagas present views of Nordic life and times up to 1100 A.D. The Saga writers sought to record their heroes' great achievements and to glorify the virtues of courage, pride, and honor, focusing in the later Sagas on early Icelandic settlers. The best-known Icelandic writer of the 20th century is the 1955 Nobel Prize winner Halldor Kiljan Laxness. The literacy rate is 99.9%, and literature and poetry are legendary passions with the population. Per capita publication of books and magazines is the highest in the world.

Unlike its literature, Iceland's fine arts did not flourish until the 19th century because the population was small and scattered. Iceland's most famous painters are Asgrimur Jonsson, Jon Stefansson, and Johannes Kjarval, all of whom worked during the first half of the 20th century. The best-known modern sculptor, Asmundur Sveinsson (1893-1982), drew his inspiration from Icelandic folklore and the Sagas for many of his works. Today, Kristjan Johannsson and Gardar Thor Cortes are Iceland's most famous opera singers, while pop singer Bjork and progressive rock band Sigur Ros are well known internationally.

HISTORY

Iceland was settled in the late 9th and early 10th centuries, principally by people of Norse origin. In 930 A.D., the ruling chiefs established a republican constitution and an assembly called the Althingi (Alþingi) the oldest parliament in the world. Iceland remained independent until 1262, when it entered into a treaty establishing a union with the Norwegian monarchy. Iceland was then passed to Denmark in the late 14th century when Norway and Denmark were united under the Danish crown.

In the early 19th century, national consciousness was revived in Iceland. The Althingi had been abolished in 1800 but was reestablished in 1843 as a consultative assembly. In 1874, Denmark granted Iceland limited home rule, which was expanded in scope in 1904. The constitution, written in 1874, was revised in 1903. The Act of Union, a 1918 agreement with Denmark, recognized Iceland as a fully sovereign state united with Denmark under a common king. Iceland established its own flag, but Denmark continued to represent Icelandic foreign affairs and defense interests.

German occupation of Denmark in 1940 severed communications between Iceland and Denmark. Consequently, Iceland moved immediately to assume control over its own territorial waters and foreign affairs. In May 1940, British military forces occupied Iceland. Responsibility for Iceland's defense passed to the United States in July 1941. Following a plebiscite, Iceland formally became an independent republic on June 17, 1944. In October 1946, the Icelandic and U.S. Governments agreed to terminate U.S. responsibility for the defense of Iceland, but the United States retained certain rights at Keflavik. Iceland became a charter member of the North Atlantic Treaty Organization (NATO) in 1949. After the outbreak of hostilities in Korea in 1950, and pursuant to the request of NATO military authorities, the United States and Iceland agreed that the United States should again make arrangements for Iceland's defense. A bilateral defense agreement signed on May 5, 1951 remains in force, even though the U.S. military forces are no longer permanently stationed in Iceland. Iceland is the only NATO country with no standing military of its own.

GOVERNMENT

Politics of the Iceland take place in the framework of a parliamentary representative democratic republic, whereby the President is the head of state, while the Prime Minister of Iceland serves as the head of government in a multi-party system. Executive power is exercised by the government. Legislative power is vested in both the government and the parliament, the Althingi. The judiciary is independent of the executive and the legislature.

Iceland is arguably the world's oldest assembly democracy.[1] The Economist Intelligence Unit has rated Iceland as "full democracy" in 2016

The president, elected to a 4-year term, has limited powers. When Iceland became a republic in 1944, the post of president was created to fill the void left by the Danish king. Although the president is popularly elected and has limited veto powers (he can force a public referendum on a proposed law by refusing to sign it), the expectation is that the president should play the same limited role as a monarch in a traditional parliamentary system. President Olafur Ragnar Grimsson has referred legislation to referendum three times (one time the legislation was withdrawn before the referendum could be held), and the current government is considering appointing a constitutional assembly to propose changes to the constitution.

The prime minister and cabinet exercise most executive functions. The parliament is composed of 63 members, elected every 4 years unless it is dissolved sooner. Suffrage for presidential and parliamentary elections is universal for those 18 and older, and members of the parliament are elected on the basis of parties' proportional representation in six constituencies. The judiciary consists of the Supreme Court, district courts, and various special courts. The constitution protects the judiciary from infringement by the other two branches.

Principal Government Officials

The current cabinet (in office since 11 January 2017), consists of the following ministers:[4]

Minister	Ministry	Since	Incumbent	Party	Image
Prime Minister (Forsætisráðherra)	Prime Minister's Office (Forsætisráðuneytið)	30 November 2017	Katrín Jakobsdóttir	LG	

Minister for Foreign Affairs (Utanríkisráðherra)	Ministry for Foreign Affairs (Utanríkisráðuneytið)	30 November 2017	Guðlaugur Þór Þórðarson	IP	
Minister of Finance and Economic Affairs (Fjármála- og efnahagsráðherra)	Ministry of Finance and Economic Affairs (Fjármála- og efnahagsráðuneytið)	30 November 2017	Bjarni Benediktsson	IP	
Minister of Justice (Dómsmálaráðherra)	Ministry of the Interior (Innanríkisráðuneytið)	30 November 2017	Sigríður Á. Andersen	IP	
Minister of Transport and Local Government (Samgöngu- og sveitarstjórnarráðherra)	Ministry of the Interior (Innanríkisráðuneytið)	30 November 2017	Sigurður Ingi Jóhannsson	PP	
Minister of Fisheries and Agriculture (Sjávarútvegs- og landbúnaðarráðherra)	Ministry of Industries and Innovation (Atvinnuvega- og nýsköpunarráðuneytið)	30 November 2017	Kristján Þór Júlíusson	IP	
Minister of Education, Science and Culture (Mennta- og menningarmálaráðherra)	Ministry of Education and Culture (Mennta- og menningarmálaráðuneytið)	30 November 2017	Lilja Dögg Alfreðsdóttir	PP	

Minister of Tourism, Industry and Innovation (Iðnaðar- og viðskiptaráðherra)	Ministry of Industries and Innovation (Atvinnuvega- og nýsköpunarráðuneytið)	30 November 2017	Þórdís Kolbrún R. Gylfadóttir	IP	
Minister of Social Affairs and Equality (Félags- og jafnréttismálaráðherra)	Ministry of Welfare (Velferðarráðuneytið)	30 November 2017	Ásmundur Einar Daðason	PP	
Minister of Health (Heilbrigðisráðherra)	Ministry of Welfare (Velferðarráðuneytið)	30 November 2017	Svandís Svavarsdóttir	LG	
Minister for the Environment and Natural Resources (Umhverfis- og auðlindaráðherra)	Ministry for the Environment and Natural Resources (Umhverfis- og auðlindaráðuneytið)	30 November 2017	Guðmundur Ingi Guðbrandsson	LG	

Ambassador to NATO--Thorsteinn Ingolfsson
Ambassador to the EU--Thorir Ibsen

Iceland maintains an **embassy** in the United States at the House of Sweden, 2900 K Street, NW, #509, Washington, DC 20007-1704 [tel. (202) 265-6653], and a consulate general at 800 Third Ave, 36th floor, New York, NY 10022 [tel. (212) 593-2700]. Iceland also has 25 honorary consulates in major U.S. cities.

POLITICAL CONDITIONS

Iceland has a left–right multi-party system. Following the 2013 parliamentary election, the biggest parties are the centre-right Independence Party (*Sjálfstæðisflokkurinn*) and the Progressive Party (*Framsóknarflokkurinn*). Other political parties with seats in the Althing are the centre-left Social Democratic Alliance (*Samfylkingin*), Left-Green Movement (*Vinstrihreyfingin – grænt framboð*), Bright Future (*Björt framtíð*), and the Pirate Party of Iceland (*Píratar*). Many other parties exist on the municipal level, most of which run only locally in a single municipality.

Iceland was the first country in the world to have a political party formed and led entirely by women. Known as the Women's List or Women's Alliance (*Kvennalistinn*), it was founded in 1983 to advance the political, economic, and social needs of women. After participating in its first parliamentary elections, the Women's List helped increase the proportion of female parliamentarians by 15%. Although it disbanded in 1999, merging with the Social Democratic Alliance, it left a lasting influence on Iceland's politics: every major party has a 40% quota for women, and in 2009 nearly a third of members of parliament were female, compared to the global average of 16%.

In 2011 Iceland was ranked 2nd in the strength of its democratic institutions and 13th in government transparency. The country has a high level of civic participation, with 81.4% voter turnout during the most recent elections compared to an OECD average of 72%. However, only 50% of Icelanders say they trust their political institutions, slightly less than the OECD average of 56% (and most probably a consequence of the political scandals in the wake of the Icelandic financial crisis).

ICELANDIC PARLIAMENTARY ELECTION, 2017

Parliamentary elections were held in Iceland on 28 October 2017. On 15 September 2017, the three-party coalition government collapsed after the departure of Bright Future over a scandal involving Prime Minister Bjarni Benediktsson's father writing a letter recommending a convicted paedophile have his "honour restored".[1] Bjarni subsequently called for a snap election,[2] which was officially scheduled for 28 October 2017 following the dissolution of the Althing.

Though many opinion polls in the run-up to the election indicated an increase in support for the Left-Green Movement, the Independence Party retained its position as the Althing's largest party.[3] Following the election, four-party coalition talks led by the Left-Greens ensued; however, after the Progressive Party rejected the possibility, a three-party coalition led by the Left-Greens including the Independence Party and Progressive Party was negotiated. After formally receiving the mandate to form a coalition on 28 November, Left-Green leader Katrín Jakobsdóttir was designated Prime Minister to lead the new government on 30 November.

RESULTS

The Independence Party retained its position as the Althing's largest party. However, the Independence Party's parliamentary representation decreased by five seats to 16 and it lost its governing majority. The Left-Green Movement retained its position as the Althing's second largest party, increasing its representation by one seat to 11. The Social Democratic Alliance saw a large increase in support, doubling its vote share from 2016, and will enter the new parliament with seven members. The Progressive Party held steady at eight seats while the newly formed Centre Party, founded by former Progressive Prime Minister Sigmundur Davíð Gunnlaugsson, won seven seats. The Pirate Party, which entered the election as the Althing's third largest party, lost four seats and was reduced to six seats. Entering the Althing for the first time, the People's Party obtained four seats. The Reform Party, one of the members of the outgoing government, lost three seats and was left with four seats. In line with all pre-election polling, Bright Future did not meet the 5% threshold and was therefore not returned to the Althing.

Party		Votes	%	Seats	+/–
Independence Party	D	49,543	25.2	16	–5
Left-Green Movement	V	33,155	16.9	11	+1
Social Democratic Alliance	S	23,652	12.1	7	+4
Centre Party	M	21,335	10.9	7	New
Progressive Party	B	21,016	10.7	8	0
Pirate Party	P	18,051	9.2	6	–4
People's Party	F	13,502	6.9	4	+4
Reform Party	C	13,122	6.7	4	–3
Bright Future	A	2,394	1.2	0	–4
People's Front of Iceland	R	375	0.2	0	0
Dawn	T	101	0.1	0	0
Invalid/blank votes		5,531	–	–	–
Total		201,777	100	63	0

GOVERNMENT

Iceland is a representative democracy and a parliamentary republic. The modern parliament, *Alþingi* (English: Althing), was founded in 1845 as an advisory body to the Danish monarch. It was widely seen as a re-establishment of the assembly founded in 930 in the Commonwealth period and suspended in 1799. Consequently, "it is arguably the world's oldest parliamentary democracy."

It currently has 63 members, elected for a maximum period of four years. The president is elected by popular vote for a term of four years, with no term limit. The elections for president, the Althing and local municipal councils are all held separately every four years.

The president of Iceland is a largely ceremonial head of state and serves as a diplomat, but may veto laws voted by the parliament and put them to a national referendum. The current president is Ólafur Ragnar Grímsson. The head of government is the prime minister (currently Sigmundur Davíð Gunnlaugsson) who, together with the cabinet, is responsible for executive government. The cabinet is appointed by the president after a general election to the Althing; however, the appointment is usually negotiated by the leaders of the political parties, who decide among themselves after discussions which parties can form the cabinet and how its seats are to be distributed, under the condition that it has a majority support in the Althing. Only when the party leaders are unable to reach a conclusion by themselves within a reasonable time span does the president exercise this power and appoint the cabinet personally. This has not happened since the republic was founded in 1944, but in 1942 regent Sveinn Björnsson, who had been installed in that position by the Althing in 1941, appointed a non-parliamentary government. The regent had, for all practical purposes, the position of a president, and Sveinn would later become the country's first president in 1944.

The governments of Iceland have always been coalition governments, with two or more parties involved, as no single political party has ever received a majority of seats in the Althing throughout the republican period. The extent of the political power possessed by the office of the president is disputed by legal scholars in Iceland; several provisions of the constitution appear to give the president some important powers, but other provisions and traditions suggest differently. In 1980, Icelanders elected Vigdís Finnbogadóttir as president, the world's first directly elected female head of state. She retired from office in 1996. In 2009, Iceland became the first country with an openly gay head of government when Jóhanna Sigurðardóttir became prime minister

There are five political parties represented in parliament:

Social Democratic Alliance: Formed in 2000 from three leftist parties--the Social Democratic Party, the People's Alliance, and the Women's List--the SDA was created to challenge the long-dominant Independence Party. Though this effort failed initially, under the leadership of Ingibjorg Solrun Gisladottir, the SDA eventually formed a coalition government with the Independence Party (IP) in 2007. It is now the senior member in a government coalition with the LG. The party has worked to reconcile the widely varying foreign policy views of its members, which range from strong support for NATO membership to pacifism and neutrality. The SDA is also the most openly pro-EU of Iceland's political parties.

Left Green Movement: The LG was founded in 1999 by a group of politicians who did not agree with the planned merger of the leftist parties in Iceland that resulted in the SDA. The Left Greens won a respectable 9% of the vote (5 seats) in 2003, but in the 2007 election they improved significantly, with 14% of the total vote (9 seats). The LG captured 22% of the vote and 14 seats in the 2009 election and joined the SDA as the junior partner in the coalition government. As its name implies, the party is focused on a Nordic socialist model of governance with a strong emphasis on environmental issues. It formally opposes EU membership for Iceland but is open to change should the Icelandic public demand it.

Independence Party: The IP was formed in 1929 and is the center-right political party in Iceland. Iceland's recent political upheaval follows nearly 2 decades of relative stability under the IP, much of it marked by an Independence-Progressive coalition that was in power from 1995-2007. Longtime IP leader David Oddsson was Prime Minister from 1991-2004, making him the longest-serving prime minister in Europe. The IP elected parliamentarian Bjarni Benediktsson to follow former Prime Minister Geir Haarde as Party Chairman in late March 2009, after Haarde announced in January his intent to leave politics while undergoing treatment for esophageal cancer. Following the economic collapse of 2008, the IP undertook a thorough review of its policy on joining the EU, concluding that the question should be decided by a national referendum at the conclusion of accession negotiations with Brussels. Party support plummeted to 24% (16 seats) in the elections in April 2009, from 37% (25 seats) in the 2007 elections.

Progressive Party: The centrist agrarian Progressive Party has been a party to government for over 30 of the past 40 years. Its support dropped from 23% (15 seats) in the 1995 parliamentary election to 12% (7 seats) in 2007. The party, however, rebounded slightly in 2009 receiving 15% of the vote and nine seats in parliament. The Progressive Party has faced internal instability in the past few years, and power struggles have led to frequent change in the party's leadership. Current Chairman Sigmundur David Gunnlaugsson was elected at the party's national congress in January 2009, following the sudden resignation of Gudni Agustsson in November 2008. Agustsson himself had replaced Jon Sigurdsson after the party's disastrous showing in the 2007 elections.

Citizens' Movement: The Citizens' Movement was the only new party to successfully use protests about the government's management of the economic crisis in 2008-2009 to launch itself into prominence. Subsequently, internal strife has torn the party apart. All four members resigned from the party; one is now an independent member of Parliament and the other three formed a parliamentary group called The Movement, which has no constituency.

Iceland's current President is Olafur Ragnar Grimsson, a former political science professor who led the far-left People's Alliance in 1987-1995 and served as Finance Minister in 1988-91. Although Grimsson won office with only a 41% plurality in 1996, he was not challenged for re-election in 2000 and was re-elected again on June 26, 2004. In 2008, Grimsson was again re-elected by default. This follows a well-established tradition of giving deference to sitting presidents. Once in office, a president can generally count on serving as many terms as he or she likes, assuming good behavior. Reflecting the belief that the president is "above politics," presidential candidates run for election as individuals--since 1952, political parties have played no role in nominating or endorsing candidates.

PRIME MINISTER - KATRÍN JAKOBSDÓTTI

28th Prime Minister of Iceland

Incumbent	
Assumed office 30 November 2017	
President	Guðni Th. Jóhannesson
Preceded by	Bjarni Benediktsson
Chair of the Left-Green Movement	
Incumbent	
Assumed office 24 February 2013	
Preceded by	Steingrímur J. Sigfússon
Minister of Education, Science and Culture	
In office 2 February 2009 – 23 May 2013	
Prime Minister	Jóhanna Sigurðardóttir
Preceded by	Þorgerður Katrín Gunnarsdóttir
Succeeded by	Illugi Gunnarsson
Personal details	
Born	1 February 1976 (age 42) Reykjavík, Iceland
Political party	Left-Green Movement
Spouse(s)	Gunnar Örn Sigvaldason
Children	3 sons
Alma mater	University of Iceland

Katrín Jakobsdóttir (pronounced [ˈkʰaːtʰrin ˈjaːkʰɔpstouhtɪr]; born 1 February 1976) is an Icelandic politician serving as the 28th and current Prime Minister of Iceland since 2017. She is the member of the Althing for the Reykjavík North constituency since 2007. She became deputy chairperson of the Left-Green Movement in 2003 and has been their chairperson since 2013. Katrín was Iceland's Minister of Education, Science and Culture and of Nordic Co-operation from 2 February 2009 to 23 May 2013

PARLIAMENTARY RESOLUTION ON A NATIONAL SECURITY POLICY FOR ICELAND.

145th Legislative Session, 2015-2016 Parliamentary document 1166 – 327th matter No. 26/145

The Althingi hereby resolves to commission the government to adopt the following national security policy so as to ensure Iceland's independence, the sovereignty and integrity of its borders, the security of its citizens and the protection of its system of government and the fundamental structures of society.

The policy is to be based on the proposals of the parliamentary committee on the formulation of a national security policy for Iceland which the Althingi commissioned the minister for foreign affairs to establish under Parliamentary Resolution No. 46/139 of 16 September 2011.

The Icelandic government's national security policy is to be based on the obligations set out in the United Nations Charter, its guiding principles being the fundamental values of the nation, democracy and respect for law as the basis of the state, international law, humanitarian considerations and the protection of human rights, universal equality and sustainable development, disarmament and the peaceful solution of disputes. A fundamental premise of the policy should be Iceland's position as an island nation with a small population that has neither the capacity nor the desire to maintain an army and ensures its security and defence through active collaboration with other nations and within the framework of international organisations.

The policy is to address global, social and military risks and be manifested in an active foreign policy, public security and collaboration with other states on defence.

The national security policy is to embrace the following points of emphasis, which shall be accorded equal weighting:

1. To secure Iceland's broad security interests through active international collaboration on the basis of international law, with the peaceful resolution of disputes, disarmament, respect for human rights and a state based on the rule of law, gender equality and the struggle against inequality, hunger and poverty as its guiding principles.

2. That particular attention be given to Iceland's environmental and security interests in the Arctic in international collaboration and domestic preparedness.

3. That membership of the North Atlantic Treaty Alliance shall continue to be a key pillar in Iceland's defence and the principal forum of Western collaboration in which Iceland participates on a civil basis in order to promote its own security and that of other NATO member states.

4. That the 1951 Defence Agreement between Iceland and the United States of America continue to guarantee the defence of Iceland and that work will continue to develop collaboration on the basis of the agreement, taking account of military threats and also other risk factors in which mutual defence and security interests play a substantial role.

5. To deepen and develop still further Nordic cooperation on security and defence and other neighbour-state collaboration on local interests and participation in international cooperation in this field.

6. To ensure that Iceland has the defence structures, equipment, capacity and expert knowledge needed to meet the challenges it faces in the field of security and defence and to fulfil its international obligations.

7. That official policy on civil protection and security, as formulated by the Civil Protection and Security Council, form part of Iceland's national security policy and that it take account of the threats connected with climate change, natural disasters, food security, health security and epidemics.

8. To enhance cybersecurity through continuing development of Iceland's own capacity in this area and in collaboration with other states.

9. That official policy take account of other threats that call for full attention, such as terrorism, organised crime and threats to the nation's financial and economic security.

10. That Iceland and its economic zone be declared a nuclear-free zone, taking account of international obligations, with a view to contributing to disarmament and peace.

11. That special legislation be enacted establishing a national security council to assess the situation and the outlook in the field of security and defence on a regular basis, monitor the implementation of the national security policy, reflect the broad vision expressed in the policy and have a review of the policy made at least every five years.

Approved by the Althingi on 13 April 2016.

ECONOMY

Currency	Icelandic króna (ISK) = 0.007 EUR
Fiscal year	Calendar year
Trade organisations	EFTA, OECD, WTO
	Statistics
GDP	$17 billion
GDP rank	111th (nominal) / 145th (PPP)
GDP growth	1.9%
GDP per capita	$51.000 14th (nominal) / 22nd (PPP)
GDP by sector	services: 71.7% industry: 22.4% agriculture: 6.0%
Inflation (CPI)	1.9% (Change in past 12 months)
Population below poverty line	8%- income below 1200€/ monthly(2015)
Gini coefficient	.23
Labour force	0.2 million (April 2015)
Labour force by occupation	services: 73% industry: 22.2% agriculture: 4.8%
Unemployment	2.9% (June 2015)
Main industries	Fish processing, aluminum smelting, ferrosilicon production, geothermal power, hydropower, tourism
Ease-of-doing-business rank	12th (2015)
	External
Exports	$5.1 billion (
Export goods	Fish and fish products: 40%, aluminum, animal products, ferrosilicon, diatomite
Main export partners	Netherlands 37.5% United Kingdom 14.4% Spain 9.7% Germany 7,7% France 6.4%
Imports	$4.6 billion
Import goods	Machinery and equipment, petroleum products, foodstuffs, textiles
Main import partners	Norway 15.78%

	United States 9.59% Germany 8.46% China 8.20% Brazil 7.66% Denmark 6.39% Netherlands 5.12% United Kingdom 4.57% Sweden 4.19% other 30.05%
	Public finances
Public debt	$16.3 billion (31 December 2012 est.)
Revenues	$5.5 billion (2012 est.)
Expenses	$5.8 billion (2012 est.)
Economic aid	~$20 million (0.24% GDP)
Credit rating	Moody's Investors Service Baa2 (Foreign) Baa1 (Domestic) Outlook: Stable Standard & Poor's BBB- (Foreign) BBB- (Domestic) Outlook: Positive Fitch BBB (Foreign) BBB+ (Domestic) Outlook: Positive
Foreign reserves	US$9.1 billion

The **economy of Iceland** is small and subject to high volatility. In 2011, gross domestic product was US$12.3bn. With a population of 321,000, this is $38,000 per capita, based on purchasing power parity (PPP) estimates. The financial crisis of 2007–2010 produced a decline in GDP and employment, although the magnitude of this decline remains to be determined.

Iceland has a mixed economy with high levels of free trade and government intervention. However, government consumption is less than other Nordic countries. Geothermal power is the primary source of home and industrial energy in Iceland.

In the 1990s Iceland undertook extensive free market reforms, which initially produced strong economic growth. As a result, Iceland was rated as having one of the world's highest levels of economic freedomas well as civil freedoms. In 2007, Iceland topped the list of nations ranked by Human Development Indexand was one of the most egalitarian, according to the calculation provided by the Gini coefficient.

From 2006 onwards, the economy faced problems of growing inflation and current account deficits. Partly in response, and partly as a result of earlier reforms, the financial system expanded rapidly before collapsing entirely in a sweeping financial crisis. Iceland had to obtain emergency funding from the International Monetary Fund and a range of European countries in November 2008.

Iceland, a stable democracy with a dynamic consumer economy, suffered an economic crisis in October 2008. The banking sector collapsed, and the Icelandic Government turned to the International Monetary Fund (IMF) for assistance.

In the years before the crisis, Iceland enjoyed an economic boom with several years of strong economic growth spurred by economic reforms, deregulation, and low inflation. The economy suffered an initial setback in spring 2006 when credit rating agencies and other international financial firms released a number of reports raising questions about the activities and stability of Iceland's major banks and the state of the Icelandic economy. These reports were widely covered in the international financial press, causing a marked drop in the value of shares listed on the Icelandic stock exchange and of the Icelandic krona (ISK), but the market recovered temporarily.

The financial sector was hit hard by the global credit crisis beginning in 2007. In the first 6 months of 2008, the Icelandic krona began devaluing and inflation rose to nearly 12%. Difficulties increased as Icelandic banks could not get financing on the global market and, with liabilities estimated at approximately 10 times GDP, they were forced to turn to their lender of last resort, the Central Bank of Iceland. The Financial Supervisory Authority took possession of the three large commercial banks, and Iceland turned to the IMF for a $5 billion loan package that included bilateral loans from the Nordics and other countries. A letter of intent sent to the IMF outlined the strategy for the recovery of the economy. Its main components were to stabilize the currency, establish trust in Iceland's monetary policy, revise fiscal policy to meet the increased debt burden, and restructure the banking system. The Executive Board of the IMF approved the loan package in November 2008, subject to Iceland following the proposed economic recovery program, and subsequently disbursed the first tranche of the loans. Several reviews of the program had been conducted as of January 2011, allowing Iceland to draw disbursements.

The financial crisis resulted in a dramatic rise in unemployment from less than 2% to 9.3% in March 2010, and widespread business closures and bankruptcies. Political turmoil resulted in the resignation of the cabinet and installation of an interim government in January 2009 and early elections, as well as the replacement of the Central Bank and Financial Supervisory Authority leadership. At the end of 2008, inflation was at 18.6% and the currency had depreciated by roughly 90%. Inflation has since subsided to a large degree, dropping to 2.5% in December 2010. The government has made good progress in restructuring the banking system. Following the takeover of the three big commercial banks, new banks were established around Icelandic assets, transferred from the old banks. The majority shares of two of the new banks have been sold to private investors, while the government still holds a majority stake in the third one. The old banks are still in receivership.

In April 2010, the Special Investigatory Commission (known informally as the Truth Commission) released a 2,000-page report on the banking meltdown. The report detailed the banks' questionable practices, all while the banking sector exploded exponentially in size. It provided the basis for investigation by the Special Prosecutor, who has since arrested some suspects and frozen their assets. In response to the report, three members of parliament took temporary leaves of absence in 2010; two of them returned to parliament in 2011. A parliamentary review committee established to determine whether ministerial responsibilities were breached recommended that four government ministers be indicted and tried by the Court of Impeachment. In September 2010, parliament voted to indict only one, former Prime Minister Geir Haarde, who will stand trial in the Court of Impeachment.

As a small and undiversified economy, Iceland depends heavily on imports for consumption and industry. Its main exports are aluminum and marine products. Aluminum exports exceeded marine product exports in value for the first time in 2008. The tourism industry is the third-largest provider of foreign currency to the economy. Other important exports include ferro-silicon alloys, equipment and electronic machinery for fishing and fish processing, and pharmaceuticals. The vast majority of Iceland's exports go to the European Union (EU) and the European Free Trade Association (EFTA) countries, followed by the United States and Japan. The U.S. is by far the largest foreign investor in Iceland, primarily in the aluminum sector. In February 2011, a U.S. company signed an investment agreement with the Government of Iceland to build a silicon metal facility in southwest Iceland. The agreement represents the largest new foreign direct investment in Iceland since the economic collapse of 2008. A Trade and Investment Framework Agreement (TIFA) with the United States was signed in January 2009.

Iceland's relatively liberal trading policy was strengthened by accession to the European Economic Area in 1994 and by the World Trade Organization (WTO) Uruguay Round agreement, which also brought significantly improved market access for Iceland's exports, particularly seafood products. The agricultural sector, however, remains heavily subsidized and protected. Iceland became a full member of the European Free Trade Association in 1970 and entered into a free trade agreement with the European Community in 1973. Under the European Economic Area agreement, which took effect January 1, 1994, there is basically free cross-border movement of capital, labor, goods, and services between Iceland, EU, and EEA countries. However, following the financial turmoil in fall 2008, movements of capital to and from Iceland were restricted by the Rules on Foreign Exchange issued by the Central Bank. These rules are intended to be temporary measures to strengthen and stabilize the exchange rate of the Icelandic krona. In August 2009, the Central Bank published a strategy on how to lift the restrictions. In November 2009, the first step of the strategy, permitting the inflow of foreign currency for new investments and the outflow of capital converted to foreign currencies from such investments was implemented. Subsequent phases will be introduced as conditions allow, but the Central Bank of Iceland has been acquiring ISK-denominated assets held by foreign entities in order to make it easier to lift capital controls.

Iceland has no railroads. Organized road building began around 1900 and has greatly expanded in the past decade. The current national road system connects most of the population centers along the coastal areas and consists of about 13,000 kilometers (8,125 mi.) of roads, of which about 4,800 kilometers (2,982 mi.) are paved. Regular air and sea service connect Reykjavik with the other main population centers.

Iceland has felt the economic impact of the April to May 2010 Eyjafjallajokull volcano eruption. In the short term, tourism and transportation were disrupted. In the longer term, the ash and flooding hurt some of Iceland's most productive agricultural lands, including the area that produces about 12% of Iceland's dairy products, 15% of its cattle, and 17% of its horses.

DEFENSE

The U.S. and Iceland signed a bilateral agreement in 1951 stipulating that the U.S. would make arrangements for Iceland's defense on behalf of NATO and provide for basing rights for U.S. forces in Iceland. In March 2006 the U.S. announced it would continue to provide for Iceland's defense but without permanently basing forces in the country; Naval Air Station Keflavik closed in September 2006 after half a century. The Government of Iceland expressed disappointment, and even opposition politicians opposed to the U.S. military presence criticized the manner of the closing, but bilateral discussions ensued to explore new ways of ensuring the country's security, with an emphasis on a "visible defense."

Negotiations concluded with a technical agreement on base closure issues (e.g., facilities return, environmental cleanup, residual value) signed on September 29, 2006, and a "Joint Understanding" on future bilateral security cooperation (focusing on defending Iceland and the North Atlantic region against emerging threats such as terrorism and trafficking) signed by the Secretary of State and Icelandic Prime Minister and Foreign Minister in Washington on October 11, 2006. The United States also cooperated with local officials to mitigate the impact of job losses at the Air Station, notably by encouraging U.S. investment in industry and tourism development in the Keflavik area. The Government of Iceland formed a public corporation to oversee redevelopment of the former base site. In fall 2007 the university-level "Keilir Atlantic Center of Excellence" began its operations with a focus on aviation, science and energy technology, and innovation. Former base housing is now rented by roughly 1,100 university students (at Keilir as well as institutions in Reykjavik) and commercial redevelopment of other areas of the former base is proceeding.

Cooperative activities in the context of the new agreements began almost immediately after the closure of the base, with the arrival of the amphibious ship USS Wasp in October 2006 as the first U.S. Navy port visit since 2002. Subsequent activities have included joint search and rescue, disaster surveillance, and maritime interdiction training with U.S. Navy and U.S. Coast Guard units, a port call by the U.S.-led NATO Standing Maritime Group 1, and U.S. deployments to support the NATO air surveillance mission in Iceland. The U.S. and Iceland jointly led planning and execution of Northern Viking air defense exercises in 2007 and 2008, and planning for subsequent joint endeavors is underway. Additionally, the U.S. Coast Guard's First District (Boston) and the Icelandic Coast Guard signed an agreement in 2008 to develop a joint training and exchange program, with the first activity--a joint search and rescue exercise--taking place in August 2008. In 2010 the Icelandic Coast Guard contributed a Bombardier Dash 8 fixed-wing aircraft to serve as a command and control platform and oil-spotting resource as part of the Deepwater Horizon response effort in the Gulf of Mexico.

In 2008, the Government of Iceland passed its first defense budget ($20 million) and established the Icelandic Defense Agency (IDA). The IDA oversaw support of cooperative defense activities, military exercises in Iceland, and maintenance of defense-related facilities, including the operation of the Iceland Air Defense System radar sites. The Government of Iceland, however, dissolved the short-lived IDA in January 2011. The responsibilities of the IDA are currently split between the Icelandic Coast Guard and the National Commissioner of the Icelandic Police, both of which are under the Ministry of the Interior.

The Government of Iceland contributes financially to NATO's international overhead costs and provides support to International Security Assistance Force (ISAF) operations in Afghanistan. Iceland hosted the NATO Foreign Ministers' Meeting in Reykjavik in June 1987 and again in May 2002. Iceland hosted the NATO Military Committee in April 2007 and the NATO Parliamentary Assembly in October 2007.

FOREIGN RELATIONS

Iceland maintains diplomatic and commercial relations with practically all nations, but its ties with other Nordic states, with the United States, and with the other NATO member states are particularly close. Icelanders remain especially proud of the role Iceland played in hosting the historic 1986 summit in Reykjavik between President Ronald Reagan and Soviet leader Mikhail Gorbachev, which set the stage for the end of the Cold War.

Iceland has greatly increased its international profile since the early 1990s. From the mid-1990s until 2007, Iceland opened a number of missions overseas, including in all five permanent member countries of the UN Security Council in anticipation of its (ultimately unsuccessful) bid for a rotating seat on the UN Security Council in 2009-2010. The buildup also included missions to the Council of Europe in Strasbourg and to the Organization for Security and Cooperation in Vienna. In 1998, it bolstered its delegation to NATO, assigning a permanent representative to the military committee for the first time ever. However, in the wake of the economic crisis in fall 2008, the Ministry for Foreign Affairs announced budget cuts resulting in the closure of four overseas missions. Iceland currently has 20 missions in 16 countries.

European Union (EU) membership was one of the top campaign issues in the 2009 parliamentary elections. The parliament voted in favor of applying for EU membership in July 2009, and Iceland was granted candidate status on June 17, 2010. Formal accession negotiations began at an intergovernmental conference in Brussels on July 27, 2010 and are expected to last several years. After the negotiations are concluded, the Icelandic people will determine by national referendum whether the country joins the EU. Icelanders also have a strong emotional bond with the Baltic states, and Iceland prides itself on being the first country to have recognized these countries' claim for independence in 1991.

Notwithstanding its status as an unarmed nation, Iceland has been eager to do its part to contribute to the maintenance of international peace and security. One of the niches it is helping to fill is in civilian peacekeeping and crisis management. It took a significant step forward in this area in 2001 by launching its Icelandic Crisis Response Unit (ICRU). In setting up the ICRU, the Ministry for Foreign Affairs established a roster of over 100 experts in various occupations (police officers, nurses, doctors, lawyers, engineers, journalists, etc.) who are specially trained and prepared to deploy to trouble spots abroad on short notice. Due to financial constraints, Iceland has had to dramatically reduce the number of deployed peacekeepers serving worldwide, although the country was one of the first on the ground after the devastating 2010 Haiti earthquake.

Membership in International Organizations
Iceland is a member of the following organizations: Arctic Council, Barents Euro-Arctic Council; Council of Baltic Sea States; Council of Europe; European Economic Area; European Free Trade Organization; EFTA Court; EFTA Surveillance Authority; North Atlantic Treaty Organization; Organization for Security and Cooperation in Europe; Organization for Economic Cooperation and Development; International Criminal Police Organization; International Council for the Exploration of the Sea; International Hydrographic Organization; International Maritime Satellite Organization; International Union for the Publication of Custom Tariffs; Nordic Council; North-East Atlantic Fisheries Commission; North Atlantic Salmon Conservation Organization; the International Whaling Commission; and the North Atlantic Marine Mammal Commission.

It also is a member of the United Nations and most of its related organizations, specialized agencies, and commissions, including the International Monetary Fund, World Trade Organization, World Tourism Organization, Food and Agricultural Organization, International Atomic Energy Agency, International Civil Aviation Organization, International Fund for Agricultural Development; Industrial Development Organization; International Labor Organization, International Maritime Organization, International Telecommunications Union, UN Educational, Scientific, and Cultural Organization, Universal Postal Union, World Health Organization, and World Meteorological Organization; World Intellectual Property Organization; International Bank for Reconstruction and Development; International Development Association; International Finance Corporation Multilateral Investment Guarantee Agency and International Center for Settlement of Investment Disputes; UN Conference on Disarmament; Economic Commission for Europe; UN High Commissioner for Refugees; Office for the High Commissioner for Human Rights; Commission of Human Rights; UN Conference on Trade and Development.

U.S.-ICELANDIC RELATIONS

U.S. policy aims to maintain close, cooperative relations with Iceland, both as a NATO ally and as a friend interested in the shared objectives of enhancing world peace; respect for human rights; economic development; arms control; and law enforcement cooperation, including the fight against terrorism, narcotics, and human trafficking. Moreover, the United States endeavors to strengthen bilateral economic and trade relations.

Principal U.S. Officials
Ambassador-- Robert C. Barber

Robert C. Barber was confirmed by the United States Senate on December 12, 2014, and sworn in by Vice President Biden on January 8, 2015, as the U.S. Ambassador to the Republic of Iceland. Prior to this, he was a partner at Looney & Grossman LLP, a law firm in Boston, Massachusetts, where he focused primarily on issues of start-up, small and medium-size companies and commercial litigation, and served many of these companies in the role of outside general counsel.

Deputy Chief of Mission--Samuel Watson
Political Officer--Joshua Rubin
Economic/Commercial Officer--Meredith Rubin
Management Officer--Michael Greer
Information Management Officer--Phil Bunch
Public Affairs Officer--Laura Gritz
Consular Officer--Kristyna Rabassa
Regional Security Officer--Marco Fernandez

The U.S. Embassy in Iceland is located at Laufasvegur 21, Reykjavik [tel. (354) 562-9100]. The Embassy's web site is **http://iceland.usembassy.gov/**.

TRAVEL AND BUSINESS INFORMATION

TRAVEL ALERTS, TRAVEL WARNINGS, TRIP REGISTRATION

The U.S. Department of State's Consular Information Program advises Americans traveling and residing abroad through Country Specific Information, Travel Alerts, and Travel Warnings. **Country Specific Information** exists for all countries and includes information on entry and exit requirements, currency regulations, health conditions, safety and security, crime, political disturbances, and the addresses of the U.S. embassies and consulates abroad. **Travel Alerts** are issued to disseminate information quickly about terrorist threats and other relatively short-term conditions overseas that pose significant risks to the security of American travelers. **Travel Warnings** are issued when the State Department recommends that Americans avoid travel to a certain country because the situation is dangerous or unstable.

For the latest security information, Americans living and traveling abroad should regularly monitor the Department's Bureau of Consular Affairs Internet web site at http://travel.state.gov, where current Worldwide Caution, Travel Alerts, and Travel Warnings can be found. The travel.state.gov website also includes information about passports, tips for planning a safe trip abroad and more. More travel-related information also is available at http://www.usa.gov/Citizen/Topics/Travel/International.shtml.

The Department's Smart Traveler app for U.S. travelers going abroad provides easy access to the frequently updated official country information, travel alerts, travel warnings, maps, U.S. embassy locations, and more that appear on the travel.state.gov site. Travelers can also set up e-tineraries to keep track of arrival and departure dates and make notes about upcoming trips. The app is compatible with iPhone, iPod touch, and iPad (requires iOS 4.0 or later).

The Department of State encourages all U.S. citizens traveling or residing abroad to register via the State Department's travel registration website or at the nearest U.S. embassy or consulate abroad (a link to the registration page is also available through the Smart Traveler app). Registration will make your presence and whereabouts known in case it is necessary to contact you in an emergency and will enable you to receive up-to-date information on security conditions.

Emergency information concerning Americans traveling abroad may be obtained by calling 1-888-407-4747 toll free in the U.S. and Canada or the regular toll line 1-202-501-4444 for callers outside the U.S. and Canada.

PASSPORTS

The National Passport Information Center (NPIC) is the U.S. Department of State's single, centralized public contact center for U.S. passport information. Telephone: 1-877-4-USA-PPT (1-877-487-2778); TDD/TTY: 1-888-874-7793. Passport information is available 24 hours, 7 days a week. You may speak with a representative Monday-Friday, 8 a.m. to 10 p.m., Eastern Time, excluding federal holidays

ICELAND LEGAL SYSTEM BASICS

Iceland is a Republic with a parliamentary government. The President, members of the Althingi and local authorities are elected in general elections held every four years.

The Althingi was established in 930 AD and was a key element of Iceland's existence as an independent state for several centuries after the settlement. However, in 1262-1264 Iceland came under the authority of the Norwegian crown and towards the end of the 14th century royal succession brought both Norway and Iceland under the control of the Danish crown. Iceland remained under the rule of Denmark until the 20th century. In 1903 it received home rule and parliamentary government, in 1918 the Act of Union made Iceland a sovereign state unified with Denmark through the person of the monarch. The country then received full independence when the union with Denmark was dissolved in 1944. The Republic's present Constitution dates from the same year, though many of its provisions are much older and can be traced back to 1874 when the country received its first constitution.

The Icelandic legal system is heavily influenced by the systems in the other Nordic countries, especially that of Denmark. The Nordic legal systems share several common features with continental European legal systems. Nevertheless, the legal systems of the Nordic countries have evolved distinct characteristics.

THE LEGISLATIVE POWER

According to the Constitution (Art. 2), the Althingi and the President of Iceland jointly exercise legislative power. In reality it is the Althingi which holds the power of legislating while the President gives parliamentary bills formal consent, see Art. 26 of the Constitution. Since the establishment of the Republic of Iceland in 1944, the President has only once refused consent, in the summer of 2004. The bill was on the ownership of media and was very controversial.

The Althingi consists of 63 elected members who sit in a single chamber. Parliamentary elections must be held at least every four years, the next one being in May 2007. There are now five parties represented in the Althingi (the Independence Party, Social Democratic Alliance, the Progress Party, the Left-Green Movement and the Liberal Party).

All proposed legislation must be submitted within six months of the commencement of the parliamentary session, i.e. before 1st April, but a majority of Althingi can admit a bill which has been submitted after this deadline. According to the Constitution, Art. 44, no draft legislation may be adopted until it has received three readings by the Althingi. Bills are generally referred to committee between the first and second readings. Once the bill has been adopted and confirmed by the President it has to be published, see Art. 27 of the Constitution.

THE EXECUTIVE POWER

The President and other governmental authorities exercise executive power, see Art. 2 of the Constitution. However, the executive power of the President is of a more formal than actual nature. Art. 13 and 19 of the Constitution stipulate that the President entrusts his authority to Ministers and that his signature validates a legislative act or government measure when countersigned by a Minister. According to Art. 15 of the Constitution, the President appoints and dismisses individual ministers. This has to be seen in the light of the rule of representative government.

The President is bound to follow the will of the majority of Parliament. He has the obligation to invite the Party which is most likely to be able to form a Government. If it proves to be impossible to form a Government that has a majority of seats in Parliament, a Government based on a minority can be formed or a Government of members outside of Parliament. The latter scenario has only happened once since the establishment of the Republic, during 1942-1944. Since 1995 there have been successive coalition governments of the Independence Party and the Progressive Party.

The President distributes assignments between ministers according to Art. 15 of the Constitution. The distribution is enacted through the Act on the Government Offices of Iceland No. 73/1969 (only in Icelandic). There it is stipulated that the Government Offices of Iceland are to be divided into the following ministries; the Prime Minister's Office, the Ministry of Justice and Ecclesiastical Affairs, the Ministry of Social Affairs, the Ministry of Finance, Statistics Iceland, Ministry of Health and Social Security, Ministries of Industry and Commerce, Ministry of Agriculture (homepage only in Icelandic), Ministry of Education, Science and Culture, Ministry of Communications, Ministry of Fisheries,Ministry for the Environment, and the Minstry for Foreign Affairs. Each ministry typically consists of a central department with a number of ministerial agencies under its jurisdiction.

According to Art. 78 of the Constitution some public tasks are to be delegated to local municipalities. The extent and circumstances of the delegations is defined by the Local Government Act No. 45/1998. According to the recent reform of the structure of local and regional governance, Iceland is now divided into 79 local municipalities. Each municipality is governed by an elected body of locally elected representatives.

THE JUDICIARY

The Constitution stipulates in Art. 2 that judges exercise judicial power and according to Art. 59 the organization of the judiciary can only be established by law. The main Act on the organization of the judiciary is Act No. 15/1998 on Courts. The judicial court system of Iceland comprises 8 District Courts, of which the Reykjavík District Court is by far the largest, and the Supreme Court (Hæstiréttur Íslands). Additionally, there are two Special Courts; the Labour Court (*in Icelandic* Félagsdómur) which deals with trade union matters and industrial disputes according to the Act on Trade Unions and Industrial Disputes, No. 80/1938 (unofficial English translation), see Section IV of the Act. The decisions of Félagsdómur are available online (only in Icelandic) since the year 2000. The other Special Court is the Court of Impeachment (*in Icelandic* Landsdómur) which has competence if Ministers, in pursuance of their official tasks, are impeached, see Art. 14 of the Constitution and Act No. 3/1963 (not translated). Landsdómur was established in 1905 but has never been convened.

In order to guarantee the independence of the judiciary it is stipulated in Art. 61 of the Constitution that in the performance of their official duties, judges shall be guided solely by the law. In the same Article it is further stipulated that those judges who do not also have administrative functions cannot be discharged from office except by a judicial decision, nor may they be transferred to another office against their will, except in the event of re-organization of the judiciary.

The district courts in Iceland have jurisdiction in civil as well as criminal cases. The judges of the district courts are 38 in number and are appointed to their offices for an indefinite period of time by the Minister of Justice, see Art. 12 of Act No. 15/1998. The Judicial Council, which is established according to Act No. 15/1998, deals with matters pertaining to the district courts, see Art. 13.-15. It was established in 1998 to secure to a greater extent the independence of the Judiciary from the executive power. The Judicial Council's authority only extends to the district courts.

The Supreme Court is the only court of appeal and has nationwide jurisdiction. It is composed of nine judges, commissioned for an indefinite period of time by the President of Iceland as proposed by the Minister of Justice, see Art. 4 of Act No. 15/1998. Judgments in criminal cases may be referred to the Supreme Court without any restriction while the appeal of civil judgments is dependent on minor requirements related to the minimum interests at stake.

LEGAL RESOURCES

Iceland has a civil law legal system and thus Icelandic law is characterized by written law. Major sources of law in Iceland include the*Constitution*, *statutory legislation*, and *regulatory statutes*. Other legal resources are *precedent* and *customary law*. The recognition of*tradition of culture* (*in Icelandic* eðli máls) does bear significantly on Icelandic law in a variety of contexts. Act No. 15/2005 stipulates how official material, including adopted Acts, are published.

THE CONSTITUTION

The Constitutional Act represents the highest national legal authority. Iceland received its first Constitution in 1874 and the current Constitution of 1944 (Act. No. 33/19944) can be traced back to it. The Constitution is composed of seven Chapters, with a total of 79 Articles: Chapter One provides for Iceland's status as a Republic with a parliamentary government, and the separation of the three principal branches of the government;

Chapter two stipulates the election and powers of the President; Chapter three and four set out the composition and mandate of the parliament; Chapter five addresses the organization and role of the judiciary; Chapter six lays down that the Evangelical Lutheran Church shall be the State Church in Iceland; Chapter seven includes thirteen human rights provisions, including the right to equal treatment, freedom from interference with privacy and right to freedom of opinion and belief.

The Constitution has been revised seven times. Fundamental changes were made to the human rights chapter of the Icelandic Constitution with Constitutional Act No. 97/1995. The bill accompanying the Act made several references to the European Convention on Human Rights as well as to other Council of Europe and United Nations human rights instruments to which Iceland is a party. Further amendments to the Constitution are envisioned. Early in 2005 the office of the Prime Minister appointed a committee to consider revisions of the Constitution. The committee was to finish its task at the end of 2006. Proposals to amend or supplement the Constitution may be introduced at regular as well as extraordinary sessions of the Althingi. If the proposal is adopted, the Althingi shall immediately be dissolved and a general election held. If the Althingi then passes the resolution unchanged, it shall be confirmed by the President of the Republic and come into force as constitutional law (see Art. 79). The Constitution is available in English Translation.

STATUTORY LAW

Except with respect to constitutional issues, legislation enjoys primacy as a source of law. With the increasing complexity of economic and social life, the amount and importance of legislation has even increased. The area of private law is dominated by a range of individual statutory acts and the area of general criminal law is governed by the General Penal Code No. 19, February 12, 1940 (official translation). New general revised acts have been adopted in principal areas of law, such as the Act on Customs (Act No. 88/2005) and the Act in Respect of Children (Act No. 2003). In the last few years, numerous pieces of legislation have been adopted in certain fields of law, such as in banking, communications, corporations and intellectual property rights.

Legal Acts are published in the Legal Gazette (Stjórnartíðindi), section A. Since 2005 publication has been in electronic form. All Acts are also accessible on the Althingi's homepage under the heading "Lagasafn" but as with the Legal Gazette they are only in Icelandic. Official and unofficial translations of certain Acts can be found on the web-pages of the relevant ministries, accessible through the portalwww.government.is.

REGULATORY LAW

Frequently, statutory acts give the administration the authority to issue regulations. As sources of law, statutory acts prevail over regulations.Public executive regulations and directives are published in the Legal Gazette, section B. They are also available online on www.reglugerd.is, only in Icelandic. Official and unofficial translations of certain regulations can be found on the web-pages of the relevant ministries, accessible through the portal www.government.is.

PRECEDENTS

Being a civil law country, court practice in Iceland does not have the same authoritative role as in Common Law countries. The Supreme Court has no duty to follow its earlier decisions, and the district courts are not obligated to adhere to earlier decisions of the Supreme Court. However, in matters of legal uncertainty, the decisions of the Supreme Court have considerable authority for the disposition of future cases. In certain areas of law which did or do not have extensive statutory legislation, e.g., tort, the decisions of the Supreme Court are a source of law of central importance.

Since the beginning of the year 2006, the decisions of the district courts in Iceland have been published online (only in Icelandic) on theJudicial Councils (in Icelandic) webpage. The decisions of the Supreme Court are also published online on the Courts homepage (in Icelandic).

CUSTOMARY LAW

In Iceland, a custom can acquire the force of law, i.e., become a source of law. For instance, customary law has been an important source of law in Constitutional matters.

TRADITION OF CULTURE (*IN ICELANDIC* EÐLI MÁLS)

Tradition of culture refers to considerations of fairness, justice and feasibility as to needs of the society and resembles to some extent the legal term *equity*. Some commentators consider the use of this source of law as distinctive for Nordic legal traditions. In particular, when other sources of law have not been able to establish a rule of law, courts in Iceland have in some cases relied on Tradition of Culture.

STATEMENTS AND DECISIONS BY ADMINISTRATIVE AUTHORITIES

In some areas of law statements by an administrative organ can carry considerable authority. For instance, in the area of administrative law, the statements of the parliament´s Ombudsman (*in Icelandic* Umboðsmaður Althingis) carry considerably authority. The Ombudsman´s statements are published and are also available on his website. Similarly, in the area of tax law, the decisions of the Internal Revenue Board can carry considerable weight.

THE EEA AND ITS EFFECT ON ICELANDIC LEGISLATION

Iceland is a member of the European Economic Area (EEA). The Agreement on the EEA, which came into force in 1994, extends the Single Market of the European Union (EU) to three out of the four EFTA countries, namely Iceland, Norway and Liechtenstein.

Membership of the EEA has affected Icelandic legislation considerably. The EEA Agreement is based on the primary legislation of the EU, as developed over the past 30 years and on the relevant succeeding secondary legislation (Acquis Communautaire). To achieve homogeneity between the EEA and EU, the agreement incorporates hundreds of acts, largely identical to the relevant parts of the EC legislation, and these acts are made part of the internal legal order of the contracting parties. Importantly, this process is continuous; each month a number of pieces of EC legislation, relevant for the EEA, are incorporated in the agreement by decision of EEA Joint Committee.

The decisions of the EEA Joint Committee are published in the EEA Supplement to the Offical Journal of the European Union a weekly legal gazette containing EEA-related texts from EFTA and EU bodies.

INTERNATIONAL LAW

With respect to the relation between municipal law and international law, Iceland adheres to the principle of dualism. Therefore, ratified international treaties do not assume the force of domestic law, but rather are only binding according to international law. The Supreme Court of Iceland has sought to interpret Icelandic law, as far as possible, in conformity with Iceland's international obligations. The Court has made several references to international obligations undertaken by Iceland, and it has interpreted both the Constitution and other laws in coherence with such obligations. Interestingly, these references include also instruments which have not been incorporated into Icelandic law, such as the United Nations Convention on the Law of the Sea and the International Covenant on Civil and Political Rights.

The European Convention on Human Rights was incorporated into Icelandic law by Act No. 62/1994. Following its incorporation, its provisions can be directly invoked in court as domestic legislation. Other major human rights instruments ratified by Iceland, such as the International Covenant on Civil and Political Right and Convention on the Rights of the Child, have not been incorporated into Icelandic law.

STRATEGIC INFORMATION AND DEVELOPMENTS

ECONOMIC STRATEGY

Economic prosperity rests on a successful implementation of an ambitious long term strategy for the economy. The Ministry of Finance and Economic Affairs plays a central role in the formulation and implementation of the Government's economic policy, taking into consideration both the domestic and international macroeconomic situation and developments.

The Ministry prepares economic analyses, monitors economic indicators, communicates with foreign rating agencies and participates in economic and financial cooperation through various international organisations.

An efficient domestic financial market fosters economic stability and a high standard of living. The Ministry drafts legislation in this sector, taking into account financial stability and consumer protection in financial markets. The majority of domestic financial market legislation applies the harmonised rules of the European Economic Area (EEA). These have undergone major changes by the European Union since the financial turmoil of 2008. Iceland is obliged to transpose into Icelandic law the European rules which are annexed to the EEA Agreement.

THE PUBLIC FINANCES

The Ministry of Finance and Economic Affairs is responsible for implementing the Public Finances as a whole on the basis of the Public Finance Act. Among the focal points are working procedures in shaping public financial policy, i.e. the finances of both central and local government, through a fiscal policy statement and a fiscal strategy plan. The strategy plan covers the upcoming five-year period and is updated each spring.The Act also includes a framework for the procedure and preparation of the corresponding state budget together with annual budgets of the various ministries.

At the first meeting of the Icelandic Parliament's autumn session the Minister of Finance and Economic Affairs submits the Government's budget for the coming calendar year. The budget seeks parliamentary approval for expenditures in a total of 34 expenditure areas, over 100 expenditure functions and any and all obligations of Group A Treasury entities. In drafting the annual budget the government is restricted to the expenditure framework approved by the Althingi in its fiscal strategy for the 34 expenditure areas.

The Central Government's revenues are comprised primarily of taxes and fees charged and collected based on various Acts. Preparing draft legislation amending such Acts to reflect the current Government's policy is another task of the Ministry, which also assesses the underlying assumptions and impact on the economy. No payments can be made from the Treasury which have not been authorised in the budget or supplementary budget.

The Althingi debates the budget bill in three readings. Parliamentarians discuss the premises for expenditures in each field, the distribution of budget allocations to individual functions and the emphases which are laid out in the budget for the activities of each function. At the same time the Althingi will debate the premises for the Government's taxation policy and income generation. Between readings the Budget Committee reviews the bill.

Allocations to institutions and projects are shown in a special appendix to the bill which will accompany the budget legislation once adopted.

FISCAL PLAN 2019-2023 IMPROVED SOCIAL INFRASTRUCTURE, LOWER TAXES AND AND BETTER PUBLIC SERVICES

The first Fiscal Strategy Plan of the coalition Government formed by the Left-Green Movement, the Independence Party, and the Progressive Party, reflects the Government's commitment to ensure that society as a whole will enjoy the benefits of the ongoing economic growth phase while strengthening social stability and the quality of life for the future.

The plan ensures that the policy of maintaining a fiscal surplus will continue, while promoting responsibility and steadfastness in public sector activities. The increased strength of the Treasury, lower interest costs, and the prospect of diminishing demand pressures in the economy put the Government in a good position to follow up on its goals of stepping up investment in social infrastructure and further supporting social welfare services.

Since 2013, the outstanding debt of the Treasury has been lowered from ISK 1.500bn to less than ISK 900bn, or by a total of ISK 600bn. Lower debts along with the resulting reduction in interest costs have contributed towards a growing fiscal space. In addition, GDP has doubled from 1998 and is now higher than ever before. In spite of significantly increased allocations to all key spending areas, the public consumption of the central government will remain constant relative to GDP over the period, at around 11.2%. The increase in allocations therefore aligns well with the economy's capacity to finance improved services for the public at large.

SUBSTANTIAL INVESTMENT IN INFRASTRUCTURE

Investment will grow markedly in 2019, or by just over ISK 13bn, and will peak in 2021. Over the period as a whole from 2019 until 2023, investments in all expenditure areas is projected to total ISK 338bn.

Large-scale investment in transportation infrastructure will be financed in part with a temporary increase in dividend payments from State-owned financial institutions. In all, investment allocations are projected at ISK 124bn over the period, and for three years beginning in 2019 a special annual contribution of ISK 5.5bn will be added. The nationwide installation of fibre-optic cable connections is scheduled for completion in 2020.

Total investment in hospital services is estimated at nearly ISK 75bn, most of it for the construction of the new Landspítalinn hospital on Hringbraut. Construction of a new treatment centre for the hospital will begin in 2018, and the bulk of construction will take place in 2020-2023.

The fiscal plan also provides for further development of infrastructure and other projects pertaining to popular wilderness areas and other tourist destinations.

Other large investments include the purchase of helicopters for the Coast Guard and construction of nursing homes as well as the House of Icelandic Studies.

BETTER SERVICES

Allocations to healthcare will total about ISK 249bn per year by the end of the period. The aggregate amount will have increased by about ISK 40bn from 2018, or more than 19%, in real terms. Apart from the construction of Landspítalinn hospital and real growth in the healthcare system, particular emphasis is placed on mental health services, on strengthening primary healthcare centres, and on reducing patients' co-payments.

Allocations to social and housing affairs and benefit payments for the elderly and disabled will total about ISK 226bn through 2023. The cumulative increase in allocations totals ISK 28bn, a 14% increase in real terms. Changes are planned in the benefit system for disability pensioners so as to improve their living standards and promote participation in the community. It is also planned to increase maximum childbirth leave payments and lengthen the childbirth leave period.

In education and culture, allocations to university-level education will increase markedly. Contributions to universities were increased by more than ISK 2bn in the budget for 2018, and an additional increase of over ISK 2.8bn is planned for the period covered by the fiscal plan. The contribution per student increases as well, both at the high-scool and university level. In the area of arts and culture, significant funds will be devoted to an action plan for language technologies, in addition to the large allocations made in the 2018 budget. The country's main libraries will be strengthened, and professional artists' stipends and project funds will be supported.

Allocations to environmental affairs will be increased by nearly ISK 4bn over the period, an increase of 35% from the 2017 budget. Preparatory work for the establishment of a national park in the central highlands will move foreward, land patrolling will be supported strongly, and allocations for the reduction of greenhouse gas emissions will be increased in line with the objective of making Iceland carbon-neutral by 2040.

In addition to an increase of ISK 900m for public security and criminal justice in the 2018 budget, it is now planned to increase allocations by nearly 14% in 2019. It is planned to improve border control and integrate border administration, in part based on Iceland's obligations under the Schengen agreement. In addition, allocations for law enforcement and the operation of the Coast Guard will be increased by over ISK 800m.

TAXATION MEASURES

In the field of foreign affairs, it should be noted that allocations for development aid will increase from 0.26% of GNI this year to 0.35% by 2022. Contributions to the EEA development fund also increase over the period, and increases for defence cooperation with the US and membership of NATO are also planned.

The Government's aim is to continue to reduce the taxburden, make taxation fairer, and ensure effective tax monitoring. The Government intends to consult with the main social partners about plans to reduce the tax rate in the lower bracket of the income tax by 1 percentage point, in stages, and simultaneously to undertake a comprehensive review of the personal income tax system, alongside a review of benefits systems. Of particular concern is public support for families with children and housing support, with targeted financial assistance to less well-off households.

The payroll tax is to be lowered by 0.25% in 2019, from 6.85% to 6.6%. Further reduction will depend on, among other things, the results of consultation with the social partners concerning changes in labour market benefits funded with payroll tax, and the Treasury overall balance.

Value-added tax on books will be eliminated at the beginning of 2019, and a year later, payments of royalties collected by recognised rights-holders' associations will be taxed as assets and not as income.

The special bank tax will be reduced from 0.376% to 0.145% over the period. Tax concessions for research and development costs will be increased in 2019, with the aim of removing the ceiling on them later in the period. The tax base for investment tax will be reviewed with the aim of taxing real returns. The impact of those changes will emerge in 2020.

At the beginning of this year, the carbon tax on fuel was increased by 50%. It is planned to increase it by 10% in 2019 and another 10% in 2020. Ways to collect fees from tourists will be explored. The aim is to generate revenue from 2020 onwards.

Good cooperation with the labour market and continued debt reduction

The economy is well balanced at present, after strong growth in recent years. According to official economic forecasts and analysis, the outlook is for slower growth in coming years. The Government emphasises successful cooperation with the social partners so as to preserve economic stability and enhance social welfare. In this way, it will be possible to work towards favourable results from wage negotiations in coming years, so as to preserve the unusually strong real wage growth that has been achieved in recent years, through moderate pay rises that will continue to deliver increased purchasing power to households.

The fiscal plan assumes that there will be a continuing surplus on central and local government operations in each year covered by the plan, in accordance with the Fiscal Policy Plan that was presented together with the 2018 fiscal budget and has now been approved by Parliament. Treasury debt has been reduced markedly from the 2012 peak.

The objective is to lower total public sector debt from 36% of GDP in 2018 to less than the legally stipulated ceiling of 30% of GDP by end-2019, a year earlier than envisaged in the Fiscal Policy Plan,and that the debt level will have declined to 22% of GDP at the end of 2023.

MEDIUM-TERM DEBT MANAGEMENT STRATEGY 2018 - 2022

This strategy, which lays down objectives and criteria for Government debt management during the period 2018-2022, is presented on the basis of the fiscal plan in accordance with the Article 38 of the Act on Public Sector Finances, no. 123/2015. The strategy is to be presented annually. The Medium-Term Debt Management Strategy is presented over a horizon of five years and is based on the previous Strategy, issued in autumn 2016.

The Medium-Term Debt Management Strategy 2018-2022 (MTDS) lays down the government's plans for financing its activities during this period. The aim is to map out a clear debt management policy with quantitative targets. The strategy thereby creates a framework for debt management measures, and its principal objective is to ensure that the Treasury's financing need and payment obligations are met at the lowest possible cost that is consistent with a prudent risk policy. It is also intended to encourage further development of efficient primary and secondary markets for domestic Government securities.

The strategy describes debt management objectives and guidelines, the current composition of the debt portfolio, inherent risk factors, and contingent liabilities. It also describes the institutional structure of debt management and explains how information disclosure to market agents and investors is carried out.

The Ministry of Finance and Economic Affairs is responsible for the central government's debt management, formulates its debt management strategy, and makes decisions regarding securities issuance. Government Debt Management, a special department within the Central Bank of Iceland, is responsible for executing the Treasury's debt management strategy in accordance with an agreement between the two parties.

Benchmark issues of Treasury bonds are structured so that each series is large enough to ensure effective price formation in the secondary market. Each year it will be ensured that there is effective price formation with two-, five-, and ten-year benchmark Treasury bonds. In order to reduce refinancing risk, the aim is to keep the redemption profile of Treasury securities as even as possible. The average time to maturity should be at least five years and no longer than seven years.

The Treasury has borrowed in foreign currencies in order to expand the Central Bank's foreign exchange reserves. The foreign borrowing strategy is aimed at securing regular access to international capital markets and appealing to a diversified investor base. Attempts shall be made to maintain 1-2 benchmarks in market issues at any given time so as to facilitate domestic firms' access to foreign credit if market conditions and the Treasury debt position permits.

At year-end 2016, gross Treasury debt was equivalent to 46% of GDP. The aim is to reduce total debt over the period to approximately 25% of GDP by end-2022. Net debt – that is, debt net of interest-bearing assets, excluding stability contributions – amounted to 32% of GDP at the end of 2016. The aim is to reduce it to below 15% of GDP by year-end 2022. Fiscal policy formation assumes that total general government debt – that is, debt excluding pension obligations and accounts payable, and net of cash and bank deposits – will fall from 50% of GDP at the end of 2015 to 23% of GDP by the end of 2022.

1 DEBT MANAGEMENT OBJECTIVES AND GUIDELINES

The Government's overall debt management objectives are as follows:

1. To ensure that the Treasury's financing need and payment obligations are met at the lowest possible long-term cost that is consistent with a prudent risk policy;

2. To establish a sustainable debt service profile that is consistent with the Government's medium-term debt service capacity and minimises refinancing risk;

3. To maintain and encourage further development of efficient primary and secondary markets for domestic Government securities;

4. To broaden the Government's investor base and diversify funding sources.

In order to meet the demand for new Treasury issues and to increase the liquidity of benchmark series, efforts will be made to exchange non-marketable Treasury debt for benchmark series insofar as market conditions permit. Such exchanges must be consistent with the objective of minimising the Treasury's interest expense in the long run, while ensuring a prudent degree of risk.

1.1 DEBT MANAGEMENT GUIDELINES

The debt portfolio is structured so as to minimise overall risk and encourage the development of a well-functioning market that can attract a diverse group of investors and set pricing benchmarks for other financial products.

The Treasury emphasises the issuance of nominal debt, as nominal Treasury bonds form the basis of an effective domestic bond market. Issuance of indexed Treasury bonds is irregular and is determined by the financing need and the circumstances prevailing at any given time. New Treasury loans taken in foreign currencies are used primarily to expand the Central Bank's foreign exchange reserves or to refinance outstanding market issues.

The guidelines for the composition of the Treasury's debt portfolio are as follows:

Non-indexed debt	60-80%
Indexed debt	10-20%
Foreign loans	10-20%

Benchmark issues will be structured so that each series is large enough to ensure effective price formation in the secondary market. The number and size of the series shall take account of Treasury debt. The goal is for each series to have a final size of ISK 40-70 bn, except for two-year bonds, whose minimum final size will be ISK 15 bn.

The average time to maturity of the debt portfolio shall be at least five years and no longer than seven years.

The Government's domestic deposits with the Central Bank of Iceland shall average about ISK 40 bn.

1.2 QUANTITATIVE TARGETS

Clear, quantitative targets for debt management demonstrate the sustainability of Treasury debt. The targets are based on the fiscal plan for 2018-2022, the outlook for Treasury performance, the economic outlook, and the overall state of the economy. In accordance with the fiscal plan for 2018-2022, the targets are as follows:

- The ratio of Treasury debt to GDP shall be about 25% by 2022,

- Total general government debt according to the debt rule shall be 23% by year-end 2022.

These targets are subject to revision of macroeconomic and fiscal assumptions. They will be updated as necessary.

2 DOMESTIC BOND ISSUANCE

The Treasury's financing need will be met through issuance of Government securities in the domestic market and a reduction in the Treasury's deposits with the Central Bank of Iceland. This section focuses on medium-term financing needs and Treasury deposits. It also discusses Treasury securities issuance, including the redemption profile policy, average duration, and the build-up of benchmark issues.

2.1 FINANCING NEED

The Treasury's estimated financing need is based on the assumptions in the National Budget for 2017 and on the assumptions presented by the Ministry of Finance and Economic Affairs in Fiscal Policy 2018-2022 [Icelandic: Ríkisfjármálaáætlun 2018-2022.]

The net borrowing requirement is either positive or negative. A positive balance indicates a surplus on Treasury operations and financial activities, which can be utilised to reduce debt. A negative balance reflects a deficit on Treasury operations and financial activities, which must be financed through borrowing or a decrease in cash and cash equivalents.

Table 1 shows the net financing balance according to Treasury estimates for 2018-2022. According to the estimates, the net financing balance will be positive in the next few years.

Net borrowing requirement (ISK m)

2018	2019	2020	2021	2022
34,600	23,600	34,100	38,700	25,800

Table 1

2.2 DEPOSITS

The Medium-Term Debt Management Strategy for 2017-2021 introduced the concept of active liquidity management and noted that the objective was to adopt it in Q4/2016. Active liquidity management entails allowing the Treasury to take and grant short-term loans in the market so as to smooth out fluctuations in its deposit accounts. The aim is that deposit balances should average as close to ISK 40 bn as possible, instead of the previous reference balance of ISK 60-70 bn. Conditions could arise that necessitate higher balances for a short period – for instance, when large Treasury bond maturities are drawing near – and with active liquidity management, it is possible to lend a portion of the deposits while building them up so as to earn interest income on them.

The first loan agreements were made in Q1/2017, and the frequency of such agreements has been gradually increasing. At the same time, estimates of the Treasury's liquidity position have become more accurate, as they are based on estimated daily revenues and expenses, together with payment flows from revenues and loans granted. The loan agreements to date have been for amounts ranging from ISK 1 bn to ISK 7 bn, with maturities of 1-26 days, and as many as five contracts have been in effect simultaneously.

Treasury deposits with and without liquidity management

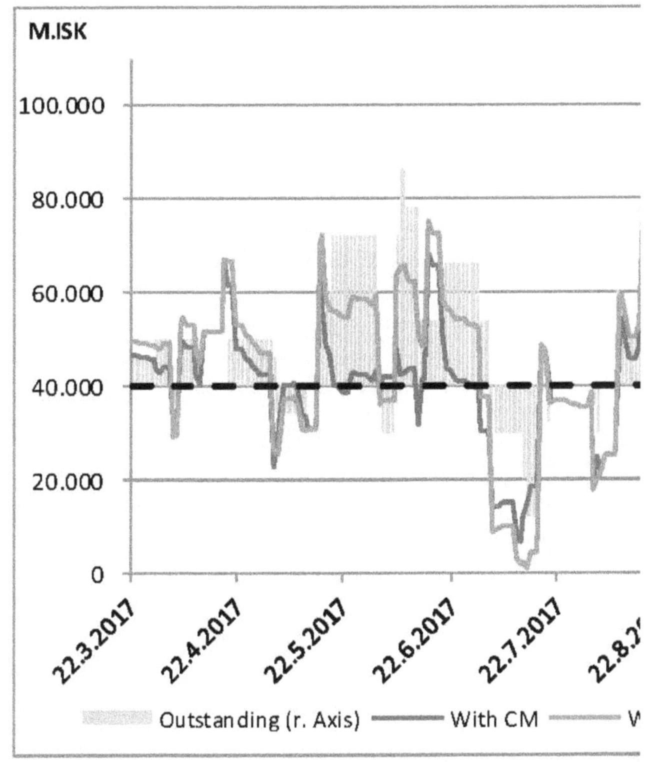

Chart 1

There is much to be gained by developing methods to
at the same time, there is increased security in being
balance is too low.

Chart 1

There is much to be gained by developing methods to achieve more efficient use of capital, and at the same time, there is increased security in being able to take short-term loans if the cash balance is too low.

2.3 STRUCTURE OF GOVERNMENT SECURITIES

This section focuses on the structure and set-up for issuance of Government securities in the domestic market.

2.3.1 STRUCTURE OF BENCHMARK SERIES

Benchmark series will be structured so that each series is large enough to ensure effective price formation in the secondary market. The number and size of the series shall take account of Treasury debt. Each year, effective price formation for two-, five-, and ten-year benchmark bonds will be ensured.

By definition, when a ten-year series is first auctioned, it will mature after approximately eleven years. Bonds will be sold in the series until nine years remain to maturity, whereupon issuance is suspended. The bond is reopened at about six years to maturity and is offered for sale until about four years remain to maturity (five-year series). Finally, the bond is reopened at two years

to maturity (two-year series). Effective price formation will be ensured in series falling under the two-, five-, and ten-year benchmark series categories each year, and each year's issuance in each series will be determined by current financing needs and the size of the series concerned. Nominal and inflation-indexed Treasury bonds with other maturities will be issued irregularly, depending on the Treasury's financing need and the conditions prevailing at the time.

The goal is for each series to have a final size of ISK 40-70 bn, except for two-year bonds, whose minimum final size will be ISK 15 bn. Attempts will be made to expedite the build-up of the series until they reach a size sufficient to ensure effective price formation in the secondary market. The size of bond series will also be determined by the Treasury's financing need at any given time. This goal pertains primarily to issuance of new series, although efforts will be made in coming years to adapt outstanding series to it if the opportunity presents itself.

Treasury bills will be issued for up to six months, with the final maturity to be announced in the issuance calendar for each year. Monthly issuance of Treasury bills will vary, depending on investor demand and the Treasury's financing need at any given time. With more active liquidity management, there is the possibility that the Treasury will issue shorter bills in order to address fluctuations in its current account.

Benchmark issuance

Series	Maturity	Issuing amount	Frequency of issue
Treasury bills	Up to 6 months	Variable	Variable
Nominal Treasury bonds	2 years	ISK 40-70 billion if initially issued with a longer maturity; ISK 15-70 billion if issued for only 2 years	Annually
Nominal Treasury bonds	5 years	ISK 40-70 billion	Annually
Nominal Treasury bonds	10 years	ISK 40-70 billion	Annually
Nominal Treasury bonds	Other	ISK 40-70 billion	Irregular
Inflation-linked Treasury bonds	Other	ISK 40-70 billion	Irregular

Table 2

2.3.2 TREASURY BOND ISSUANCE FROM 2018 ONWARDS

According to the National Budget, issuance for 2017 was estimated at ISK 45 bn. An example of Treasury bond issuance in coming years is shown in Table 3. It should be noted that the table is only for illustrative purposes, and actual issuance plans may be subject to change. The table includes Treasury securities already issued, with the identifier codes of the series concerned. The identifier RB 17 0206 means that the bond is a nominal bond maturing on 6 February 2017. For Treasury bonds that have not yet been issued, the first number indicates the maturity year and the second number indicates the length of the bond; i.e., two-, five-, or ten-year benchmark series. The shaded cells show when the series are open. Issuance in series with other maturities will be irregular, depending on the Treasury's financing need and investor demand.

Sample issuance calendar

Year	2017	2018	2019	2020	2021	2022	2023	2024	2025
	RB	RB	RB	RB	RB	RB	RB	RB	RB
0	**17 0206**	18-2 yr	**19 0226**	**20 0205**	21-2 yr	**22 1026**	23-2 yr	24-2 yr	25-2 yr
1	18-2 yr	**19 0226**	**20 0205**	21-2 yr	**22 1026**	23-2 yr	24-2 yr	**25 0612**	**26 0612**
2	**19 0226**	**20 0205**	21-2 yr	**22 1026**	23-2 yr	24-2 yr	**25 0612**	**26 0612**	**26 0612**
3	**20 0205**		**22 1026**			**25 0612**			28-5 yr
4		22 1026			25 0612			28-5 yr	
5	22 1026			25 0612			28-5 yr		
6			25 0612			28-5 yr			**31 0124**
7		**25 0612**			28-10 yr			**31 0124**	
8	**25 0612**			28-10 yr			**31 0124**		
9			28-10 yr			31 0124			34 - 10 yr
10		28-10 yr			31 0124			34 - 10 yr	
11	28-10 yr			31 0124			34 - 10 yr		

Treasury bond 2 yr **Treasury bond 5 yr** **Treasury bond 10 yr**

Table 3

2.3.3 REDEMPTION PROFILE

One of the objectives of Treasury debt management is to ensure that the redemption profile of Treasury securities is as even as possible. In order to reduce refinancing risk, the aim is to keep the size of each series at or below ISK 70 bn upon maturity. Until 2016, the maximum size of each series was set at ISK 100 bn. In view of the significant reduction in the Treasury's domestic issuance need, which stems both from improved performance and from irregular revenues that will be used to pay down debt, the maximum size of each series has been lowered to ISK 70 bn; instead, the emphasis on ensuring price formation with two-, five-, and ten-year benchmark series will continue. The new maximum size applies primarily to new benchmark series, although attempts will be made in coming years to reduce the size of outstanding bonds with buybacks and exchange auctions to the extent that market conditions permit. Figure 2 shows the redemption profile of domestic liabilities at year-end 2016, excluding Treasury bills.

Domestic redemption profile

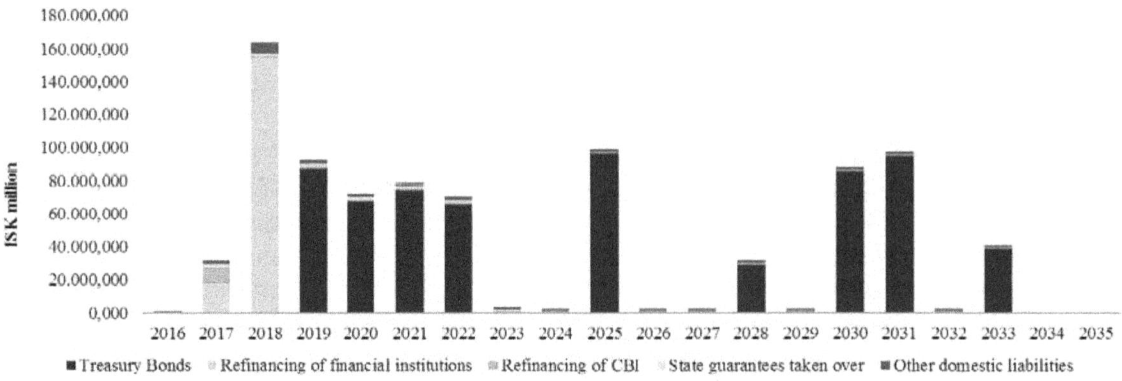

Chart 2

In 2008, the Treasury issued a five-year inflation-indexed bond to recapitalise the Central Bank of Iceland after the collapse of the banks. The bond was later converted to a nominal amortisation bond. The outstanding balance was ISK 28.5 bn at the end of 2016 and ISK 18.5 bn at the time the spring plan was issued. The bond was paid off in full at the end of May.

The Treasury's largest single maturity is in 2018, when RIKH 18 1009 matures. The series, a special issue undertaken to capitalise the financial institutions, is offset by share capital. The outstanding balance of the bond was ISK 171.7 bn at the end of 2016. In the coming term, it is planned to continue reducing it prior to maturity so as to reduce refinancing risk.

3 FOREIGN BOND ISSUANCE

New Treasury loans taken in foreign currencies are used primarily to expand the Central Bank's foreign exchange reserves or to refinance outstanding market issues. The structure of Treasury debt provides the flexibility to borrow funds in foreign currencies and requires that foreign debt constitute 10-20% of the loan portfolio. The need for foreign borrowings is met as it occurs, and when decisions are made, it is important to consider exchange rate risk, but also the Treasury's role in ensuring that Iceland has access to foreign capital markets.

The strategy for foreign debt financing aims at maintaining regular access to international credit markets and facilitating access to a diverse investor group. To this end, the Treasury aims to issue bonds in foreign markets on a regular basis. The main purpose of such issuance is to refinance outstanding marketable instruments. However, the flexibility for foreign borrowing provides an opportunity to finance specific projects in the future or to use the funds for a specific purpose. Government issuance in foreign markets facilitates domestic firms' access to foreign credit and provides an important benchmark for borrowing terms. The aim is to maintain 1-2 such benchmarks in foreign bond issues if market conditions and the Treasury debt position permit. Regular issuance of marketable bonds in the international capital markets is also intended to enhance name recognition of the Republic of Iceland as an issuer.

At the beginning of this year, there were two outstanding foreign Treasury bonds: a USD 1 bn bond maturing in 2022 and a EUR 750m bond maturing in 2020.

3.1 DEPOSITS

The Treasury's foreign deposits amounted to ISK 186 bn at the end of 2015. They are part of the Central Bank's foreign exchange reserves. It has been considered necessary to maintain large reserves in view of the risk that could accompany liberalisation of the capital controls. The Central Bank's non-borrowed reserves have grown substantially in the recent past, and foreign capital inflows have been strong. Because of this, it was possible to take the next step in liberalising the capital controls; i.e., lifting controls on residents. Since that step was taken in March 2017, there has been no significant pressure on the capital account in the form of sizeable outflows of foreign currency. With the liberalisation of the capital controls, the need for sizeable foreign exchange reserves will diminish in the coming term.

3.2 REDEMPTION PROFILE

Figure 2 shows the redemption profile of Treasury foreign debt as of end-2016. The largest maturities in coming years are in 2020 and 2022. The Government's foreign loans consist of two market issues, one in US dollars (from 2012) and the other in euros (from 2014). The Treasury buyback of US dollar bonds, which took place after the publication of the fiscal plan, is discussed in Section 4.1.2.

Foreign redemption profile

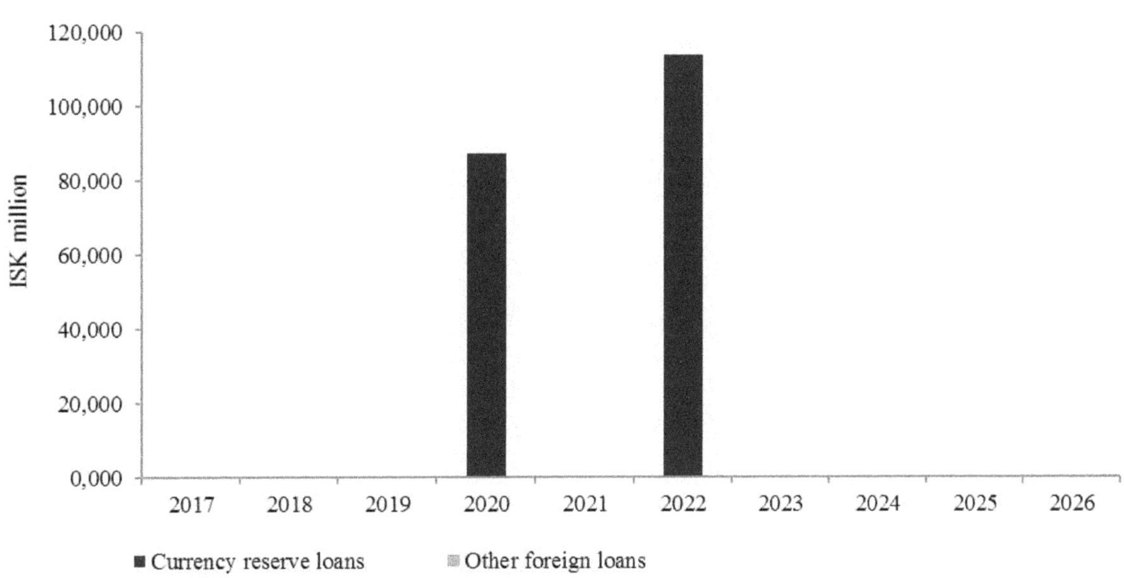

Chart 3

4 TREASURY DEBT POSITION

This section describes the Treasury debt position and loan portfolio structure as of end-2016. It also reviews the debt repayment profile and provides information on the Treasury's investor base. Figure 3 shows developments in the Treasury's debt and debt ratio, net of pension liabilities, from 2009-2016, and outlines expected developments through 2022. It closes with a discussion of deviations from the fiscal plan presented this past spring.

Developments in Treasury debt

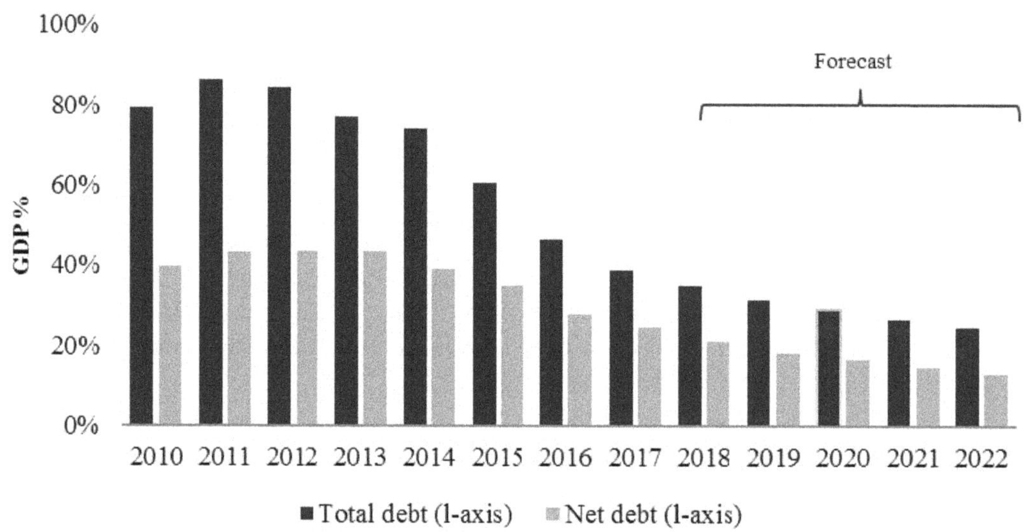

Chart 4

4.1 TREASURY DEBT STATISTICS

Treasury debt totalled ISK 1,128 bn at year-end 2016, or about 46% of GDP. The aim is to reduce it in stages to less than 30% of GDP by year-end 2021. The long-term target is to keep it below 25% of GDP. Table 4 gives a breakdown of Treasury debt at year-end 2016.

Net debt amounted to 25% of GDP at end-2016. The aim is to reduce it to below 20% of GDP in the next few years. Net debt consists of total debt excluding interest-bearing assets, receivables, and cash.

Article 7 of the Act on Public Sector Finances, no. 123/2015, stipulates that the objectives of fiscal policy and fiscal planning concerning the public sector's performance and balance sheet shall satisfy certain conditions. One of them is that total debt, excluding pension obligations and accounts payable and net of cash balances and deposits, may not exceed 30% of GDP. If the debt ratio according to the fiscal rule rises above 30%, the excess portion must decline by an average of at least 5% (1/20) per year over each three-year period. At the end of 2016, the general government debt ratio was 41%. It is assumed that it will fall rapidly in coming years, however, as Treasury debt is paid down. According to the fiscal plan, the 30% target will be reached by year-end 2019.

Treasury debt at year-end 2016

		Amounts in ISK m	
Domestic			
	Marketable bonds		
		Treasury bills	19,440
		Treasury bonds, inflation-linked	202,523
		Treasury bonds, nominal	454,411
		Recapitalisation of financial institutions	171,714
	Non-marketable debt		
		Recapitalisation of Central Bank	28,500
		Other domestic liabilities	49,934
		Domestic liabilities, total	926,522
Foreign loans			
	Foreign reserve loans		
		Foreign reserve loans	201,949
		Other foreign loans	
		Foreign liabilities, total	201,949
		Total liabilities	1,128,471

Table 4

4.1.1 DOMESTIC BORROWING

Marketable securities include Treasury bills, indexed and nominal Treasury bonds, and a special benchmark bond issued to finance capital injections and subordinated loans to financial institutions. The special issue matures in 2018, and the outstanding amount at year-end 2016 was approximately ISK 172 bn. This series bears variable interest in order to reduce the interest rate risk on the banks' liabilities. As of year-end 2016, outstanding marketable securities totalled ISK 668 bn.

Non-marketable securities include the five-year inflation-indexed Treasury bond issued to recapitalise the Central Bank of Iceland after the collapse of the banks in 2008. The outstanding balance of the bond was ISK 28.5 bn at year-end 2016, and the bond was paid off in full in spring 2017. In addition to these loans is other non-marketable debt, which is due in large part to the Treasury's acquisition of Reykjavik and Akureyri's stakes in the National Power Company of Iceland (Landsvirkjun). The Treasury's issue in connection with the acquisition of Landsvirkjun is an indexed annuity bond maturing in 2034. At year-end 2016, other outstanding non-marketable securities totalled ISK 50 bn.

4.1.2 FOREIGN LOANS

At the time the fiscal plan was issued, foreign loans taken by the Treasury to strengthen the Central Bank's foreign exchange reserves consisted of two market issues, one in US dollars and the other in euros. In 2014, the Treasury issued a foreign-denominated bond in the amount of EUR 750 m. The proceeds of the issue were used to prepay the outstanding balance of the bilateral loans from the Nordic countries. About 60% of the principal had been paid in 2012.

In 2011, the Treasury re-established its access to foreign credit markets with the issuance of a USD 1 bn bond with a five-year maturity. That bond matured in 2016 and has been paid in full. In 2012 it reconfirmed its market access with another issue, also for USD 1 bn, but with a ten-year maturity. This past spring, following the issuance of the fiscal plan, the Treasury bought back a large share of the 2012 issue, or USD 877 m nominal value. In the autumn, the Treasury bought an additional USD 31 m, leaving the outstanding balance of the bond at USD 92 m as of end-2017.

4.1.3 TREASURY DEBT STRUCTURE

Figure 4 shows marketable and non-marketable Treasury debt as of year-end 2016, including loans taken to expand the foreign exchange reserves. The debt falls into three categories: nominal (59%), inflation-indexed (18%), and foreign-denominated (23%). As is discussed in Section 4.1.2, the Treasury paid off a large share of its foreign debt during the spring; therefore, the share of foreign debt has fallen and will be 11% at the end of the year.

Debt portfolio structure

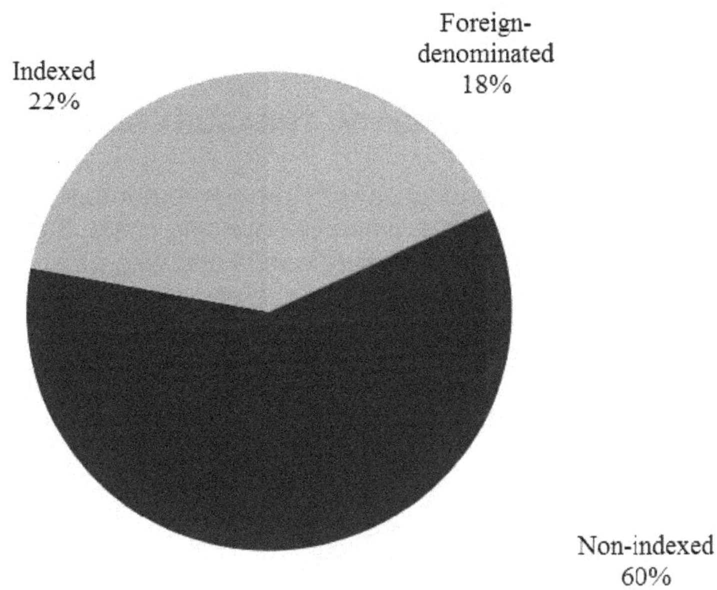

Chart 5

4.1.4 REDEMPTION PROFILE

Figure 5 shows the redemption profile for Treasury debt as of year-end 2016, together with assumptions in the National Budget for 2017. The largest maturity dates are in 2018, 2020, and 2022.

Redemption profile, Government loans

Chart 6

4.1.5 AVERAGE TIME TO MATURITY

The aim is to maintain an average weighted time to maturity of five to seven years for Treasury securities. The average duration is managed with issuance of securities of varying maturities. If domestic market conditions permit, it is also possible to use interest rate swaps and buybacks and/or hold exchange auctions to ensure that the average time to maturity remains within the defined guidelines. As of year-end 2016, the average time to maturity was 6.3 years.

4.2 INVESTORS IN DOMESTIC TREASURY SECURITIES

The Treasury issues Government securities with various maturities. The objective is to appeal to a broad base of investors and minimise financing costs. Figures 6 and 7 give a breakdown of the holders of domestic Treasury bonds and bills as of year-end 2016. 1

1 The breakdown of Treasury bond owners includes securities loans.

Owners of Treasury securities

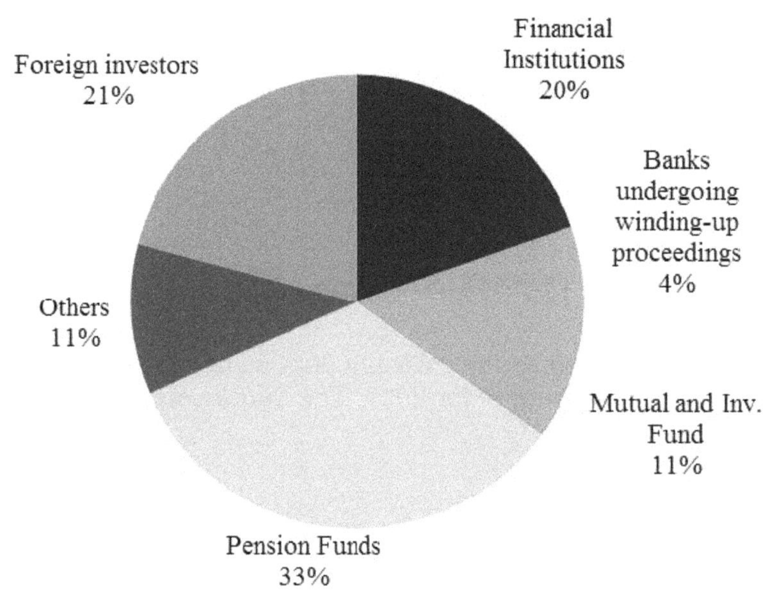

Chart 7

Chart 6

Pension funds, foreign entities, and financial institutions owned four-fifths of domestic Treasury securities, holding 33%, 21%, and 20%, respectively, of outstanding Treasury securities at the end of 2016. The pension funds' holdings were largely in longer securities: RIKB 25, RIKB 31, and RIKS 30. Foreign investors' holdings are mainly in RIKB 19, RIKB 25, and Treasury bills. The financial institutions' largest asset is RIKH 18 1009, the bond issued to recapitalise the new banks. Mutual funds and investment funds own about 11% of domestic Government securities, and other investors own about 11%.

Owners of Treasury securities

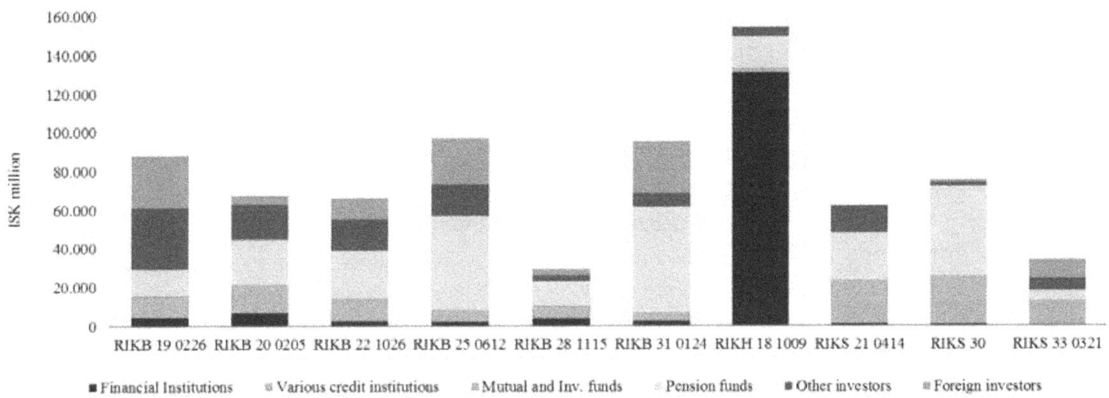

Chart 8

4.3 STABILITY CONTRIBUTIONS AND ALLOCATIONS TOWARDS REDUCTION OF DEBT

The composition agreements of the failed banks' estates were all confirmed at the end of 2015 and in early 2016, and in all instances the conditions for the stability contributions were satisfied. An agreement was made with five estates for the payment of a stability contribution to the Treasury. The stability contributions made by the estates can be classified broadly as liquid assets, transferred assets, and cash sweep assets, plus the holding in Íslandsbanki and a bond with collateral in Arion Bank. Lindarhvoll ehf., a company established by the Ministry of Finance and Economic Affairs, oversees the administration, appropriation, and sale of assets other than the holding in Íslandsbanki. The assets must be processed by end-2018, but estimates are that Lindarhvoll's activities will be largely completed by the end of 2017. Revenues from the stability contributions are used to reduce Treasury debt, upon consultation with the Central Bank, as the measures taken must not increase the money supply or jeopardise financial stability. Transferred assets are assets that the Treasury received upon confirmation of the composition agreements. They include listed and unlisted equity and debt securities, loan assets, and other financial claims. Cash sweep assets will be in the custody and administration of the estates. As these assets are processed and sold, the proceeds will revert in cash to the Treasury's account with the Central Bank.

The stability contributions are assessed at ISK 384 bn. The largest single asset is the holding in Íslandsbanki, with an assessed value of 185 bn. The bond issued by Kaupthing to the Treasury, with collateral in shares in Arion Bank, is valued at ISK 84 bn. By law, the stability contributions are intended first to cover the revoked bank tax, which would otherwise have been levied on the estates, in the amount of ISK 34 bn for 2016 and 2017. The remainder, together with other revenues that accrue from assets in coming years, will be used to pay down Treasury debt, as is provided for in the Act on a Stability Tax, no. 60/2015. Deposits to the Treasury's stability account have totalled just over ISK 140 bn since the beginning of 2016. Of that total,

ISK 34 bn have been used to cover lost bank tax and another ISK 110 bn to pay down Treasury debt. The Central Bank of Iceland bond was paid off in the spring, and just over ISK 80 bn have been used to buy back RIKH 18.

With the allocation of stability contributions towards debt reduction, the Treasury's debt ratio will improve markedly in coming years. Other things being equal, this can be assumed to have a positive impact on credit ratings. Moody's upgraded the sovereign by two notches in early September 2016. Other credit rating agencies have also upgraded the sovereign this year. The reduction of debt will also have a favourable impact on the Treasury's interest expense, which is still onerous, although it will decline in coming years, according to the fiscal plan. Reducing interest expense will provide the scope to allocate funds differently in the future.

The objectives of the fiscal plan assume that all irregular Treasury revenues will be used to reduce debt. If additional irregular revenues should accrue – such as from asset sales – this will provide even greater scope to reduce debt, thereby reducing interest expense.

5 RISK MANAGEMENT

The debt portfolio has certain inherent risks related to market volatility, such as changes in the interest rate, exchange rate, and inflation, and additional risks related to contingent liabilities. There is also substantial refinancing risk in the current portfolio. The management of these risks is covered in this section.

5.1 MARKET RISK

Financial market volatility, whether due to fluctuations in interest rates, exchange rate movements, or changes in inflation, results in fluctuations in the market value of the debt portfolio. These risks, generally referred to collectively as market risk, are discussed in greater detail in the following sections.

Effective risk management aims to reduce risk while simultaneously minimising the interest expense of the portfolio. These goals can be achieved through effective Treasury debt management and targeted use of derivative products.

5.1.1 INTEREST RATE RISK

Interest rate risk is the risk that the Treasury's financing costs will rise due to changes in interest rate terms. Interest rate risk depends on the structure of the debt portfolio. Variable interest rates create the risk that interest rates will rise, thus increasing the Treasury's interest expense. Fixed interest rates on long-term loans create the risk that the Treasury will not benefit from the savings that would accrue in the event of a reduction in market rates.

Figure 9 shows the interest rate composition of the debt portfolio as of end-2016. The majority of domestic and foreign Treasury bonds (about 72%) bear fixed interest rates, and their payment flows are known throughout their duration. Approximately 28% of the total debt portfolio bears variable rates; therefore, payment flows will change in line with changes in the base interest rate on the loans concerned. Interest rate swaps can be used in order to manage the Treasury's interest rate risk and, for instance, increase the weight of variable-rate debt.

Interest rate composition – year-end 2016

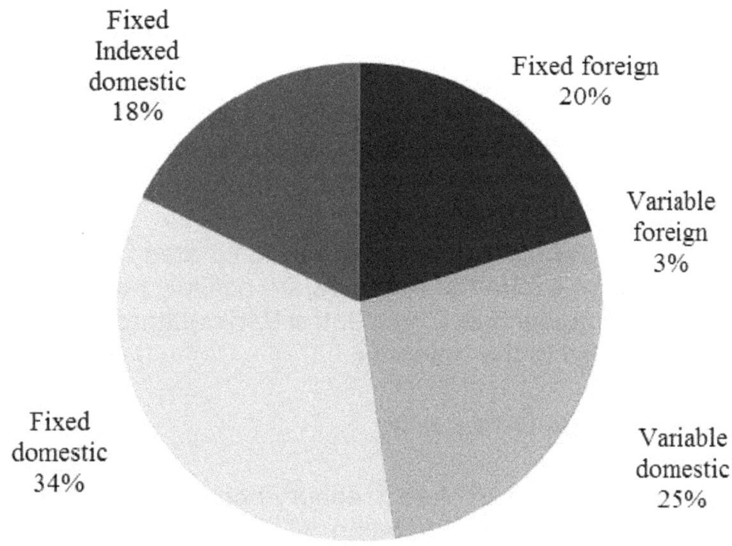

Chart 9

5.1.1.1 Interest Rate Swaps

The objective of Treasury debt management is to minimise long-term interest expense while pursuing a prudent risk policy. Interest rate swaps can serve as a means of minimising interest expense. Domestic market agents have shown some interest in having the Treasury take the initiative in this area, as it would enable them to diversify their offerings to individuals and companies to include non-indexed interest rates on longer-term products.

Given that the intention is to retire the Central Bank of Iceland bond and RIKH 18 in coming years, the need to issue interest rate swaps has increased significantly. With the retirement of these loans, the share of variable interest rates in the Treasury portfolio falls from 28% to 3%. With interest rate swaps, it is possible to affect the Treasury's interest expense, the ratio of variable to fixed interest rates, and the weight of indexation in the portfolio, as well as steering the duration of the portfolio. In MTDSs issued in recent years, it has been stated that the Treasury may use such swaps if it is considered beneficial for the Treasury. The Treasury concluded a swap agreement for fixed versus variable interest in connection with the eurobond issue in summer 2014, but this is its only outstanding interest rate swap agreement. In view of recent developments in foreign interest rates, this has proven to be a success.

It has been decided to begin preparations for the issuance of interest rate swap agreements in the domestic market in coming months. The agreements will be managed by Government Debt Management. The Treasury will be authorised to conclude such agreements for up to ISK 20-40 bn per year. The main objective with the agreements is to manage the Treasury's interest rate risk. Decisions on issuance will be determined by market conditions at any given time.

5.1.2 EXCHANGE RATE RISK

Exchange rate risk is the risk that the Treasury's debt position will deteriorate due to changes in the exchange rate of the Icelandic króna versus other currencies. The Treasury's direct exchange

rate risk is limited because the foreign currency and foreign-denominated bonds it owns offset foreign Treasury debt. The foreign exchange reserves are actively managed according to set currency composition guidelines. The Central Bank attempts to minimise the exchange rate risk attached to the reserves.

5.1.3 INFLATION RISK

Inflation risk is the risk that indexation on index-linked Treasury bonds will raise the Treasury's financing costs as a result of increased inflation. At year-end 2016, the Treasury's indexed debt amounted to ISK 203 bn, or around 18% of its debt portfolio.

Inflation risk can be managed with derivatives. The share of inflation-indexed debt in the overall portfolio is deliberately kept low due to the risk that inflation will rise if the króna should depreciate when the capital controls are lifted. It should be borne in mind, however, that the Treasury holds a number of inflation-indexed assets, such as loans to the Icelandic Student Loan Fund. This mitigates inflation risk to some extent.

5.2 REFINANCING RISK

One of the greatest risks to the debt portfolio centres on refinancing. To reduce refinancing risk, the Ministry of Finance and Economic Affairs aims to keep the redemption profile of Government securities as smooth as possible over the long term.

The largest Treasury bond maturities in the years to come – and therefore the greatest refinancing risk in the portfolio – will be in 2018, 2020, and 2022, as is mentioned above. Work will be done to reduce refinancing risk with buybacks or exchange auctions prior to maturity.

5.3 CONTINGENT LIABILITIES

Contingent liabilities are financial obligations that could fall on the Treasury; for example, due to State guarantees or administrative decisions that entail involvement in the financing of municipalities or corporations that are of key importance in Icelandic society. The scope of this risk is discussed in Sections 7.3.1 – 7.3.3.

5.3.1 State Guarantees

State guarantees represent the Treasury's greatest indirect liability. State guarantees are governed by Act no. 121/1997. The Treasury may not grant State guarantees without statutory authorisation from Parliament.

State guarantees and related matters are administered by the State Guarantee Fund, which compiles information on the position of the undertakings benefiting from guarantees and assesses the risk attached to the guarantees. The Central Bank oversees State guarantees according to an agreement with the Ministry of Finance and Economic Affairs. The State

Guarantee Fund notifies the Ministry of Finance and Economic Affairs if a guarantee is likely to fall on the Treasury. Table 5 shows the status of State guarantees at the end of December 2016. 2

2 *Market Information*, February 2017. (http://www.lanamal.is/en/news/market-information)

State guarantees, year-end 2016

Year end 2015	ISK million	%
Housing Finance Fund (HFF)	821.180	79%
Landsvirkjun	195.048	19%
Others	22.949	2%
Total	1.039.177	

Table 5

5.3.1.1 Housing Financing Fund (HFF)

The Housing Financing Fund (HFF) operates in accordance with the Act on Housing Affairs, no. 44/1998. With statutory amendments and changes in the authorities' focus, the Fund's role was changed from being primarily a lending institution to being an agency responsible for administering housing affairs. The Fund was in severe difficulties during the aftermath of the financial crisis, and the Treasury had to contribute ISK 52 bn in capital to strengthen its capital ratio. The HFF's operating performance has improved vastly with improved economic conditions, and its capital ratio is now at an all-time high of 7.3%, well above the targeted minimum. If the capital raio is low, the HFF has more difficulty responding to risks in its operations, and the Treasury's financial risk will be greater as a result. The risks facing the HFF are credit risk, prepayment risk, liquidity risk, interest rate risk, inflation risk, refinancing risk, and operational risk. Of these, credit risk is the most important, owing to the risk of default. In the recent term, prepayments of outstanding loans from the Fund have subsided. The Fund cannot pay off the debt offsetting these prepayments; therefore, the risk lies in investing liquid assets in order to generate acceptable returns. In most instances, prepayment of HFF loans has a negative impact on the Fund's interest rate differential, and therefore on its performance.

The HFF's operating results for 2016 were positive in the amount of ISK 4.2 bn. Total assets amounted to ISK 787 bn at the end of the period, including issued loans amounting to ISK 578 bn. Its capital totalled ISK 23.5 bn at the end of June. Interest-bearing assets outside the loan portfolio, including liquid assets, increased between years, to ISK 197 bn at the end of 2016. The HFF's position has been improving in recent years, and it is not deemed likely that the Fund will need further capital contributions in the years to come.

5.3.1.2 LANDSVIRKJUN

Landsvirkjun's operations have been successful in the recent term. The company's equity ratio has strengthened in recent years and is now close to a historical high, at 45.4%. Its net liabilities have declined significantly since 2012, and this, together with improved borrowing terms, have had a positive impact on its performance. Its net debt totalled USD 1,960 million at the end of 2016. In recent years, Landsvirkjun's financing has been without a Treasury guarantee, and its older debt, which does still bear a guarantee, is rapidly declining as debt is paid off. The company's profit before depreciation and financial items totalled USD 302 m in 2016, and cash

from operations amounted to USD 230 m. Landsvirkjun's financial risk consists of market risk, liquidity risk, and counterparty risk. Its market risk is primarily of three types, relating to developments in aluminium prices, interest rates, and currency exchange rates. The company has worked systematically to reduce its market risk through derivatives contracts, modifications to the loan portfolio, and amendments to electrical energy contracts. Its counterparty risk is primarily due to electrical energy contracts with manufacturers and derivatives contracts entered into for hedging purposes. The risk is limited by the company's requirements concerning counterparty quality.

5.3.2 MUNICIPALITIES

While there is no legally mandated State guarantee on local authorities' debt, their financial position could generally threaten individual their ability to carry out their tasks, and their overall debt level poses a risk to the economy and the Treasury. The high level of indebtedness and weak financial position of some municipalities therefore gives cause for concern.

In 2011, Parliament passed the Local Government Act, which provides for increased discipline and sets clearer rules for local authorities' finances, as well as requiring increased supervision and information disclosure on financial affairs. First of all, the new legislation stipulates that municipal consolidations' combined Part A and Part B revenues and expenditures must be in balance over each three-year period. Second, total debt and obligations may not exceed 150% of revenues. It is clear that many municipalities will need several years to adapt their debt position to this maximum. The Act provides for a maximum adaptation period of ten years. It is important that the municipalities use this time well so that their finances become sustainable as soon as possible. According to the Act, decisions on municipal investment, development, or other contractual obligations exceeding 20% of the current year's tax revenues are subject to an impartial appraisal of the impact on the municipality's financial position.

The aim of the Act on Public Sector Finances, no. 123/2015, is to promote sound economic policy and strong, responsible management of public sector finances. The Act entails significant changes, and the public sector must comply with a fiscal rule that applies to both the overall balance and public sector debt.

5.3.3 PUBLIC-PRIVATE PARTNERSHIPS

Public-private partnerships can entail financial risk for the Treasury, even in the absence of a State guarantee. Public-private partnerships are governed by the Regulation on Service Agreements, no. 343/2006. The purpose of the Regulation is to define the role and responsibilities of entities that manage long-term projects for individual ministries and public institutions. According to the Government Financial Reporting Act, agreements of this kind must be approved by Parliament. While such partnerships usually represent little direct financial risk for the Treasury, circumstances can develop where the projects need capital in excess of current budgetary allocations. The main public-private partnerships currently underway are the operation of the Harpa Concert and Conference Centre and the construction of the Vaðlaheiðargöng tunnel.

6 INSTITUTIONAL STRUCTURE

In each year's National Budget, Parliament authorises the Ministry of Finance and Economic Affairs to borrow funds and issue State guarantees. The Act on Government Debt Management stipulates that the Ministry is responsible for and implements debt management and State guarantees. The Ministry has also concluded an agreement with the Central Bank of Iceland, providing for specified advisory services and execution in connection with Treasury debt management. The agreement contains explicit provisions on division of tasks and responsibilities so as to ensure that debt management decisions are taken independent of the Central Bank's monetary policy.

6.1 MINISTRY OF FINANCE AND ECONOMIC AFFAIRS

The Ministry of Finance and Economic Affairs oversees Treasury debt management. It takes decisions on issuance volume, planned bond auctions, and liquidity management. It also determines yields and amounts of accepted bids in Treasury auctions. Moreover, the Ministry determines the structure, maturity, and characteristics of new issues, as well as deciding on buybacks and/or swap agreements.

6.2 CENTRAL BANK OF ICELAND

The Ministry of Finance and Economic Affairs and the Central Bank of Iceland have concluded an agreement providing for specified advisory services and execution in connection with Treasury debt management. 3 The purpose of the agreement is to promote more economical, efficient, and effective debt management based on the Ministry's debt management strategy.

3 The Government Debt Management Agreement of 18 October 2010, based on the agreement of 4 September 2007.

A special department within the Central Bank of Iceland, Government Debt Management, is mandated by the Ministry of Finance and Economic affairs to handle Treasury debt management in accordance with guidelines adopted by the Ministry. Government Debt Management is responsible for ensuring that borrowing and debt management are in compliance with the strategy set out by the Ministry.

Government Debt Management also administers State guarantees and assesses the Treasury's risk due to such guarantees. It provides the Ministry with opinions on State guarantees and grants them if authorised by Parliament.

On behalf of the Ministry of Finance and Economic Affairs, Government Debt Management handles the regular disclosure of information on the Treasury's domestic and foreign liabilities to market agents, and publishes information on auction dates and planned issuance volume for the year based on the Treasury's estimated financing need. It also issues press releases on debt management on behalf of the Ministry of Finance and Economic Affairs.

6.3 CONSULTATIVE COMMITTEE ON DEBT MANAGEMENT

The Ministry of Finance and Economic Affairs appoints a Consultative Committee on Debt Management whose members represent the Ministry and the Central Bank.

The Consultative Committee serves as a forum for the exchange of views on the situation and outlook for capital markets, and on the Treasury's domestic and foreign borrowing and borrowing plans. It is intended to encourage improvements in the domestic credit market as it deems appropriate.

The Committee makes proposals to the Ministry of Finance and Economic Affairs on the structure of individual bond series and their maturity and volume, as well as arrangements for market making and auctions. It also proposes risk management guidelines for the Treasury's domestic and foreign debt portfolios. The Committee discusses and adopts proposals for the Treasury's issuance schedule in domestic and foreign markets. The schedule specifies the issuance volume, issuance dates, and planned borrowing actions for the year. It must be approved by the Ministry of Finance and Economic Affairs and is then announced to market agents. The Committee meets on a regular basis, or as often as is deemed necessary.

7 INFORMATION DISCLOSURE TO THE MARKET

The Ministry of Finance and Economic Affairs and Government Debt Management attempt to maintain effective communication with market participants through regular information disclosure and meetings with primary dealers and investors. All news releases are published on the NASDAQ Iceland Exchange and Bloomberg and are distributed to the media and market agents. The exchange uses the data vendor GlobeNewsWire to distribute press releases to foreign media and market participants.

Publications on debt management issued by the Ministry of Finance and Economic Affairs and Government Debt Management include the following:

- Medium-Term Debt Management Strategy
- Annual Government Debt Management Prospect
- Quarterly Government Debt Management Prospect
- Auction announcements
- Planned auction dates
- Market Information

7.1 MEDIUM-TERM DEBT MANAGEMENT STRATEGY

The Ministry of Finance and Economic Affairs prepares the Medium-Term Debt Management Strategy (MTDS), which is revised and published annually. It includes the following topics:

- Debt management objectives
- Debt management guidelines
- Issuance policy
- Structure of Treasury debt
- Risk management
- Contingent liabilities

7.2 ANNUAL GOVERNMENT DEBT MANAGEMENT PROSPECT

The Annual Government Debt Management Prospect is designed to provide market participants with general information on Treasury issuance for the upcoming year. It is published following parliamentary approval of the National Budget and includes the following information:

- Total issuance volume for the year
- Issuance policy for the year
- Buybacks
- Bond swap auctions

7.3 QUARTERLY GOVERNMENT DEBT MANAGEMENT PROSPECT

At the end of each quarter, Government Debt Management issues the Prospect for the upcoming quarter. The Quarterly Prospect includes the following information:

- Planned Treasury bond issuance for the quarter
- Planned Treasury bill issuance
- Summary of issuance in the previous quarter
- Actions to be taken in the upcoming quarter

7.4 AUCTION ANNOUNCEMENTS

Press releases on individual auctions are published by the Nasdaq Iceland exchange at least one business day in advance. The press releases state which series are to be auctioned each time. The results are published after each auction, on that same day.

7.5 PLANNED AUCTION DATES

The planned dates for Treasury bill and Treasury bond auctions are published on the Government Debt Management website each December. This information is also distributed directly to market participants.

7.6 MARKET INFORMATION

Government Debt Management publishes a monthly newsletter entitled Market Information. The newsletter contains important information on Treasury debt and State guarantees. Market Information is distributed to the media and to market participants and is published on the Government Debt Management website. It includes the following information:

- Highlights from the previous month
- Results of Treasury auctions
- Treasury debt statistics
- Position of Treasury benchmark securities
- Structure of Treasury debt
- Redemption profile for Government debt
- Owners of Treasury securities

- Securities loans
- State guarantees

7.7 GOVERNMENT DEBT MANAGEMENT WEBSITE

Government Debt Management publishes a website, www.lanamal.is, which includes information on Treasury debt management, market prices, yields, and historical statistics on Treasury securities, as well as issue prospectuses. The following information can also be found there:

- Medium-Term Debt Management Strategy
- Annual Government Debt Management Prospect
- Quarterly Government Debt Management Prospect
- Auction announcements
- Market Information
- Press releases
- The Republic of Iceland's sovereign credit ratings

Information on Government debt can also be found on the Ministry of Finance and Economic Affairs website: www.fjr.is.

7.8 PRIMARY DEALERS IN TREASURY SECURITIES

Government Debt Management monitors primary dealers on a daily basis to ensure that they fulfil their market-making obligations in the secondary market. Meetings are held with them at least quarterly, and more often if necessary.

7.9 INVESTORS

Representatives from Government Debt Management and the Ministry of Finance and Economic Affairs meet regularly with investors to acquaint them with points of emphasis in Treasury debt management.

STATE OWNERSHIP STRATEGY

1. Care shall be taken to ensure equal treatment in relations between owners and between the owner and the company.

2. The scope of responsibility and separation of governance between the owner and the company, and between the Board of Directors and management, shall be clearly defined.

3. Those managing the company shall follow well-conceived and open governance practice.

4. The company's Board of Directors shall work independently and bear responsibility for its activities and operations towards the owner.

5. The company shall operate in accordance with the ownership strategy and performance benchmarks of the owner.

6. The company shall pursue those social objectives aimed at by the owner in its ownership.

7. The company's Board of Directors shall be comprised of qualified individuals possessing good educational qualifications and practical experience suited to the sector in question.

8. The company shall adopt a moderate but competitive remuneration policy.

9. The company shall aim at increasing competition and reducing oligopoly through its activities.

10. The company shall ensure objectivity and equal treatment in procurement and disposition of assets and other financial measures taken.

THE ICELANDIC STATE'S OWNERSHIP STRATEGY FOR FINANCIAL SERVICES

Contents

The State's Ownership Strategy for Financial Undertakings covers those financial undertakings administered by Icelandic State Financial Investments (Icel. *Bankasýsla ríkisins*). It has been adopted by virtue of a provision in Art. 44 of Act No. 123/2015, on Public Finances, and a provision in Art. 1 of Act No. 88/2009, on Icelandic State Financial Investments. When the state adopted an Ownership Strategy for Financial Undertakings in 2009, this was the government's first ownership strategy for companies owned by the state.

In 2012 a general State Ownership Strategy was published, intended to apply generally to limited liability companies and partnerships owned by the State. The essence of both these strategies implies that state-owned companies are to be operated professionally and transparently, to ensure public confidence regarding their direction and activities.

The state's role as owner is based on recognised guidelines on good corporate governance, especially the OECD Guidelines on Corporate Governance of State-owned Enterprises 1 , as well as general criteria regarding the role and obligations of owners. Emphasis is placed on regular communication and information disclosure between the owner and the enterprise on its operations and policy formulation, which must, however, be based on a clear division of responsibility between the owner, the Board of Directors and the management. It is appropriate to view these strategies in context, but in those instances where discrepancies may arise between them the provisions of this Ownership Strategy for Financial Undertakings shall apply to those enterprises administered by Icelandic State Financial Investments.

1 More specifically: OECD Guidelines on Corporate Governance of State-owned Enterprises and the Guidelines on Corporate Governance issued by the Iceland Chamber of Commerce, NASDAQ Iceland and the Confederation of Icelandic Employers.

The State's Ownership Strategy for Financial Undertakings provides for its regular revision and updating to take into consideration developments on financial markets and in the state's ownership. Since the adoption of the first ownership strategy, material changes have been made to the legal framework of financial undertakings, supervision of their operations and guidelines on corporate governance. Major changes have also occurred in their operating and economic environment.

Extensive changes occurred in the Treasury's involvement in commercial banks and savings banks following the financial system collapse in the autumn of 2008, with further changes occurring to the state's holdings in financial market enterprises since that time. Mention could be made, for instance, of the considerable reduction in the number of savings banks owned by the state, with their acquisition or takeover by other financial undertakings, and the acquisition by the Icelandic state of all share capital in Íslandsbanki. This has created, at least provisionally, a situation where practically all the share capital in two of the country's three largest banks, Landsbankinn hf. and Íslandsbanki hf., is owned by the state. Due to this an accord was reached with the Icelandic Competition Authority to encourage active financial

market competition and ensure that financial undertakings owned by the state would be operated as independent competitors.

Financial undertakings also have a special status in the national economy, performing an important systemic role as one of the basic pillars of the society. This makes it extremely important that ownership of financial undertakings is in capable hands and in recent years the legislator has set stringent requirements concerning the eligibility of parties holding controlling interests in such enterprises.

In view of the above-mentioned developments, a decision was taken to review the ownership strategy. The strategy takes into consideration the special position of financial undertakings compared to other state-owned enterprises, both with regard to the administrative arrangements for ownership by the state and the state's objectives and future vision for its ownership. The strategy is also based on benchmarks set out in the previously mentioned general state ownership strategy.

The State Ownership Strategy for Financial Undertakings is divided into four chapters:

1. State objectives in ownership of financial undertakings

2. Administrative arrangements for ownership by the state, i.e. responsibility of each party and their relationship

3. Principles adopted by the state as owner

4. Requirements and benchmarks for operations of financial undertakings in which the state has a holding

It is important that the current State Ownership Strategy for Financial Undertakings be accessible to the public and presented to the individual undertakings, their Boards of Directors and management. The same applies to other stakeholders, both in the public administration itself and in parliament, as well as private sector stakeholders. Knowledge of the state's ownership strategy is conducive to fostering stability and confidence in the financial system and those companies which it covers.

1 STATE OBJECTIVES IN OWNERSHIP OF FINANCIAL UNDERTAKINGS

It is important that the objectives of the state's ownership strategy are known, clear and foreseeable. This section lists the state's principal objectives, firstly, as owner of holdings in financial undertakings and, secondly, in the sale of holdings and longer-term ownership of specific enterprises in the future. The state does not aim to hold a majority in financial undertakings in the private sector in the longer term. It is therefore important that administration of these holdings is done professionally, soundly and on market principles, in part to maximise their sales value and dividends to taxpayers, as they comprise valuable public assets.

1.1 THE STATE'S OBJECTIVES AS OWNER

a. That the administration of ownership and activities of financial undertakings contribute to a sound and credible financial market.

• Icelandic State Financial Investments, together with the Boards of Directors and others involved in the activities of financial undertakings on behalf of the state, shall comply with recognised guidelines on corporate governance and endeavour to lead the way in good governance, business ethics and social responsibility.

• Care shall be taken to ensure equal treatment of customers, which in this context means ensuring non-discrimination and similar handling of comparable cases.

• In the sale of assets emphasis shall be placed on transparency, objectivity, equity and cost-efficiency, as well as considerations of competition.

• Procedures and methods adopted by financial undertakings for their activities and decision making shall be written, transparent and accessible to all. Procedures shall, among other things, cover investments, granting of credit, sale of assets and enforcement of claims.

b. Promoting competition in the financial market

• The exercise of the state's holding in financial undertakings shall aim at boosting and strengthening competition in the financial market, for instance, by promoting active and effective competition among financial undertakings owned by the state.

• This means complying with provisions of the accord between the Ministry of Finance and Economic Affairs, Icelandic State Financial Investments, Landsbankinn hf. and Íslandsbanki hf. and the Icelandic Competition Authority, cf. the Authority's Decision No. 9/2016, for instance, on the autonomy of financial undertakings, independence of directors and procedures regarding information disclosure.

• It must be assured that processes and access controls are in place preventing confidential information, which is made known to owners' representatives, from finding its way to other financial undertakings. Icelandic State Financial Investments shall adopt special procedural rules in this regard and publish them on their website.

• An independent selection committee, appointed by the Board of Icelandic State Financial Investments as provided for by law, shall make appointments to the Boards of Directors on behalf of the State, having regard especially to competition perspectives.

c. To maximise the long-term value for the state, having regard for risk.

• It must be ensured that those financial undertakings in which the state holds a stake return an acceptable dividend to shareholders, having regard for market circumstances.

• Profitability shall be based on cautious, long-term considerations and not short-term gain.

• The activities of financial undertakings should be based on a focused strategy and cost-efficient operations providing returns to customers and the society over the long term.

1.2 OBJECTIVES CONCERNING SALE AND LONG-TERM OWNERSHIP

a. That acceptable conditions must exist before a holding is sold.

• The state's holdings in Icelandic financial undertakings have been regarded as a temporary arrangement, although there could be reasons to continue to keep some of them in state ownership.

• Under certain circumstances it may be appropriate to sell a company in part on the market to set in motion active price formation without creating an oversupply of shares. The objective of such sale would be to obtain a higher overall value in the longer term.

• The state's holdings in financial undertakings will not be sold until circumstances on the financial market, including the legal and regulatory framework, are favourable and desirable, potential buyers exist and the undertaking concerned is ready for sale. In making this assessment consideration shall be given, for instance, to the following aspects before a final decision on sale is taken:

– that the capital structure and operations of the financial undertaking concerned are in a suitable balance;

– that the separation of risk from various business lines is acceptable; and

– the market's capacity to acquire the holding, for instance, given the supply of shares of other large enterprises, not least financial undertakings.

b. To safeguard the state's long-term interests, having regard for risk.

• Every effort shall be made to maximise the long-term value of the state's holdings in financial undertakings, taking into consideration the profitability of their operations (including return on equity and assets), dividends, the selling price of shares and other factors of significance.

• Regard shall be given to the state's primary objective of reducing Treasury debt and thereby creating additional leeway for provision of public services and investment by the state in the future. Regular and acceptable dividends from and/or sale of shares in financial undertakings are key factors in achieving this objective.

• The state's position and risk of owning a majority in Icelandic financial undertakings must be regularly assessed, e.g. with regard to the risk of financial setbacks.

c. To encourage sound long-term ownership

• Sale of the state's holdings in financial undertakings shall be aimed at promoting and strengthening financial market competition.

• Even though a major portion of the financial system is currently owned by the state, the aim is to have diverse, sound and broadly distributed ownership of Icelandic financial undertakings in the future.

• Broadly distributed ownership refers to a shareholder group which is diverse and financial undertakings that are publicly listed on an equity market.

• Sound ownership in this context refers to shareholders with holdings of over 10%, or qualifying holdings, being considered eligible to exercise such holdings by the competent supervisory bodies. It is not acceptable for shareholders, singly or in concert with others, to be able to use their influence in a manner which is detrimental to the interests of the financial undertaking concerned or other shareholders. This is especially significant in the case of systemically important financial undertakings.

• When financial undertakings are listed on an equity market efforts shall be made to repeal all special legislation concerning enterprises in majority state ownership, even though the state continues to hold a majority in such undertakings. The state's ownership strategy, however, will continue to apply to companies where the state holds a majority, and directors nominated by the state shall be guided by the principles laid down there.

• In light of the above-mentioned objectives, and with a view to achieving still more broadly distributed ownership and a more realistic valuation, it may be advisable to list the shares of financial undertakings in part or in full both in Iceland and abroad. Sale to a foreign financial undertaking with broadly

distributed ownership could satisfy the requirement for such, in addition to which partial or total foreign ownership can encourage more active and more extensive competition and offer opportunities for lowering financing costs to the benefit of the customers of the financial undertaking in question.

1.3 OBJECTIVES CONCERNING INDIVIDUAL COMPANIES

The state has holdings in four financial undertakings: the commercial banks Landsbankinn hf., Íslandsbanki hf. and Arion Bank hf. and the savings bank Sparisjóður Austurlands hf. The state's plans for each of these companies are as follows:

a. Landsbankinn hf.

• The intention is to have the state hold a sizeable stake, of 34-40%, in the bank for the long term to contribute to financial system stability and ensure its necessary infrastructure.

• The remainder of the state's holding in the bank will be sold in coming years when favourable and desirable circumstances prevail.

• The intention is to list the bank on an equity market.

b. Íslandsbanki hf.

• The Treasury acquired all shares in Íslandsbanki as part of Glitnir's stability contribution upon the settlement of its estate.

• The state's ownership of Íslandsbanki is based on Act No. 60/2015, on a Stability Tax, and therefore dividends and the selling price of the bank must be used to pay down Treasury debt.

• The intention is to sell the state's entire holding in Íslandsbanki when favourable and desirable circumstances prevail.

c. Arion Bank hf.

• The intention is to sell the state's entire holding when favourable and desirable circumstances prevail.

• As the state is a minority shareholder, the sale will likely take place in tandem with sale by the majority owner or the bank's listing on an equity market.

d. Sparisjóður Austurlands hf.

• The intention is to sell the state's 49.5% holding as soon as possible, as long-term ownership of the savings bank is not the state's objective.

2 ADMINISTRATIVE ARRANGEMENTS FOR OWNERSHIP

The Ministry of Finance and Economic Affairs is responsible for representing and acting on behalf of the state regarding its assets, companies and rights, acquiring and disposing of these, unless otherwise provided for by law.

Following the financial crisis of 2008 a decision was taken to set up a public agency, Icelandic State Financial Investments, with the principal role of exercising the state's ownership of financial undertakings which it had taken over or established as a result of the crisis. This agency is under the administration of the Minister of Finance and Economic Affairs.

The following section discusses the administrative arrangements for ownership together with the tasks of all the main parties involved in exercising and selling holdings in financial undertakings.

2.1 THE ICELANDIC PARLIAMENT *ALTHINGI*

Each year Althingi decides in its budget for the following year whether authorisation is to be given to sell state holdings in financial undertakings as provided for by law. Such authorisation or, as the case may be, special legislation on the sale of individual holdings serves as a basis for the Treasury to be able to sell holdings in such companies.

The parliamentary Budget Committee and Economic and Trade Committee are involved at the initial stage in the sale of holdings in financial undertakings, as the committees are by law expected to give their opinion on a report from the Minister of Finance and Economic Affairs on any proposed sales process.

Althingi supervises generally how the government is performing its ownership role and can in this connection request information.

2.2 MINISTRY OF FINANCE AND ECONOMIC AFFAIRS

The Ministry of Finance and Economic Affairs acts on behalf of the state regarding its holdings in financial undertakings and is responsible for their sale, although Icelandic State Financial Investments in other respects administers these holdings.

The Ministry adopts a specific ownership strategy for financial undertakings owned by the state and is responsible for such. The ownership strategy sets out the emphases on which the state bases administration of the holdings by Icelandic State Financial Investments and for the operation, management and practices of individual financial undertakings by their Boards of Directors and management. The ownership strategy also contains the general and specific aims of the state regarding the operation, future ownership and disposition of its holdings in these undertakings.

As the Ministry of Finance and Economic Affairs is also responsible for financial market matters and regulation in various related areas the Ministry must keep the state's role as owner of financial undertakings clearly separated from its other tasks in connection with financial markets, policy formulation, legislation and supervision.

If Icelandic State Financial Investments makes a proposal for the sale of holdings in a financial undertaking and such proposal is approved by the Minister, the latter shall prepare a special report on the proposed sales process and submit it to the relevant parliamentary committees. The report shall include information on the primary objectives in selling the holding, what sales procedure will be followed and how this will be arranged in other respects.

The committees are in accordance with law granted a suitable time limit for commenting on the contents of the report, after which the Minister shall take an independent decision as to whether to initiate a sales process for the holding. The Minister may amend individual aspects of the proposed sales process, for instance, to take into consideration comments on the report from the Budget Committee or Economic and Trade Committee.

Once bids for the holding have been received, together with a grounded assessment by Icelandic State Financial Investments of these, the Minister shall take a decision as to whether a bid shall be accepted or rejected, and shall sign the purchase contract.

2.3 ICELANDIC STATE FINANCIAL INVESTMENTS

The purpose and objectives of this agency are laid down in Act No. 88/2009, on Icelandic State Financial Investments. Its purpose is to exercise the state's holdings in financial undertakings in accordance with legislation, good business and corporate governance practice, and the state's current ownership strategy. The final authority in Icelandic State Financial Investments rests with a three-person Board of Directors appointed by the Minister, to which all major decisions are to be referred. The Director General of Icelandic State Financial Investments is appointed by the Board of Directors and is responsible to it for the agency's activities and operations.

Icelandic State Financial Investments shall emphasise the development of a strong domestic financial market and its continuing vitality, encourage active and appropriate competition in this market and ensure transparency in all decision-making with regard to the state's involvement in financial activities and effective information disclosure to the public.

The agency's principal task is to handle relations between the state and financial undertakings in which it holds stakes in connection with its ownership role. These should, in the main, take place through the Boards of Directors of the financial undertakings. Due to arm's length considerations in legislation, these parties are not expected to communicate directly with the Ministry of Finance and Economic Affairs or the Minister in connection with decisions regarding the state's ownership or operations of the companies. This shall not, however, prevent financial undertakings from informing the Ministry or the Minister on strategic matters.

Icelandic State Financial Investments exercises the Treasury's vote at shareholders' meetings of the companies and nominates directors on the owner's behalf. It is responsible for enforcing this ownership strategy towards financial undertakings owned by the state and shall monitor compliance with it in order to achieve its objectives. In carrying out such enforcement

Icelandic State Financial Investments can receive general suggestions from customers but does not deal with cases concerning individual customers of financial undertakings.

The agency shall, on behalf of the owner, conclude agreements with state-owned financial undertakings for specific and general objectives in their operations, in addition to carrying out other specified statutory task in connection with the administration of the state's holdings in financial undertakings.

Icelandic State Financial Investments takes the initiative in the sale of state holdings in financial undertakings, cf. Act No. 155/2012, on the Sales Process for the State's Holdings in Financial Undertakings. It is expected to evaluate the circumstances and prepare and draft a proposal to the Minister on the sale of individual financial undertakings. In this connection Icelandic State Financial Investments shall define the tasks of the financial undertaking concerned and arrangements for information disclosure and the parties' collaboration. In preparation for sale, special consideration shall be given to the principles laid down in Art. 3 of the Act on a sales process.

Should the Minister, acting on a proposal from Icelandic State Financial Investments, decide to commence a sales process for a financial undertaking or part of it the agency shall handle the sales process of the holding on behalf of the state as decided by the Minister. Icelandic State Financial Investments shall prepare the sale, seek bids for the holding, assess the bids, supervise the negotiations with outside consultants and potential buyers and see to drafting of agreements. It is important that outside consultants satisfy suitable eligibility/qualification requirements, including regarding relevant experience of directing sales and/or listing processes for state holdings in similar financial undertakings in Europe.

Icelandic State Financial Investments shall regularly inform the Minister of the progress of the sales process for financial undertakings. Once bids for a holding are available Icelandic State Financial Investments shall deliver to the Minister a grounded assessment of the bids received.

Icelandic State Financial Investments shall report to the Minister of Finance and Economic Affairs on the situation of financial undertakings having regard to the objectives and emphases set out in statutes and this ownership strategy.

Act No. 88/2009, on Icelandic State Financial Investments, provides for the agency to conclude its activities within five years of its establishment, following which it shall be abolished. The agency has not, however, completed its tasks and it is assumed that a bill would be presented to parliament on its abolition should large financial undertakings in majority state ownership be sold or listed on an equity market.

2.4 SELECTION COMMITTEE FOR BOARDS OF DIRECTORS OF FINANCIAL UNDERTAKINGS

The Board of Directors of Icelandic State Financial Investments shall appoint a three-person selection committee to appoint two or three persons for each position of director of a financial undertaking to be filled. The Board of Icelandic State Financial Investments shall take a decision on the selection of individual directors based on the selection committee's nominations. The selection committee's criteria and qualification requirements, as well as

procedures laid down by Icelandic State Financial Investments for its work, shall be commensurate with the task, publicly available and accessible on the agency's website.

2.5 BOARDS OF GOVERNORS AND BOARDS OF DIRECTORS

Financial undertakings are operated on commercial premises, on the responsibility of their Boards of Directors/Governors and managers, like other companies. References to the Board of Directors of financial undertakings in this ownership strategy includes both Boards of Governors and Boards of Directors. The role of Boards of Directors of financial undertakings is to direct the progress of the undertakings in accordance with the statues, rules, Articles of Association and guidelines which govern their activities, including agreements on specific and general objectives in their operations which they have concluded with Icelandic State Financial Investments.

Persons elected to the Boards of financial undertakings to represent the state's holding shall following the criteria and objectives laid out in this ownership strategy. The same applies to the management of those financial undertakings majority owned by the state.

2.6 CENTRAL BANK OF ICELAND

In planning the sale of a financial undertaking the Minister must by law seek the opinion of the Central Bank of Iceland on equal treatment of bidders, the probable impact of the sale on the foreign exchange market, foreign reserves and liquid assets in circulation.

2.7 FINANCIAL SUPERVISORY AUTHORITY

The Financial Supervisory Authority is an independent supervisory institution responsible for financial market supervision. The Financial Supervisory Authority operates in accordance with the Act on Official Supervision of Financial Activities and among other things is to ensure that the activities of financial undertakings comply with currently applicable acts, regulations and rules. The Financial Supervisory Authority's responsibilities include assessing whether a party intending to acquire or increase a qualifying holding is eligible to own the holding, having regard to the sound and prudent operation of the financial undertaking. A qualifying holding under current legislation is 10% of more of share capital/voting rights.

3 CORE PRINCIPLES OF THE OWNERSHIP STRATEGY

Financial undertakings owned by the state must comply with those Acts and Regulations which apply to its activities.

The Boards of Directors of these companies are, just as Boards of Directors of other companies are, responsible for the company's operations and activities.

In view of their public ownership, it is important that the companies' emphases in their governance and activities support and work to achieve the owner's objectives in ownership. To accomplish this the owner's involvement in formulating policy and objectives for the company must be clear and unequivocal, however, without restricting the normal authority of the Board of Directors or reducing the responsibility of the Board for the company's operations. A clear strategy of the owner concerning the company defines plainly the Board's role and responsibility towards the owner.

To achieve the required balance between the owner's objectives in the company's operations, general perspectives of the Board and managers regarding its operations, and the specific considerations arising from public ownership of the company certain core principles are set out here which the company's owner has decided shall serve as guidelines for its operations and tasks. The rules are intended, firstly to provide a framework for exercising ownership of the company; secondly, to prescribe the owner's routes of communication with the company; thirdly, to provide guidance to the company's directors and managers in their work on behalf of the company; and, fourthly, to make the owner's principles regarding the company's management and corporate governance accessible to the public.

Those core principles laid down here by the owner are based on views of good and successful operation of publicly owned companies. The rules are further developed and explained in the section on governance, requirements and performance benchmarks.

Core principles of the ownership strategy

4 GOVERNANCE, REQUIREMENTS AND PERFORMANCE BENCHMARKS

This section lays down more detailed requirements and benchmarks set by the owner for the activities, based on the core principles of the ownership strategy. The requirements and benchmarks apply to the following aspects: management and organisation, governance, policy formulation and future vision, company operations, procedures and working practices, information disclosure and relations with the owner.

4.1 MANAGEMENT AND ORGANISATION

a. The role of management and the Board of Directors is to safeguard the company's interests in every respect and ensure the implementation of this ownership strategy.

b. Icelandic State Financial Investments shall make every effort to select on behalf of the owner directors with varied educational background and extensive and practical knowledge and experience of operations suitable for the company in question, to ensure the Board consists of a professional and diverse team of directors.

c. In selecting directors regard must be had for considerations of gender equality and to ensure that the work of directors and managers does not create conflicts of interest with their other work.

d. The company's Board of Directors shall work independently, in accordance with acts and rules applying to financial undertakings and bear the responsibility for the company's activities and operations towards its owner.

e. The company's Board of Directors takes the lead in formulating its policy and setting objectives for the company in accordance with this ownership strategy.

f. The company's Board of Directors has an independent duty to monitor and supervise its operations and activities on behalf of the owner.

g. The company's Board of Directors shall have an overview of its activities and provide appropriate control of its management.

h. The CEO is appointed by the Board and responsible to it for the company's activities.

4.2 CORPORATE GOVERNANCE

a. Issues affecting the company shall be raised at a shareholders' meeting, which is the formal venue for Icelandic State Financial Investments to involve itself in the company's affairs on behalf of the owner.

b. Icelandic State Financial Investments implements decisions, which it has taken on behalf of the owner, at shareholders' meetings.

c. The Board of Directors and employees of Icelandic State Financial Investments shall neither be involved in the day-to-day operations of the undertakings nor influence their decisions except through the normal channels of communication

arising from the legal form of each undertaking or as agreed in accords between the companies and Icelandic State Financial Investments, cf. the provision in Art. 4 of the Act on Icelandic State Financial Investments.

d. The company shall ensure equal treatment of all its shareholders.

e. The limits of responsibility between Icelandic State Financial Investments, on behalf of the owner, and the company's Board of Directors shall be clear and all communications, information disclosure and supervision shall be based on the provisions of this ownership strategy and generally recognised rules on the activities of independent companies.

f. In its work the company's Board of Directors shall follow recognised guidelines on corporate governance, including guidelines of the Financial Supervisory Authority on internal governance of financial undertakings, and as appropriate the Basel Committee on Banking Supervision Guidance on Corporate Governance for Banks.

g. The company's Board of Directors shall adopt written protocols providing in detail for the role and work of the Board of Directors, division of duties among directors and the Board's relationship with company management. There must be a clear demarcation between the Board of Directors and management of financial undertakings, ensuring that the distinction between their respective authority and responsibility is clear.

h. The company's Board of Directors and management shall make every effort to work in accordance with the criteria, values and business ethics generally expected to apply to publicly owned companies.

i. Transactions between the owner and the company or between the company and other state-owned companies shall be transparent and on market terms.

j. Larger financial undertakings owned by the state shall, in accordance with this ownership strategy, establish the necessary work processes to follow standards, rules and guidelines comparable to those required of enterprises listed on NASDAQ Iceland.

4.3 POLICY FORMULATION AND FUTURE VISION

a. The company's Board of Directors shall have a clear vision for its future and objectives for its operations. In addition to those objectives and emphases set out in this ownership strategy, the company shall adopt clear and ambitious targets for its operations.

b. The company shall adopt an information policy based on the principle of making public information which need not specifically be kept secret due to material interests of the company or its customers.

c. The company shall set out a detailed policy on environmental issues, sustainable development and corporate social responsibility and make this public.

d. The company's Board of Directors shall adopt a human resources policy in consultation with its employees.

e. The company's Board of Directors shall adopt a remuneration policy for the company to be approved at an AGM.

f. The company shall publicly disseminate its future vision, strategy and performance on its website or by other means.

4.4 COMPANY OPERATIONS

a. Investments made and financial risk taken in the company's operations shall be managed with a view to making its operations financially stable in the short and long term.

b. In its budgets the company shall aim at acceptable profitability commensurate with the risk in its operations and the objectives laid out in this ownership strategy.

c. The company shall make every effort to adopt new products and innovations and ensure continuous development in its activities to maintain its competitiveness.

4.5 WORKING PRACTICES AND PROCEDURES

a. Care shall be taken to ensure transparency and non-discrimination in the company's management and activities.

b. Its operations shall be characterised by well-conceived and open management practices.

c. Both managers and employees shall be hired based on their qualifications following a transparent, objective and pre-determined hiring process.

d. Decisions taken concerning the company's general operations shall wherever possible aim at increasing competition and reducing oligopoly in the society.

e. Special attention shall be given to work procedures for procurement of goods and services, taking care to ensure cost-efficiency, non-discrimination and transparency.

f. Care shall be taken to ensure non-discrimination, objectivity, cost-efficiency and transparency in the sale or disposal of the company's assets. As a general principle such assets are to be sold in an open sales process from which no derogations may be made without unequivocal grounds for so doing. Competition aspects shall also be considered. The Board of Directors shall set procedural rules for the sale of assets and make them public and accessible.

4.6 INFORMATION DISCLOSURE, PERFORMANCE MEASUREMENT AND RELATIONSHIP WITH OWNER'S REPRESENTATIVES

a. Icelandic State Financial Investments shall, on behalf of the owner, conclude agreements with financial undertakings on specific and general targets, cf. the provision of Art. 4 of Act No. 88/2009.

b. Dividends paid by state-owned financial undertakings are part of state revenues. It is important to take this into consideration in the budgets of state-owned financial undertakings and in agreements between the companies and Icelandic State Financial Investments concerning the companies' dividend policy.

c. Icelandic State Financial Investments shall, on behalf of the owner, meet regularly with company representatives to go over the company's performance and how successfully it has achieved the objectives for its operations.

d. Any major changes in its activities proposed by the company must be presented to Icelandic State Financial Investments on behalf of the owner.

e. If there is seen to be specific cause for so doing, notice shall be given of other upcoming company matters deemed appropriate that the owner be informed of even if no decision is called for on its part.

f. The company shall take care not to discriminate between owners in its information disclosure.

g. The company shall publish financial data as provided for by the Act on Financial Undertakings and comply with standards, rules and guidelines comparable to those required of enterprises listed on NASDAQ Iceland.

h. If the Board of Directors of a financial undertaking or individual directors decide they cannot comply with the provisions of this ownership strategy, Icelandic State Financial Investments must be informed thereof without delay. This shall also be done if the Board of Directors becomes aware that this strategy has not been followed in the company's operations, in which case information on what the response to this will be must furthermore be provided.

IMPORTANT DEVELOPMENT TRENDS

BASIC INFORMATION

Since 2012, the country has continued to recover from the severe economic crisis that started in 2008. GDP growth averaged 3.8% for 2012-16, while GDP per capita reached nearly US$60,000 in 2016. Growth during this period was driven by tourism-related services while the contribution to GDP from the traditional fishing, fish processing, and aluminium sectors declined.

With a small open economy and limited range of natural resources, trade is critically important to Iceland's economy and exports and imports of goods and services were the equivalent of over 90% of GDP in 2016. The main goods exported were fish and fish products, and aluminium and products thereof which together accounted for over three-quarters of the value of goods exports in 2016. However, a surplus in trade-in-goods in 2012 became a deficit in 2014 as imports increased while exports declined due to lower aluminium prices and lower quantities of fish exports. The EU is the main destination for exports (nearly three-quarters) and source of imports (nearly half) . The deficit in trade-in-goods was more than compensated by the rising surplus in trade-in-services, primarily due to increased tourism. Tourism is now Iceland's largest export sector, and tourism services (transport and travel) were responsible for nearly 80% of Iceland's services receipts in 2016, which resulted in a tourism-services-related surplus of ISK 300 billion.

Practically, all the temporary restrictions on certain types of cross-border capital transfers and foreign exchange transactions that were introduced following the collapse of the banking sector have been removed. A capital account liberalization strategy was introduced in 2015 and controls were progressively reduced. In March 2017, the restrictions on foreign exchange transactions and cross-border movement of domestic and foreign currency were largely lifted.

Iceland is an active Member of the WTO but has a mixed record for notifications with no TBT, import licensing or preferential rules of origin notifications and only two SPS notifications were made in the period 2012 to 2016. On the other hand, several notifications from Iceland were distributed in the first half of 2017, including on domestic support for agriculture for the years 2013-15, new public procurement rules, and state trading enterprises.

As a member of the European Free Trade Association (EFTA) and the European Economic Area (EEA), many of Iceland's trade and trade-related policies and laws are closely related to those of the European Union and Iceland is part of the Internal Market with free movement of goods, services, capital and workers. However, some issues such as trade policy and taxation are not incorporated into the EEA and agriculture is covered by bilateral arrangements. In 2015, a new bilateral agreement on trade in agricultural goods between Iceland and the EU was concluded which eliminated or reduced tariffs on a range of products, increased the quantities in some existing tariff quotas, and created new tariff quotas. As part of the agreement, Iceland is to apply the same level of protection as the EU for GI products registered in the EU.

Iceland is a party to 32 reciprocal preferential agreements, mostly through the EFTA, with three new agreements having entered into force during the review period (Bosnia and Herzegovina, certain Central American states (Costa Rica and Panama), and the GCC) . In addition, during the review period, Iceland concluded an FTA on its own behalf with China.

Since 2012, several projects have been implemented to improve customs procedures, including the introduction of a risk management system, and the introduction of a quality control system. In addition, work is under way on the establishment of an authorized economic operator programme, a single window system, implementation of the revised single administrative document, and an electronic system for the clearance of vessels. The instrument of ratification of the Trade Facilitation Agreement was submitted to the WTO on 31 October 2016.

In a significant development, Iceland eliminated tariffs on all non-agricultural products, with tariffs on clothing and footwear eliminated on 1 January 2016 and tariffs on remaining products eliminated on 1 January 2017. As a result, nearly 90% of tariff lines are now duty-free compared to 70% in 2012. In addition, tariffs on some agricultural products were also reduced. As a result, the overall average tariff fell from 8.3% in 2012 to 4.6% in 2017. However, tariffs on several agricultural product groups, particularly meat, dairy, plants, and flowers, remain high and often take the form of complex non-*ad valorem* duties. Nevertheless, the average applied tariff on agricultural products declined to 20% in 2017 compared to 29% in 2012 although tariffs are much higher on some products, such as dairy products. About 95% of tariff lines are bound and the unbound tariffs apply to a wide variety of products including some fuels, fertilizers, and machinery products all of which now have duty free applied rates. It was not possible to calculate the *ad valorem* equivalents for bound tariffs given the complex nature of some of them. However, there were no cases of applied rates exceeding bound rates.

Tariff quotas are used for a number of agricultural products either under the WTO Agreement on Agriculture, FTAs, or autonomously. In many cases, the current applied tariff for tariff lines subject to WTO tariff quotas is the same as, or lower than, the bound in-quota tariff and, therefore, the quota is not used.

Iceland has never used or initiated investigations for anti-dumping or countervailing duties, nor has it ever used the special agricultural safeguard although its customs legislation does provide for them and Iceland reserved the right to use the SSG on 390 tariff lines. There is no legislation on global safeguards although safeguard provisions are generally included in the free trade agreements to which Iceland is a party. According to Iceland’s notifications to the WTO, export subsidies for agricultural products have not been used since 31 August 1998.

Although a number of amendments have been made during the review period to the laws relating to SPS measures they remain strict and are justified on the grounds that Iceland's domestic animals are highly susceptible to exotic pests and diseases. Imports of some products are prohibited and others are subject to controls and licensing requirements. In general, Iceland applies the EU's rules on food and imported food must comply with requirements that are at least equivalent to those applicable in the EU.

Incentives for regional investment are provided for under new legislation; the previous legislation expired at the end of 2013. Some of the projects approved under the expired legislation had been found by the EFTA Surveillance Authority to be incompatible with the EEA Agreement. Under the new legislation, tax incentives apply for investments outside the Reykjavik area which are limited to 15-35% of the initial investment depending on the size of the enterprise with the higher limits applying to smaller enterprises. In addition, there are incentives for research and investment through tax credits and grants.

Although there have been no substantive changes to the legislation on competition policy during the review period, the Icelandic Competition Authority (ICA) has been actively implementing the law and, in the 2012-17 period, has prevented one merger, imposed conditions on a further 25 mergers, and has fined 17 companies a total of over €22 million for collusion or abuse of dominant position. In addition, in an opinion issued in 2015, the ICA found that due to the slot allocation arrangements at Keflavik Airport Icelandair has enjoyed a *de facto* priority for the most important slot times.

The legal framework for public procurement was significantly revised during the review period with a new Act on Public Procurement and other laws and regulations (including new thresholds) introduced to bring legislation into line with EEA rules. The new Act, which applies to the State, local authorities, their institutions and other public entities, sets out to ensure equal treatment of economic operators, encourage efficiency in public sector operations through active competition and to promote innovation and development in public procurement of supplies, works and services. Iceland has been a party to the WTO Agreement on Government Procurement (GPA) since 2001 and has completed the procedures for becoming a party to the revised GPA, which entered into force for Iceland on 6 April 2014.

In addition to changes in legislation on various aspects of intellectual property (IP), including on geographical indications (GIs), the trademark law, and a new fee structure, more changes are foreseen to bring national laws into line with the EEA. Furthermore, the Intellectual Property Policy, 2016-22, issued in 2016, put forward a number of proposals to review laws, promote the role of IP in the economy, and improve procedures for registration and enforcement of IP rights. The new act and regulation on GIs apply to food, wine, spirit drinks, and some other products. The product name may be protected if the product originates from a specific area, has qualities or characteristics of the area, and the production, processing and preparation of the product takes place in the area. The name must be registered by the Icelandic Food and Veterinary Authority (MAST) . In addition, as part of the agreement with the EU on trade in agricultural products, Iceland is to provide protection for a list of 1,150 EU GIs.

Agriculture represents a small part of GDP and employment but remains historically, socially, and culturally important for Iceland, as well as being relatively highly protected and subsidized. Imports (at US$492 million in 2016) exceeded exports (US$95 million) . Domestic policies were revised under new agreements between the Government and the farmers' association for the period 2017-26. For dairy and beef, the production quota system remains but is to be reviewed in 2019 to consider the feasibility of abolishing it; headage payments continue and milk payments are to be increased; and support entitlements (basic payments to all active dairy and cattle farmers) are to be phased out.

For sheep, support entitlements are also to be phased out while quality assurance payments are to be increased and headage payments introduced. Under these and other changes, the total support to agriculture is to decrease slightly over the duration of the agreements. During 2012 to 2016, support to agriculture in ISK terms increased under the Green, Blue, and Amber Boxes of the WTO and for the 2012 to 2015 period under the OECD's total and producer support estimates (TSE and PSE) . The dairy sector is the most heavily supported; in 2016, it accounted for ISK 18.5 billion out of a total of ISK 21.3 billion in Amber Box support and, together with beef, ISK 0.7 billion in the Blue Box. Overall, the PSE was nearly ISK 26 billion in 2015 or 56% of gross farm receipts, the third highest among OECD countries.

Although the contributions of fishing and fish processing to GDP have declined, they remain relatively very important and represented 4.6% and 2.7% respectively in 2016. Total exports of fish and fish products were US$1,925 million in 2016, representing 43% of exports of goods, while imports were US$134 million. Fisheries policy has not changed significantly over the past few years. Based on stock assessments by the Marine and Freshwater Research Institute (MRFI), total allowable catches (TACs) are established which are allocated to individual vessels under the individual transferable quota (ITQ) systems. In addition, a number of effort and gear restrictions apply, discards of commercial species are prohibited, and a vessel owner may not leave port without an adequate quota for the trip. According to the OECD, the Fisheries Support Estimates (FSE) for 2012 to 2014 was negative indicating a net average annual contribution of ISK 4.4 billion from the fisheries sector as fees were greater than the estimates of support. The FSE was positive for 2015 when general services support was greater than cost recovery charges. Foreign ownership of fishing operations and fish processing is limited to 25% direct and 49% direct plus indirect ownership although up to 33% direct foreign ownership may be permitted in some cases.

Hydro and thermal power sources are abundant in Iceland and electricity prices for industrial consumers are the lowest in the EEA. As a result, energy intensive industries, such as aluminium production, have been established and aluminium and alloys thereof represent over one-third of total exports of goods (US$1.5 billion) . Investment and ownership of energy exploitation rights and the production and distribution of energy are limited to EEA and EFTA residents, while Landsnet, a private company, has the exclusive right to provide transmission services.

Since the financial crisis, the banking system has stabilized and recovered. Currently there are four commercial and four savings banks (compared with nine in 2012) . Two of the commercial banks are wholly state-owned, while a third has a minority government stake. The restructuring of the banks has also resulted in the ratio of non-performing loans to total loans declining from a peak of 20% in 2010 to 2.1% in 2016. In June 2015, the authorities announced a plan to unwind the estates of the failed banks and the remaining offshore ISK holdings (mainly bank deposits, treasury securities and equity interests) . In June 2016, the Central Bank held the first of three voluntary euro auctions for offshore ISK holders with the exchange rate based on a sliding scale related to the size of the bid. Direct state assistance to the financial sector was the equivalent of about 34% of GDP. However, recoveries were estimated to be about 43% of GDP (mainly bank equity and subordinated debt, and stability contributions from the estates of the failed banks) .

Thus, the State is estimated to have made a net gain in excess of 9% of GDP. During the review period, several regulatory changes were introduced including the establishment of new bodies to assess the financial system, systemic risk, and financial stability and formulate policies. In addition, several other measures, including new liquidity rules, funding ratios, capital buffers, and rules relating to consumer mortgage credit were introduced.

Tourism has increased considerably since 2010 and, in 2016, represented about 10% of GDP and nearly 40% of export receipts for goods and services. Total spending on tourism-related activities increased from ISK 93 billion in 2009 to ISK 222 billion in 2015. Apart from Iceland's unique landscape and other attractions, the increase can also be attributed to the depreciation in the ISK after the financial crisis, better and more frequent flight connections, and better marketing. Tourism also accounts for the increase in air passengers, as well as Icelandic airlines becoming a more financially viable option for transatlantic passengers and the promotion of Iceland as a transatlantic hub. The total number of passengers through Keflavik airport in 2017 is estimated to be in the region of 9 million.

Iceland has improved trading and investment conditions since 2012 and partly as a result of this the economy has recovered and is expanding rapidly. With a small population and limited natural resources, apart from energy and fish, trade remains important but the range of exports is limited to tourism, fish and fish products, and aluminium and products thereof. Therefore, the country remains vulnerable to shocks, including the appreciation of the ISK, overheating of the economy, and Brexit. However, short term exposure to external factors has been reduced: at end-2016, total external debt was US$23.4 billion compared to US$105.8 billion in 2012 and international reserves were over US$7 trillion (partly due to the unwinding of the estates of the failed banks) . Furthermore, despite uncertainties relating to Brexit, as growth picks up in the EU, Iceland's main trading partner, opportunities for trade in goods and services should continue to improve.

MAIN FEATURES OF THE ECONOMY

Iceland is a high-income developed economy with a GDP per capita of ISK 7.2 million (€53,948) and a population of 338,450 in 2016 (Table 1.1) . Fishing and fish processing remain important to the economy (contributing 7.2% to GDP in 2016), but services have continued to increase (now representing 71% of GDP), as have manufacturing (mainly aluminium) (8.4%), and construction (6.8%) . Trade is critical to the economy, with imports and exports of goods and services equivalent to about 92% of GDP. Merchandise exports continue to be concentrated in fish and fish products and aluminium manufacturing, both of which were responsible for over three quarters of merchandise exports in 2016. Furthermore, during the review period, services exports have shown robust growth, driven primarily by the tourism sector (Table 1.2) .

Iceland was one of the countries worst affected by the 2008 financial crisis with the banking system collapsing and the country going into a deep recession. 2009 to 2010, real GDP contracted by over 10%. In response, the Government enacted the Emergency Act (the Act on the Authority for Treasury Disbursements due to Unusual Financial

Market Circumstances, etc., No. 125/2008) which allowed for,*inter alia*, immediate intervention in the operations of the collapsing banks and the putting in place of capital controls. Furthermore, funding from Nordic countries and the IMF through a Stand-By Arrangement helped to shore up the economy.[1] Prudent macroeconomic management and continued openness of the economy have since helped turn the economy around. During the review period (2012-16), real GDP grew at an average annual rate of 3.8% and is estimated to grow at the same rate in 2017 (Table 1.1) . Growth has been fuelled mainly by tourism-related services (wholesale and retail trade, hotels and restaurants, and transportation and storage) (Table 1.2) . As a result of the growth, GDP per capita rose from around US$44,000 in 2012 to nearly US$60,000 in 2016 and the unemployment rate halved from 6% to 3% over the same period.

The main risks to sustained growth stem from the potential overheating of the economy which would be perpetuated by the recent large wage awards, capital account liberalization (which could result in monetary and exchange rate instability), and the uncertainty surrounding the aftermath of Brexit. To mitigate the risks from these, the right policy mix would include monetary and some fiscal tightening to cool demand.

The large wage awards (about 25% for 2015-18) could increase domestic demand and, coupled with fiscal easing, could give rise to inflationary pressures.

To keep fiscal policy in check, the parliament passed new legislation on public sector finances in December 2015. The new legislation imposes stringent rules on operational performance and developments in the debt level. The main objective of the new legislation is to provide for sound macro-fiscal policy based on comprehensive medium-term budgeting and reporting. The new medium-term fiscal framework (MTFF), the cornerstone of the new Act, is designed to address gaps in the old legal framework from budget formulation to execution. The objective is to set up a transparent and credible MTFF that serves the purpose of mapping out macroeconomic and fiscal policy-making. The Act establishes a procedural fiscal rule that maps out a five-year general government fiscal path with the following three fiscal rules: the overall result over a five-year period must always be positive, and the annual deficit may not exceed 2.5% of GDP; total debt, excluding pension obligations and accounts payable, but including cash balances and deposits, may not exceed 30% of GDP; and, if the net debt ratio rises above 30%, the excess portion must decline by an average of at least 5% per year in each three-year period.

The objective of the capital controls that were introduced as a temporary measure during the crisis was to place temporary restrictions on certain types of cross-border capital transfers and foreign exchange transactions that could cause monetary and exchange rate instability while the resurrection of the Icelandic economy and financial system was underway. The capital controls played an important role in achieving and safeguarding the objectives of the Icelandic policy response to stabilize the exchange rate, ensure medium-term fiscal sustainability, and develop a comprehensive bank restructuring strategy. According to the authorities, the controls were successful in achieving these objectives.

The Government's updated capital account liberalization strategy was presented in June 2015. The strategy proposed that the controls be lifted in stages. The first phase in the strategy involved reducing the size of outflows through the foreign exchange market in connection with the resolution of the failed banks' estates, either through voluntary composition agreements based on specific stability conditions or through taxation that would mitigate the adverse balance of payments effects. The second phase would focus on reducing the externalities associated with outflows from offshore ISK owners through an auction and secure segregation of the offshore market from the onshore market during the liberalization of restrictions on households and businesses. The third phase would focus on households and businesses.

The Act No. 37/2016 on the Treatment of Króna-Denominated Assets Subject to Special Restrictions was passed by the parliament in May 2016 enabling the authorities to segregate offshore ISK and take the next step towards lifting the capital controls. Under the provisions of the Act, offshore ISK holders were allowed to invest in the same instruments as before, with the addition of special certificates of deposit issued by the Central Bank. However, the banks holding the accounts of offshore ISK owners were required to buy equivalent certificates of deposit from the Central Bank. These instruments bear an interest rate of 0.5%, which is reviewed every 12 months. In June 2016, the Central Bank held a foreign currency single price auction in which owners of offshore ISK assets were given the option of exchanging their holdings for foreign currency. The auction price was set at ISK 190/euro and the Bank accepted all offers submitted at that rate. The auction helped to facilitate the exit of offshore ISK without negative effects on the foreign exchange market, and the outstanding stock of offshore ISK was reduced significantly.[2] The Act grants the owners of offshore ISK assets temporary authorization to withdraw and conclude foreign exchange transactions at a reference rate of ISK 220/euro; such transactions amounted to a further ISK 15.5 billion exiting. In March 2017, the Central Bank concluded agreements with several owners of offshore ISK assets subject to special restrictions pursuant to Act No. 37/2016. Under the agreement, the Bank purchased a further ISK 90 billion at an exchange rate of ISK 137.5/euro of offshore ISK assets. As a result of the above measures, the remaining offshore ISK assets are now estimated to be ISK 103.6 billion or 4.3% of GDP and the risk of large-scale outflows of offshore ISK through the foreign exchange market following the liberalization of capital controls has been mitigated.

Owners of offshore króna assets who were not parties to the March agreement were subsequently given the option of concluding a transaction with the Central Bank on the same terms. The Central Bank's offer was valid until 28 April 2017. Owners of remaining offshore ISK assets continue to have the right to sell their assets; they can make withdrawals, exchange all interest payments in the foreign exchange market, and trade in the offshore market.

Additionally, Act No. 105/2016 (amending the Foreign Exchange Act, No. 87/1992), which is aimed at lifting capital controls on individuals and businesses, entered into force on 21 October 2016. The Act authorized immediate outward FDI and easing of restrictions on long- and short-term portfolio investment up to a limit of ISK 30 million. Effective 1 January 2017, the limit was raised to ISK 100 million and expanded to include cross-border deposit transfers. The Central Bank is authorized to ease these limits until they are abolished, along with limitations on derivatives and other instruments and other remaining restrictions.

Furthermore, in June 2016, in order to pre-empt any disruptions caused by the lifting of capital controls, the Central Bank of Iceland published new Rules on Special Reserve Requirements for New Foreign Currency Inflows, No. 490/2016. The main purpose of the Temporary Provision was to provide the Central Bank with a policy instrument, generally referred to as a capital flow management measure (CFM), which is designed to temper inflows of foreign currency and to affect the composition of such inflows. The CFM aimed to reduce the risk of excessive and speculative capital inflows aimed at exploiting the wide interest rate differential between Iceland and its trading partners and to safeguard against implementation risks associated with the second and third phase of the capital account liberalization strategy. From 14 March 2017, the restrictions on foreign exchange transactions and cross-border movement of domestic and foreign currency were largely lifted.[3]

RECENT ECONOMIC DEVELOPMENTS

MONETARY POLICY

The Central Bank's main monetary policy objective is to maintain price stability. The Bank has full instrumental independence to achieve its goal. The price stability goal is defined as an annual inflation (as measured by the consumer price index) target of 2.5%. The Bank is also financially independent with direct financing of the Government by the Central Bank prohibited.

In the aftermath of the 2008 financial crisis, the inflation-targeting regime was refined (dubbed "inflation-targeting plus") . Active use of intervention in the foreign exchange market to correct excessive exchange rate fluctuations has become an important part of the post-crisis monetary policy framework, which also emphasizes the use of additional policy instruments such as macro-prudential tools and capital flow management measures to curb destabilizing capital inflows.

After the large spike in inflation following the financial crisis in 2008, inflation gradually declined towards the inflation target in early 2014. It fell further following the large decline in global oil prices in late 2014 and has remained below or close to the target for the last three years (Table 1.1) . The Monetary Policy Committee of the Central Bank of Iceland started raising interest rates again in 2015 in the face of rising risks of inflation expectations becoming unmoored following a very generous wage settlement. As inflation expectations eased back to target, the Bank has started lowering rates again. The monetary policy stance remains tight, however, as output grows strongly and spare capacity is fully absorbed.

FISCAL POLICY

The legacy of the 2008 financial crisis continues to affect Iceland's fiscal position. The crisis increased social protection expenses mainly through unemployment benefits, which peaked at 1.9% of GDP in 2009 before subsiding to 0.5% of GDP in 2015 (still higher than they were in 2008) . The crisis also imposed a debt burden on the Government resulting in increased interest payments, which rose to 6% of GDP in 2009, before falling to around 4.5% of GDP in 2015. Consequently, since the advent of the crisis, Iceland had continuously registered a fiscal deficit, which was 0.8% of GDP in 2015. In recent years, public sector wage growth and increased municipal borrowing have fuelled the deficit. On the other hand, general government gross debt, which was over 90% of GDP in 2012, had fallen to under 70% of GDP in 2015 (Table 1.1) .

The settlement of the failed banks' estates resulted in a one-off windfall gain of around 17% of GDP. As a result, Iceland registered a fiscal surplus of over 17% of GDP in 2016. The proceeds from the settlement of the banks' estates are to be used for public debt reduction, which should reduce the general government gross debt to around 50% of GDP.

The 2016 budget included a reform of the personal income tax (PIT) system. The main objectives of the reform were to lower taxes on average wage income, and also to simplify the system, increase its efficiency and make it more transparent. The personal income tax rates were reduced and the current three rate bands harmonized into two, in two phases, for an annual revenue loss of about 0.5% of GDP. The latter phase was subject to a general proviso that the changes would only be implemented if it can be considered justifiable in view of economic developments and prospects as they were assessed in mid-2016. That test was passed and the latter phase of the PIT changes came into force from the beginning of the year 2017. No specific tax measures were made to make up the revenue loss from the PIT changes.

BALANCE OF PAYMENTS

During the period under review, Iceland's current account showed a drastic turnaround. From a deficit of around 4% of GDP in 2012, the current account registered a surplus of 8% of GDP in 2016, reflecting an increasing difference between gross national savings and gross national investment (Table 1.3) .

1The improvement in the current account since the 2008 financial crisis was initially due to reduced interest payments and a surplus in merchandise trade, which has since turned into a deficit. However the increase in the surplus for services has more than compensated for the negative goods balance. The growth in the services balance was primarily due to the strong performance of the tourism sector. Between 2010 and 2015, the number of visitors to Iceland grew by an average annual rate of 22% to reach 1.3 million, and tourism-related spending more than doubled to ISK 222 billion over the same period (Section 4.3.4) . Consequently, tourism is Iceland's largest export sector, and tourism services (transport and travel) were responsible for nearly 80% of Iceland's services receipts in 2016, which resulted in a tourism-services-related surplus of ISK 300 billion in 2016 (Table 1.4) . Additionally the balance on the income account, which had reached a deficit of over ISK 300 billion in 2008, has also shown a significant improvement, albeit not as marked as the services surplus, reaching a surplus of ISK 51 billion. The improvement has come about due to reduced outlays in lieu of investment.[4]

The capital account measures capital transfers between residents and non-residents; these can include investment grants, debt forgiveness, or unusually large insurance compensation payments. The financial account includes net transactions with financial assets and liabilities that take place between residents and non-residents. Not all entries in the financial account derive from actual transactions. In certain instances, imputed values are entered into the financial account even though no transaction has taken place, so as to reflect the underlying economic relationship. Reinvested earnings, investment income earned on technical reserves, accrued unpaid interest on liabilities, interest added to the principal amount, and interest in arrears are all classified as financial account transactions. The difference between assets and liabilities is the international investment position (IIP), which indicates whether there is a net claim or a net liability *vis-à-vis* non-residents. Net direct investment, portfolio investment and financial derivatives are also included in the financial account.

During the period under review, the capital and financial account has gone from a deficit of around ISK 92 billion in 2012 to a surplus of ISK 300 billion in 2016. Iceland's net international investment position (NIIP) improved considerably in the post-crisis period, through debt repayments facilitated by the current account surplus, debt write-offs due to bankruptcies of private sector entities, and the composition agreements of the failed financial institutions' estates in late 2015. With regard to failed banks and the settlement of their estates, the underlying NIIP calculated by the Central Bank of Iceland was -131% of GDP in 2008, but that improved to -31.5% in 2015. Nearly 40% of the reduction is due to the current account surplus and GDP growth during the period, while the rest is due to asset revaluation and debt restructuring.[5] Furthermore, at the end of 2008, the failed banks owned 77% of total foreign loans. This share increased to 90% at year-end 2009 but had fallen to 64% by the end of 2014. Between 2009 and 2014, the stock of foreign lending by the deposit money banks in winding-up proceedings dropped from 63% of GDP to 11%. The main reason for this decline is that some of the loans were reclassified as foreign direct investment (FDI) at the end of 2009 because of financial difficulties among the banks' debtors, prompting a takeover of the companies concerned. At the end of 2015, foreign lending by the holding companies of the failed banks amounted to 7.4% of GDP, and had decreased further to 5.6% of GDP in 2016.

In addition to the current account surplus, the Central Bank purchased foreign currency through interventions so as to build up foreign exchange reserves in preparation for the lifting of capital controls. At the end of 2016, reserves amounted to 34% of GDP and provided import cover for nine months.

TRADE PERFORMANCE

Iceland's economy has continued to depend on trade, and trade in goods and services as a proportion of GDP exceeded 92%. During the period under review, the balance on trade in goods turned from a surplus to a deficit as exports fell and import rose, due mainly to an appreciation of the exchange rate. In contrast, the services surplus more than doubled during the review period to over ISK 260 billion in 2016. The increase was mainly due to an upsurge in tourism.

COMPOSITION OF TRADE

During the review period, the composition of Iceland's exports did not change; exports of primary products in total merchandise exports remained static at around 85% of total exports (Chart 1.1) . Within primary products, the share of agriculture, fish, and food products increased. In contrast, the share of aluminium products fell (Table A1.1) . The share of manufactures declined from over 14% in 2012 to around 13% in 2016. Within manufactures, the decline was due to reduced exports of iron and steel and chemicals.

The share of primary products in total merchandise imports declined from nearly 40% in 2012 to 31.5% in 2016. Within primary products, the decline was due to reduced imports of alumina on account of lower alumina prices (Table A1.1) . On the other hand, the share of manufacturing in total merchandise imports rose from around 60% in 2012 to 68.4% in 2016. Within manufactures, imports of transport equipment and consumer goods rose partly due to increased tourism and strong consumption growth fuelled by a rapid rise in households' purchasing power.

DIRECTION OF TRADE

Iceland's main export destination in 2016 remained the EU-28, followed by the United States, and then other EFTA countries (Norway, Liechtenstein, and Switzerland) . The shares of the EU-28 and EFTA declined negligibly during the review period, while the share of the United States and that of Asia as a whole increased

1.27. The EU-28 remains Iceland's largest import supplier, followed by EFTA and the United States. During the period under review, the EU-28 share rose significantly, as did that of Asia as a whole, while the shares of Brazil and EFTA declined sharply (Table A1.3) . The decline in the latter two is explained by declining oil and other commodity prices.

FOREIGN DIRECT INVESTMENT

During the period under review, both inward and outward FDI flows were volatile. FDI inflows peaked at over ISK 128 billion in both 2011 and 2012 (around 11% of GDP), before declining to ISK 48 billion (4% of GDP) in 2013. They have since picked up, and amounted to ISK 93 billion in 2015 (around 7% of GDP) . Consequently, the stock of inward FDI peaked at 104% in the beginning of 2012 but had fallen back to 75% of GDP by year-end 2015 because of the restructuring of a pharmaceutical company, in 2012 and again in 2015. The 2012 restructuring also explains the turnaround in the net FDI position, which was negative in 2010 and 2011 but had turned positive by year-end 2012. Furthermore, non-residents' equity as a share of inward FDI had been roughly 12% in 2011 but fell to 0 at the end of 2013 because of the restructuring of the pharmaceutical company. At year-end 2015, the ratio had risen up to 32%, due to a further restructuring of the pharmaceutical company in early 2015

In 2015, the main investor in Iceland was Luxembourg (nearly 80% of FDI stock), followed by the Netherlands and Switzerland. Most of the FDI in Iceland takes the form of inter-company loans; and Luxembourg has a large banking industry and a large cross-border fund administration industry (Table A1.4 and A1.6) . Netherlands is the largest recipient of FDI from Iceland, followed by the United Kingdom and Luxembourg (Table A1.5 and A1.7) . According to the authorities, FDI investment in the Netherlands and in Luxembourg is most often related to affiliates of domestic companies that have headquarters in these countries due to tax reasons. The FDI in the United Kingdom can to some extent be explained by investment in companies that have been acquired as a result of debt restructuring and which are being prepared for sale by their holders.

TRADE AND INVESTMENT REGIME

GENERAL FRAMEWORK

Iceland, an island nation, located strategically between Europe and North America, has excellent connectivity, both by air and sea. It possesses plentiful energy resources from geothermal and hydroelectric sources, which has allowed it to have 100% renewable energy and thus one of the most reliable power infrastructures. The country also benefits from social stability and a well-educated work force. Iceland has capitalized on these elements and has developed many energy-intensive industries and data centres, and propelled its tourism sector to the leading export earner. As a representative democracy, Iceland's people assign powers to their elected representatives in the parliament, who have legislative and fiscal powers. Iceland is governed by rule of law whereby the judiciary is autonomous and the executive is answerable to parliament.

Iceland's constitution forms the country's main legal framework and is comprised of seven sections covering the parliament, president, judiciary, church (including freedom of religion), and human rights. The current constitution dates from 1944, but has been amended eight times since. The most recent amendment[6] was in 2013 and concerned a temporary provision that applied until 30 April 2017 on rules to amend the constitution.[7] It provided that in order to amend the constitution, the parliament (Althingi) was required to vote two-thirds in favour and that a referendum would then be launched so that the electorate of the country could vote to approve or reject the amendment. These temporary provisions have since expired and are no longer relevant.

The main law for the judiciary, Act No. 15/1998 on the Judiciary, will be replaced by Act No. 50/2016 on the Judiciary, with entry into force as of 1 January 2018. Under Act No. 50/2016, the Supreme Court remains the highest court, while a court on national law and appeals (Landsréttur) has been introduced between the Supreme Court and the eight district courts. The specialized Labour Court and Courts of Impeachment remain. Most provisions of Act No. 50/2016 are to take effect from 1 January 2018, but provisional provisions I, II, IV, V and VI entered into force on 14 June 2016, as necessary for the Act's entry into force. There are no special courts for trade disputes; they are handled by the general courts.

In 2009, the Althingi instructed the Government to apply for EU membership. The European Commission commenced negotiations with Iceland in 2010, however following a change of government in 2013, Iceland's EU membership negotiations were halted. In 2015, Iceland formally informed the European Union that it had no intention of resuming the accession process and was no longer a candidate country.[8] In 2014, the Icelandic Government presented a policy on Europe, including main priorities and implementation.[9] The policy gives priority to the efficient implementation of the EEA Agreement, proactive and close collaboration with the EU, and collaboration among EFTA States for access to international markets.

A Presidential Decree was issued in January 2017 setting out the organization and administrative responsibilities of the various ministries in the Government of Iceland.[10] The decree introduced some changes of reporting or responsibility for the

Central Bank and Statistics Iceland, among others. There are several ministries involved in economic and trade-related policies; these include the Ministry of Finance and Economic Affairs responsible for customs and tax matters and the Ministry for Foreign Affairs for trade policy and agreements. However a number of other ministries have various roles in trade and economic matters, particularly the Ministry of Industries and Innovation (Table 2.1)

ORGANIZATION OF MAIN ECONOMIC AND TRADE-RELATED MATTERS, 2017

Ministries and responsibilities
Prime Minister's Office
Economic activity
Central Bank
Ministry of Industries and Innovation
Intellectual property rights
Investment
Energy and natural resources
Business and legal framework
Fisheries resources
Agriculture, food, and food safety
Industry, trade in services
Consumer affairs
Ministry of Finance and Economic Affairs
Taxation
Customs and excise
Economic policy and financial stability
Financial markets
Public procurement
Trade in alcohol and tobacco products
Ministry of the Interior[a]
Law enforcement
Transportation
Telecommunications
Ministry for the Environment and Natural Resources
Forestry and timber products
Fisheries and international trade in wild animals and plants threatened with extinction
GMOs
Ministry for Foreign Affairs
Export trade
Preparation and implementation of trade agreements
Trade fairs

a The Ministry of the Interior, as of 1 May 2017, was to be split into two Ministries: Ministry of Justice and Ministry of Transport and Local Government. Prime

In late 2015, the Althingi passed legislation to amend its law on International Development Cooperation[11] transferring all activities of the Icelandic International Development Agency (ICEIDA) to the Ministry for Foreign Affairs.[12] The reasons for these amendments were to simplify organizational aspects, improve harmonization and results, and to ensure the best use of funds. The amendments also create a new Development Cooperation Committee and a new five-year development policy plan.[13] Iceland's Strategy for Development Cooperation 2013-16 focuses on the fight against poverty and hunger and highlights human rights, gender equality, democracy, and peace and security. It gives priority to natural resources, social infrastructure, and peace-building through bilateral and multilateral cooperation.[14] A new strategy is currently being developed which is expected to be presented to the Althingi later in 2017.

There are no specific laws or regulations concerning consultations with the private sector on trade matters or trade policy matters. However, the administration regularly holds consultations with the private sector or the relevant sectors thereof on such matters.

TRADE POLICY OBJECTIVES

Iceland's Minister of Foreign Affairs reports annually to the Althingi on the matters under its competence, including international trade. In the most recent report covering the legislative period 2015-16, the Minister enumerated a number of priorities and objectives in various trade and investment areas (Box 2.1) .

Minister of Foreign Affairs, policy objectives in certain trade-related areas, 2015-16

International trade	Strengthen the network of free trade agreements: Asian countries, Mercosur, and Canada Advance TISA negotiations Finalize WTO negotiations on environmental goods Identify Iceland's interests in transnational trade agreements Facilitate further trade with China by obtaining the necessary authorizations for new product exports to China Aid Icelandic companies in foreign markets Strengthen the business environment in foreign markets, especially in relation to investment and air transport agreements Secure the important trade relationship with the UK post-Brexit
Artic and Nordic regions	Preparation for Chairmanship of the Artic Council in 2019

	Address the growing importance of foreign policy in the region Foreign ministers will continue to discuss important international and regional issues with the Nordic countries, such as security in Europe, the situation in Syria, terrorist threats and issues with refugees Increase the number of subjects and enhance cooperation and flexibility in the Nordic Council
European Economic Area	Achieve a transposition deficit below 1% and ensure that issues do not come before the EFTA Court Strengthen cooperation within stakeholder consultative groups within the EEA Focus on analysing EEA proposals in the early stages Continue to promote information about the EEA both within and outside the Government Launch a centralized database of EEA Acts
International agreements	Focus on Iceland's interest in the work on the Law of the Sea Participate in discussions on agreements to protect against uncontrolled fishing in the North Sea and protect biodiversity beyond national jurisdictions
International development cooperation	Continue work towards the framework strategy on International Development Cooperation 2013-2016 Work to prepare the International Development Cooperation framework for the period 2017-2021

Iceland's Statement of Fiscal Policy and Fiscal Strategy Plan 2017-21 was presented by the Government to the parliament in 2016 in order to better prepare Iceland for the future and to incorporate new legislation on public sector finances; it was thereafter formally approved.[15] In addition to imposing stringent rules on the level of public debt, it also provides policy aims and objectives by government unit. In terms of trade and foreign affairs, there has been an emphasis placed on promoting Icelandic interests abroad, ensuring access to foreign markets, facilitating international cooperation, promoting the image of Iceland, attracting foreign investment and tourists to Iceland, developing a network of free trade agreements, completing the TISA negotiations, actively participating in Nordic cooperation, and implementing EEA rules in a timely manner.[16] As of the first quarter of 2017, a new Plan for 2018-2022 was under discussion in the Althingi.

Iceland's 2017 budget provides for a number of priorities or direction in certain policies.[17] It notes the success of recent economic and fiscal policies leading to a cumulative surplus of ISK 96 billion during 2014-16, in part due to tax reform and cuts. Iceland is to continue working towards simplification and improving the efficiency of the tax system, notably the abolishment of the general excise in 2015, the elimination of duties on non-agricultural products in 2016-17, and simplification of the VAT system. The 2017 budget gives priority to social security, health, and education activities. For example, there has been a continued increase in spending on healthcare, higher education, and research and technology; and a new framework put in place for agriculture with support amounting to ISK 1.1 billion.[18]

The Directorate of Customs also has a policy document – Customs 2020.[19] It provides for trust, cooperation and progress in all areas of customs. There are a number of performance objectives for customs including: efficient and effective collection of taxes and fees; effective partnerships with industry and stakeholders; effective financial management; health and safety matters; and responsible information and records management.

TRADE AGREEMENTS AND ARRANGEMENTS

WTO

Iceland has been a Member of the WTO since its establishment in 1995 and was a GATT Contracting Party from 1968. It has participated in the post-Uruguay Round negotiations on telecommunications, financial services, and the ITA. More recently, it completed the WTO procedures and implemented the revised ITA product coverage, and it ratified the Trade Facilitation Agreement in October 2016. Iceland is also a party to the plurilateral Government Procurement Agreement (GPA) and completed the procedures for adopting the revised GPA in April 2014.

During the Doha Round, Iceland has made proposals or joint proposals in the areas of services; intellectual property; fisheries subsidies; and market access, including for trade liberalization of fish and fish products. More recent communications during 2015-16 have concerned sustainable development in fisheries and on effective disciplines for fisheries subsidies.[20] At the last Ministerial Conference in Nairobi, Iceland contributed to a joint ministerial statement on fisheries subsidies.[21]

2In terms of dispute settlement, Iceland has not been involved as a complainant or as a respondent in any DSB cases during the review period. However, it has been a third party to three disputes since 2012.[22]

Regarding notifications, Iceland has had mixed compliance with its notification obligations during the review period. For example, there have been no notifications on TBT, import licensing and preferential rules of origin despite Iceland having measures or completing new preferential arrangements during the period. There have only been two notifications on SPS (in 2012) . However, in early 2017 Iceland notified its state trading entity, GPA legislation and made its first notifications of statistical information under the GPA. An overview of notifications is provided (Table A2.1) .

REGIONAL AND PREFERENTIAL AGREEMENTS

To date, Iceland participates in 32 reciprocal preferential agreements, mostly through EFTA FTAs (Table A2.2) . However, in recent years, where FTAs could not be concluded with EFTA partners, Iceland has proceeded on its own and has concluded FTAs with China and the Faroe Islands.[23] As of early 2017, no plans have been made for additional bilateral negotiations. Iceland also continues to pursue FTAs as part of EFTA, as there are a number of agreements currently in the pipeline (Section 2.3.2.1) . During the review period, there have been no changes in policy with respect to FTAs.

In 2015, as part of the European Economic Area (EEA), Iceland pursued more market opening with the European Union on agriculture (both processed and unprocessed), including the protection of GIs. This will result in the further elimination of tariffs, reduction of tariffs, and greater access through TRQs when it is implemented. As of early 2017, the old agreement was still in force, pending the finalization of internal procedures for the entry into force of the new agreement.

More recently, in August 2016, Iceland, Greenland, and the Faroe Islands (West Nordic countries) signed a declaration to increase cooperation between them.[24] The Foreign Ministers of the three countries agreed in a statement to establish a working group with participants from the three countries to draft a proposal for a cooperation agreement and to assess common benefits. As of early 2017, the working group had not yet finalized its work.

Iceland is actively involved in the Trade in Services Agreement (TISA) negotiations among 50 countries to further liberalize trade in services building upon the GATS.[25] As of November 2016, 21 rounds of negotiations had taken place and Iceland had made two conditional offers. These include sector-specific commitments in professional, courier, financial, telecommunications, construction, distribution, tourism & travel, entertainment & sporting, transport, and environmental services.[26]

EUROPEAN FREE TRADE ASSOCIATION (EFTA)

Iceland has been a member of EFTA since 1970 and follows the EFTA Convention for free trade between the EFTA States and the free trade and partnerships agreements that the EFTA States have negotiated with third parties.[27] The EFTA Convention dates from 1960 and originally provided a framework for the liberalization of trade in goods, but was expanded in 2002 to cover intellectual property, agriculture, services, investment, public procurement, movement of persons, air and land transport, social security, and mutual recognition of conformity assessments.[28] Since that time, the EFTA Council has made a number of smaller amendments. During the review period, amendments were made with respect to mutual recognition, basic agricultural products, air transport, land transport, and social security.[29]

Iceland, as part of EFTA, currently participates in 25 EFTA FTAs which cover trade with 36 partners (Table A2.2) .[30] EFTA has an extensive coverage of FTAs and its members benefit from being integrated into the global economy; about 80% of their merchandise trade benefits from FTAs. As a group, EFTA countries ranked 8th in world merchandise trade and 5th in services trade in 2014.[31] During the review period, EFTA concluded new agreements that have entered into force with Bosnia and Herzegovina, Central America, and the Gulf Cooperation Council. These FTAs have generally covered the following subjects: trade in non-agricultural products, trade in services, investment, protection of intellectual property, government procurement, competition, trade and sustainable development, cooperation, and dispute settlement. Trade in unprocessed agricultural products is generally excluded from the EFTA agreements. For the agreements with Bosnia and Herzegovina and Central American States, Iceland has substantially eliminated tariff protection, however 6.7% and 5.2%, respectively, of all tariff lines remain dutiable under the agreements.[32] As of May 2017, the agreement with the Gulf Cooperation Council had not been notified to the WTO.

As of May 2017, EFTA States were pursuing FTA negotiations with Algeria, Ecuador, India, Indonesia, Malaysia, the Russian Federation, Belarus, Kazakhstan, Thailand, and Viet Nam; but negotiations were on hold with respect to Algeria, Thailand and the Customs Union of the Russian Federation, Belarus and Kazakhstan.[33] EFTA was also undergoing work to update certain existing agreements. The FTAs with Georgia and the Philippines were concluded in 2016 but had not yet entered into force as of May 2017.

EUROPEAN ECONOMIC AREA (EEA)

Iceland, as a signatory of the EEA agreement, is integrated with Norway and Liechtenstein together with the European Union to form the Internal Market, providing for the free movement of goods, services, capital and workers. The European Economic Area also provides for cooperation in competition, state aid, research and development, environment, education, consumer protection, enterprise, tourism, and social policy. Iceland, as part of the European Economic Area, is expected to incorporate EU legislation in these areas into its own legal framework following a decision by the EEA Joint Committee. In 2015, for example, the EEA Joint Committee adopted 320 decisions to incorporate 483 EU legal acts.[34] Although included in the Internal Market, trade policy, taxation, the customs union, and agricultural products are not incorporated into the EEA. Agriculture is generally covered by bilateral agreements.

In 2015, Iceland and the European Union concluded new bilateral agreements on agricultural products and GIs under the auspices of the EEA Article 19. The new agreements, which will supersede the previously applicable agreement, will increase market access for agriculture by significantly increasing the number of agricultural products granted duty-free status by Iceland to more than 800 tariff lines, and with reduced tariffs on nearly 200 tariff lines.

This results in duty-free trade on nearly all processed agricultural products and above 90% of trade of basic agricultural products. At the same time, many bilateral quotas are increased to gain better access and new ones created; the agreement now provides for Iceland to grant quotas under nine categories of products[36], and the European Union under eight categories.[37] For processed agricultural products, full liberalization was reached on the approximate 500 Icelandic tariff lines covered by Protocol 3 to the EEA Agreement, with the exception of around 20 tariff lines that will continue to be subject to customs tariffs. As for GIs, Iceland has committed to the same level of protection as the European Union for its 1,150 agricultural and foodstuff GI products.[38] The internal procedures for the entry into force of the agreements are still under way; entry into force of the agreements is envisaged at the end of 2017 at the earliest.

In 2014, pursuant to Iceland's policy on Europe, Iceland decided to give priority to the efficient implementation of the EEA Agreement.[39] In this context, a steering group was established by the Government. The steering group subsequently published its report in December 2015, where it made a number of recommendations to improve the implementation of the EEA Agreement in Iceland.[40] As part of these recommendations, Iceland, *inter alia*, planned to work on the implementing acts at an earlier stage, increase communication between the Government and parliament, and provide more resources to relieve the backlog.[41]

The EFTA Surveillance Authority (ESA) is responsible for monitoring the implementation of EEA provisions in the EEA-EFTA States; EEA-EFTA States should furthermore notify the transposition into domestic law. The ESA also has certain enforcement mechanisms, i.e. it can order repayment, impose fines, etc. As of October 2016, ESA gained new authority over financial sector supervision and can now take certain binding decisions similar to those of the European Supervisory Authorities.

According to the ESA's latest Internal Market Scoreboard from January 2017, Iceland has the largest transposition deficit of the three EEA members and the scorecard states: "Iceland's performance remains disappointing on all counts and the Icelandic Government is once again urged to take steps to improve and demonstrate its commitment to the EEA Agreement".[42] It was noted that Iceland's situation had continued to deteriorate since the last bi-annual scoreboard with a 0.2% increase in the transposition deficit. It had 18 directives and 65 regulations overdue for transposition. Most of Iceland's outstanding directives concerned technical barriers on goods and the outstanding regulations concerned mainly the categories of food and feed, animal health and welfare, and financial services.[43] The ESA had also initiated the largest percentage of infringement cases due to non-transposition against Iceland; as of December 2016, 75% of the cases were with respect to Iceland. Once the ESA has issued a reasoned opinion alleging infringement, the matter may be brought to the EFTA Court; the Court is also the forum for appeals of ESA decisions.

It was noted that the Icelandic authorities were committed to reducing the transposition deficit and it remained a firm priority of the Government. There were a number of reasons for the transposition deficit.

BILATERAL AGREEMENTS

The majority of Iceland's reciprocal trade agreements are through EFTA. However, excluding its relationship with the EU, it has three bilateral free trade agreements with China, Greenland, and the Faroe Islands.

CHINA

As of 1 July 2014, the free trade agreement between Iceland and China, the Iceland-China Free Trade Agreement, has entered into force and covers trade in both goods and services.[44] It has been described as similar to the FTA's Iceland has entered into as part of EFTA, as it abolishes the majority of tariffs on goods, and covers trade in services, and other areas such as investment, trade facilitation, competition, and intellectual property.[45] Despite large differences in the size of their economies and rank in world trade, Iceland and China continue to have growing trade interests as Iceland's imports from China have grown constantly in recent years, with the exception of 2014, where there was a slight decrease of imports from the previous year. Iceland's main and growing export to China has been seafood.[46] Exports of goods from Iceland to China doubled in value between 2014 and 2015, and increased by 15% in 2016 from the previous year.

FAROE ISLANDS AND GREENLAND

Iceland's FTA with the Faroe Islands dates from 2006 and the substantive scope covers: trade in goods, trade in services, movement of persons and right to residence, movement of capital and investment, right of establishment, competition, state monopolies, state aid, public procurement, and cooperation in other areas. National treatment and MFN provisions form an integral part of the agreement although there are some exceptions to national treatment such as for investment in the fish sector and for trade in goods subject to SPS restrictions. There have been no developments during the review period.

Iceland's agreement with Greenland dates from 1985, through the Agreement between Iceland and Denmark on trade between Iceland and Greenland, and covers trade in goods. The agreement has six articles and mainly pertains to the continued trade provisions once Greenland left the European Community and became an overseas country and territory (OCT) . This FTA has not been notified to the WTO. As part of the group of West Nordic countries, Iceland and Greenland are forging stronger ties and working towards greater cooperation (Section 2.3.2) .

NON-RECIPROCAL PREFERENCES

In 2003, Iceland notified its Generalized System of Preferences (GSP) scheme to the WTO's Committee on Trade and Development.[47] Only the poorest countries benefit from Iceland's scheme, consistent with similar tariff preferences given in the EEA.[48] Iceland's customs regulation on the GSP provides the product coverage and rules of origin of the programme.[49] Iceland's GSP programme provides for both reduced rates of duty and elimination of duties for the GSP preference products (see Section 3.1.3 for GSP origin information and 3.1.4 for GSP preferential tariffs) . According to the authorities, Iceland plans to upgrade is GSP scheme during 2017.

OTHER AGREEMENTS AND ARRANGEMENTS

As of April 2017, Iceland has concluded 95 air transport agreements.[50] The agreements generally have provisions on traffic rights, code sharing, operational flexibility, freight, and competition provisions.[51] Often there are other provisions, for example on cabotage, charter flights, or tax issues; depending on the agreement and the country concerned. There have been 34 concluded during the review period.

Iceland is also a member of the Nordic Cooperation Council, which was created in 1962 and includes Denmark, Finland, Norway, Sweden, Faroe Islands, Greenland, and the Aland Islands.[52] This regional body cooperates in a number of ways and includes agreements or provisions on the free movement of persons, tax issues, and the labour market. Among certain members, (Denmark, Iceland, Norway, and Sweden) there is also an agreement on cooperation in matters of competition and with respect to formalities for bus transport services (Denmark, Finland, Norway, Sweden) .[53] The agreement on competition dates from 2003 and provides for the strengthening of the formal cooperation between competition authorities of the parties, including for the exchange of information, notification and enforcement measures, and formal requirements.[54]

INVESTMENT REGIME

Iceland's investment regime remains principally governed by its 1991 Law on Investment by Non-Residents in Business Enterprises as amended in 2014 by Act No. 57/2014.[55] It allows non-residents to invest in business enterprises in Iceland pursuant to the provisions or limitations in the Act. In particular, it outlines investment restrictions (Section 2.4.2), provides for notification of investments to the Minister of Industries and Innovation when applicable, gives rights for the transfer and conversion of foreign currency, and sets up a Committee on Foreign Investment for monitoring and enforcement. The 2014 amendment removed the pre-existing general notification obligation for all foreign investments by limiting the obligation to foreign investments in areas where specific restrictions apply, as well as by granting exemptions to legal and natural persons from the EEA countries, the EFTA countries and the Faroe Islands. Another development during the period was the entry into force of the 2015 Act on Incentives for Initial Investments in Iceland which sets out specific investment incentives and the procedures for receiving them[56] (Section 2.4.3) . Iceland has maintained about the same number of investment contracts, i.e. less than 10 per year, under the old and new incentive regimes.

Iceland's investment policy is developed by the Ministry of Industries and Innovation, which also has role in entering into contracts for incentives. Invest in Iceland is Iceland's one-stop shop for information on investing in Iceland; it provides information on investment opportunities and the business environment. It is part of Promote Iceland, a public-private partnership created by a 2010 Act to enhance Iceland's image and attract investment, among others.[57] Promote Iceland also has advisory boards composed of representatives from government and industry to cooperate on policy, set priorities, develop new projects, and make recommendations.

INVESTMENT AGREEMENTS

Iceland has eight bilateral investment treaties (BITs) in force, with Chile, China, India, Latvia, Lithuania, Lebanon, Mexico, and Viet Nam. The agreements with Latvia and Lithuania are being evaluated as to their future need. In addition, for example, within the EFTA framework, Iceland has signed a multilateral investment agreement with the Republic of Korea, and the EFTA-Singapore FTA includes a chapter on investment.[58] In general, investment provisions are covered in Iceland's FTAs, but not investor-state dispute settlement (ISDS) mechanisms. Iceland has concluded a BIT with Egypt but it has not entered into force as of March 2017.

Iceland's BITs are generally long-standing, the last one being concluded in 2008. However, there are two draft agreements awaiting signature, and two others under discussion as of May 2017. There has been no change in policy with respect to Iceland's BITs. Iceland's BITs generally contain provisions on promotion and protection of investments, national and MFN treatment, expropriation, compensation for losses, repatriation, subrogation, and disputes.

2.40. In addition to investment agreements, Iceland has also concluded 44 agreements on the avoidance of double taxation and 36 on tax information exchange.[59]

INVESTMENT RESTRICTIONS

Iceland's investment restrictions have remained essentially unchanged since the last review, with restrictions remaining in three main sectors (fish/fish processing, energy, and air transport) and other restrictions remaining on foreign public ownership, property ownership, and with respect to companies/business establishment (Table 2.2) . There are no plans to remove these restrictions at this time according to the authorities.

While there are no official statistics available on approvals, the authorities indicate that in the majority of cases (around 95%), permission is granted for the investments requiring approval.

In March 2017, Iceland lifted the capital controls it had in place since 2008 as a result of the banking crisis.[60] Iceland's central bank has removed the restrictions on businesses pursuant to the Foreign Exchange Act. Thus, foreign investment, hedging, and foreign exchange are no longer subject to these restrictions (Sections 1 and 4.3.1) .

INVESTMENT RESTRICTIONS

Sector	Restriction	Legal reference
Fishing and fish processing	The right to operate fishing operations or fish processing is restricted to Icelandic citizens or Icelandic legal entities controlled by Icelandic entities.	Act No. 34 of 1991
Energy	Energy exploitation rights, production, and distribution of energy are restricted to Icelandic citizens, Icelandic entities, or EEA residents/legal entities.	Act No. 34 of 1991
Air transport	Icelandic airline companies limit the maximum share capital to 49% for non-residents.	Act No. 34 of 1991
Foreign public ownership	Special permission is required from the Minister of Industries and	Act No. 34 of 1991

	Innovation for investments by foreign States, municipalities, or authorities.	
Business establishment	Individuals not domiciled in an EEA or OECD country require permission from the Minister of Industries and Innovation to establish an unlimited liability company in Iceland.	Act No. 138/1994 and Act No. 2/1995
Foreign companies	Companies domiciled outside EEA or OECD countries may only operate in Iceland if permitted by treaty or when granted permission from the Minister of Industries and Innovation.	Act No. 138/1994 and Act No. 2/1995
Board membership	The manager and at least half the board members of Icelandic companies must be resident in Iceland unless a waiver is granted by the Ministry of Industries and Innovation. This does not apply to citizens of the EEA countries, the EFTA countries, or the Faroe Islands.	Act No. 138/1994 and Act No. 2/1995
Ownership of real property	Restrictions exist for the ownership of property for residents and legal entities outside EEA or EFTA.	Act No. 34 of 1991

Source: Invest in Iceland, online information. Viewed at: http://www.invest.is/doing-business/restrictions; and Ministry of Industries and Innovation, online information. Viewed at: https://eng.atvinnuvegaraduneyti.is/invest-in-iceland/investments-by-non-residents-in-iceland---restrictions/.

INVESTMENT INCENTIVES

Invest in Iceland, as Iceland's one-stop shop for information on investing in Iceland, has a number of roles, including collecting data on the business environment, arranging site visits and contacts with local authorities, arranging meetings with local business partners and consultants, lobbying the Government for improved conditions in legislation, creating task forces for specific projects, and operating the Film in Iceland Commission project. There are also regional investment promotion agencies that work to attract businesses in certain regions of Iceland; they offer local expertise and information to potential investors. Iceland has also created certain development agreements to facilitate business clusters, i.e. to increase cooperation between local businesses, universities, municipalities, and the State.

Invest in Iceland has identified 11 key sectors to promote investment in Iceland; these are: data centres, chemical industry, carbon fibre, life sciences, sodium chlorate, polysilicon, algae culture, energy dependent industries, greenhouses, fish farming, and tourism.[61] The sectors were chosen based on benchmarking studies and where Iceland has a competitive advantage. The incentives offered are non-discriminatory and apply to all sectors equally.

Among the incentives that Invest in Iceland promotes are low corporate taxes, available land, and competitive energy prices. In addition, there are a number of specific incentives available depending on the project. Pursuant to the 2015 Act on Incentives, initial investments in Iceland are eligible for certain incentives contracted through the Minister of Industries and Innovation if they meet certain criteria.[62] The requirements include, *inter alia*, that a separate company be established in Iceland, 75% of the investment cost be financed without state aid, the annual turnover be a minimum of ISK 300 million or 20-man years of employment, the investment be in operation in the specified area of Iceland for at least 10 years, etc.[63] The Act provides for several different types of incentives: granting of regional aid in amounts not exceeding 15%/25%/35% of investment costs, depending on the size of the enterprise; derogations from taxes[64] or public levies; sale or lease of land from the State or municipalities; and derogations from certain specific laws such as compulsory insurance and residence of board members of LLCs.

Incentives are granted on a case-by-case basis upon the recommendation of a Committee formed under the Minster for the purpose of examining the investment proposal. When an agreement is reached, the incentives are enumerated in a contract with the investor that gives the specific provisions. Certain sectors are not eligible for these incentives, i.e. financial institutions, insurance operations, securities, airports, and energy production (Section 3.3.2) . In 2015, there were four new investment contracts concluded under the provisions of the 2015 Act, in biotechnology, heavy industry, and fishing sectors.

Also, there are other incentives that may be given pursuant to other legislation. The 2009 Act on support for innovation enterprises[66] provides for tax credits for innovation companies involved in research and development.[67] In general, the enterprise is entitled to a special tax credit of 20% of the paid costs up to a certain cost ceiling of ISK 300 or 450 million.

In 2014, the Act was extended until the end of 2019.[69]There are also tax incentives for foreign experts hired to work in Iceland in the form of reduced tax base to 75% for personal income tax based on the provisions contained in Act No. 90/2003.[70]

Iceland also offered direct start-up grants for SMEs through the Innovation Center Iceland and through Landsbanki Iceland during the period 2012-13. The grants ranged from ISK 500,000 to ISK 10 million per year depending upon the type of project. Direct R&D grants are available through the Icelandic Centre for Research to promote innovation in Iceland.[71] A maximum grant of ISK 45 million is available to eligible companies over a three-year period. Special incentives are also made available to producers of film and TV material in Iceland whereby all costs are eligible for a 25% reimbursement by the Film in Iceland Agency.[73]

2.49. In October 2015, Iceland launched a Route Development Fund to encourage new flight routes to Iceland.[74] The Fund makes grants to eligible service providers after they make an application to the Ministry of Industries and Innovation. The maximum grant for route development is €200,000 over a three-year period and, for promotion/marketing support, a minimum of ISK 10 million for each flight route.[75]

Iceland also offers incentives pursuant to EU regulations. EU Regulation No. 651/2014 provides the legal basis for Iceland pursuant to the EEA to offer training aid, aid to SMEs, and to environmental protection investment projects.[76]

ECONOMIC AN TRADE POLICIES FOR DEVELOPMENT

MEASURES AFFECTING IMPORTS

CUSTOMS PROCEDURES AND REQUIREMENTS

Iceland's Customs Law sets out the basic framework and rules for customs procedures, including valuation, tariff classification, warehousing, rules of origin, anti-dumping and countervailing duties, etc.[77] It also contains the customs tariff and tariff quota information in its annexes. Some of these subjects and others in the Customs Law are supplemented or further clarified by regulations. Since the last review, the Customs Law has been amended sixteen times.[78] These amendments mainly concerned: the incorporation of the amendments to the excise and VAT tax legislation; changes to the rules for the allocation of tariff quotas, including rates of duty; updates to the Customs Tariff in Annex I; adoption of the World Customs Organization (WCO) Authorized Economic Operator (AEO) standard; and rules for duty-free stores and bonded warehouses.

Customs duty revenue amounted to ISK 6.06 billion in 2014, before the autonomous liberalization of customs duties on non-agricultural products in 2016 and 2017.[79] At that time, agricultural products, clothing and footwear, and other non-agricultural products amounted to about one-third of revenue each.[80]With the tariff elimination implemented in 2016-17, it is expected that customs revenue will decrease. In 2016, customs duty revenue amounted to ISK 5.2 billion and it is estimated to be ISK 2.57 billion in 2017.[81] Thus, customs revenues are relatively small and declining, accounting for about 0.3% of GDP in 2014 and 0.21% in 2016.[82]

According to the World Bank's Ease of Doing Business rankings, Iceland ranked 66th in the category trading across borders which is significantly worse than its overall rank of 20th.[83] The lower ranking for trading is mainly due to very high border compliance costs for both imports and exports. The cost to export (preparing the paperwork, border handling, customs clearance, etc.) was US$655 for Iceland compared to US$ 115-150 for OECD high-income countries. Also noteworthy was that Iceland's time to export was 2 hours, similar to OECD high-income countries, while its time to import was twelve times that amount (24 hours) .

Iceland's Directorate of Customs (Tollstjori), under the Ministry of Finance and Economic Affairs, has the responsibility for administering customs matters for the importation, transit, and exportation of goods in the customs territory of Iceland, which includes the country, islands, and skerries, including 12 nautical miles of territorial waters and airspace above these areas. Certain entities have exclusions from paying customs duties by law, including NATO, Partnership for Peace, and United States' forces.[84] Customs operates 11 customs offices and designates 23 customs ports for the loading/unloading, storage, and customs control of goods. As an island nation, customs offices are located where there are major air or sea cargo facilities. The State Customs Committee, under the Directorate of Customs, was discontinued as of early 2015, with its functions (i.e. independent administrational committee) transferred to the Internal Revenue Board.[85] As such, most disputes concerning customs (e.g. tariff classification) are now handled by the Internal Revenue Board but disputes concerning administrative matters are handled by the Ministry of Finance and Economic Affairs, and can ultimately be taken to the courts. Traders must first appeal to the Directorate of Customs for a review/re-opening before taking the matter to the Board.

During the review period, the Directorate of Customs had a number of major projects. These included the introduction of a risk management system, revision of the long-standing single administrative document (SAD), introduction of a quality control system, advances towards the establishment of an authorized economic operator (AEO) programme, and work towards a single window application and an electronic system for the clearance of vessels.[86]

Iceland commenced work on its Single Window project in 2014 by outlining the project, defining the benefits, and envisioning its future application. It is expected to be completed by 2020.[87] Iceland also worked on a risk management application that uses its electronic systems to determine risks in line with guidelines from the WCO.

In 2014, Iceland introduced a quality control system adhering to the requirements of ISO 9001 standard in order to harmonize procedures, facilitate improvements, improve efficiency and provide quality services. This work focused on the services and collection division with the introduction of a quality management system. Other aspects of the project included training and implementation of new systems. In 2015, it was completed and Iceland received this certification, thus improving work processes and predictability.

Iceland's import procedures require that upon arrival a cargo manifest be delivered to Customs; this commences the customs clearance process. The manifest is to contain information about the vessel and on the individual shipment such as ID number of importer, product description, quantity and type of packaging, cargo manifest number, etc.[88] With the development of electronic systems, i.e. electronic data interchange (EDI), the import clearance process is increasingly conducted through electronic means (about 98% of declarations) .[89] Customs clearance further requires an entry form – the SAD, with accompanying documents such as bill of lading, commercial invoice, invoices for determining c.i.f., and permits or certificates if applicable.

Iceland's new SAD was launched in 2014 and it is to replace the previous document that has been in place for over 40 years. As of May 2017, the new SAD was expected to be implemented in the near future but the exact implementation remained unclear. The new SAD was introduced to improve disclosure, breakdown and fee calculations. Furthermore, it is applicable in the EEA and more compatible with other countries' standards and formalities. The new SAD will be applicable to all types of customs clearance and is expected to better facilitate trade.

Iceland launched its AEO system in 2014 based on the WCO's SAFE framework and modelled on relevant EU legislation. This will allow trusted operators to receive certain benefits and special treatment at Customs. The AEO parameters were incorporated into the Customs Law by Act No. 112/2016 in 2016.[90]These rules provide that traders can apply for AEO status from the Directorate of Customs if they have not been guilty of a serious offence in the last three years, have been financially solvent in the last three years, have accounting and supply chain systems for adequate customs control, and have adequate internal security procedures. As of early 2017, the AEO was in a pilot phase with the framework still being established. It is expected to be operational in 2018.

Bonded warehouses, warehouses for duty-free supplies, and free zones are provided for in Articles 91-108 of the Customs Law and Regulation No. 1100/2006.[91] Bonded warehouses may be established in Iceland by legal persons[92] or registered companies granted a licence by Customs for the operation of such warehouses. Other criteria must also be met such as payment of a security bond, adequate storage and inspection facilities, knowledgeable personnel, etc. Bonded warehouses are established for the storage of goods and no commerce, sales, or industrial processing can take place through bonded warehouses except for simple repacking, labelling, assembling, testing, and cleaning that does not result in a change of customs classification of the goods.[93] Both customs cleared and uncleared goods may be stored in the warehouses provided they are in separate areas or can otherwise be sufficiently differentiated visually. Recent changes to the rules on bonded warehouses provide that owners cannot operate their own bonded warehouses, thus there are only independent operators. Iceland's rules on free zones provide for the processing of uncleared goods and domestic goods beyond what is permitted in bonded warehouses. A similar type of licensing procedure as for bonded warehouses is required by Customs to operate free zones.[94] Iceland has never had any free zones in operation although the customs legislation provides for them. According to the authorities, the bonded warehouse scheme sufficiently accommodates the import/export requirements of traders to date, thus no free zones have been established.

The Customs Law also contains rules for customs brokers. They are authorized to represent importers or exporters before the customs authorities with respect to aiding in the completion of customs documentation, completion of customs declarations, requests for customs clearance, and payment of import charges. The Customs Directorate licenses customs brokers on the condition that they are a legal person with at least two executive board members resident in Iceland or citizens of EEA/EFTA countries or Faeroese citizens. Furthermore, there shall be a day-to-day manager and employees must have attended a special course on customs matters by the Customs Academy. According to the authorities, of the 559,000 annual customs declarations, the majority (426,000) were processed through brokers.

TRADE FACILITATION

Iceland submitted its instrument of ratification of the WTO Trade Facilitation Agreement (TFA) on 31 October 2016.[95] No laws were introduced or amended to implement the agreement. There have been no TFA notifications by Iceland since that time. In October 2015, Iceland accepted the WCO's Revised Kyoto Convention (International Convention on the Simplification and Harmonization of Customs Procedures) which entered into force on 8 January 2016.[96] Iceland has also been including trade facilitation provisions in many recent FTAs.

Advance rulings are provided for customs classification in the form of binding classification opinions as set out in the Customs Law, Article 21. A request for a binding classification opinion is to be made to the Director of Customs with the accompanying documentation necessary to determine the classification of the goods. The Director of

Customs is required to reply within 30 days of receipt. The decision is binding on Customs and on the applicant for six years. A decision may be appealed to the Internal Revenue Board. The Directorate of Customs may revoke an opinion based on the provisions of administrational law or due to legislative changes.[97] There are no provisions for making binding classification opinions available to the public. There have been no advance rulings provided for origin determination to date, although it is possible to request them.

Iceland has recently put in place a risk management system (Section 3.1.1) and regularly performs post-clearance audit functions as outlined in Article 119 of the Customs Law. Post-clearance audit encompasses all types of inspection activities to determine the accuracy of import declarations. The Customs Law also contains provisions for importers to amend an import declaration after customs clearance. This option is valid for six years from the date of customs clearance pursuant to the provisions of Article 116 of the Customs Law.

Iceland has provisions for expedited shipments; these are contained in the Customs Law (Articles 22 and 36) and Regulation No. 111/2006. The Act provides that expedited shipments may be released into circulation before the customs declaration documents have been submitted and that customs brokers may deliver express consignments before payment of customs charges by providing information about the consignor and the consignment, and paying a security deposit.

There are no pre-shipment inspection requirements for the import of goods into Iceland.

CUSTOMS VALUATION

Customs valuation in Iceland is provided for in the Customs Law, Articles 14-19, and Regulation No. 1100/2006. The Customs Law provides for transaction value as the principle method of valuation, additions to the price actually paid or payable, and conditions on the use of transaction value. The Regulation provides for the sequential application of the other valuation methods based on Article VII of GATT 1994. There have been no significant changes to the customs valuation framework during the review period. According to the authorities, nearly all imports use transaction value as the methodology for valuation.

Since 2007, Iceland has required the use of an official rate of exchange for customs clearance of goods.[98] Thus, customs value is based on the official rate of exchange published by the Central Bank each weekday. These exchange rates are posted on the Customs website.[99] Iceland values goods on a c.i.f. basis for imports and f.o.b. for exports.

Iceland's Regulation on the Custody and Customs Clearance of Goods provides additional rules on customs valuation.[100] This in particular contains special provisions on the importation of vehicles classified in HS headings 8701-8706, and 8711. Icelandic Customs uses reference prices from foreign countries to determine the customs value if the transaction value deviates from the comparison value determined by Customs. According to the authorities, these deviations are rare. Customs determines the f.o.b.

price and then makes adjustments to get an approximate retail price; they also use a depreciation method from new car prices to determine used car prices.

Iceland's law on the Production, Pricing, and Sale of Agriculture Products provides for the tariff to be set for agricultural products in ISK per kg, up to a certain maximum, based on the c.i.f. price and wholesale margin of the product.[101]

Iceland has previously notified to the WTO that the Interpretative Notes of the Agreement on Implementation of Article VII of the GATT 1994 have not been included in its respective laws and regulations and that the provisions of the Decision on the Treatment of Interest Charges in the Customs Value of Imported Goods has not been implemented.[102] Iceland's current regulation on customs valuation, Regulation No. 1100/2006, has yet to be notified to the WTO.

RULES OF ORIGIN

Iceland's Customs Law sets out the basic framework for its rules of origin in Chapter XX (Article 145) . It provides for three basic methods: change in customs classification, percentage of value, and methods of production or processing, but refers to rules of origin published in the regulations. At present, there are no Icelandic regulations on rules of origin, and therefore origin determination is pursuant to the various bilateral or plurilateral agreements. For non-preferential origin determination, Iceland generally accepts what the importer has declared in the import documentation.

For preferential rules of origin, Iceland has a number of different rules depending on the agreement. For FTAs that involve parties of the Regional Convention on pan-Euro-Mediterranean preferential rules of origin (PEM Convention),[103] Iceland follows these rules.[104] Origin under the PEM Convention provides for wholly obtained goods whereby a list of products or processes identifies these goods.[105] When goods are not wholly obtained, the Convention provides for origin to be conferred when the products are sufficiently worked or processed, as determined by processes listed in Annex II by HS chapter.[106] Three main criteria are used for the determination of sufficiently worked or processed: value percentage, change of tariff heading, and specific rules. The PEM Convention also provides for bilateral and diagonal accumulation between the parties, and full accumulation between EEA partners. Previous origin rules under the EEA have been replaced by the PEM Convention and entered into force for Iceland in 2015.

Origin rules of many EFTA FTAs involving partners outside the Euro-Mediterranean area, in particular developing countries, often involves simpler rules, i.e. more use of change of tariff heading.

Iceland's recent FTA with China has defined originating goods as those wholly obtained in the territory of a Party, goods produced entirely in the territory of one or the other Party from originating goods, or goods from non-originating materials that conform to origin determination in the Agreement. Annex IV lists the rules by HS heading; these mainly concern a change in tariff classification or regional value content rules, however, a process requirement or other rule specified in the Annex may also be used. The agreement also allows for accumulation between the parties, provides for *de minimis* origin rules, and lists operations that do not confer origin.

For GSP, Iceland follows UNCTAD conventions for origin determination. The first criterion provides for "wholly obtained products" and secondly, if the wholly obtained criterion is not met, then sufficient working or processing is required. The Regulation lists the criterion for wholly obtained products and references the processes for sufficient work through the EEA Agreement which in turn references the PEM Convention rules of preferential origin. There are also provisions for insufficient working or processing; accessories, spare parts, and tools; and sets. Per UNCTAD guidance, Iceland either requires GSP Certificate of Origin Form A or an invoice declaration declaring origin per Iceland's rules for GSP eligibility.

Iceland's last notification to the Committee on Rules of Origin was in 2012 for the notification of preferential rules of origin pursuant to the free trade agreement between Ukraine and the EFTA States.[107]Certain other preferential rules of origin were notified in 1997 for EFTA free trade agreements in force at that time.[108]

TARIFFS

Iceland's Customs Law provides the main legal framework for tariffs. Its annexes contain the applied tariffs by HS code and the basic information on tariff quotas (TQs) . In addition, a number of regulations supplement the information on quotas by providing more detailed information. The main changes to the legal framework for tariffs during the period were the changes in tariff nomenclature and rates, as outlined in detail below, and new regulations to adjust quota quantities or rates of duty.

NOMENCLATURE AND WTO BINDINGS

Since 1 January 2017, Iceland has implemented the latest (HS2017) Harmonized System (HS) changes from the WCO in its customs tariff, as contained in Annex 1 to the Customs Law. This Annex is updated periodically to keep the tariff current, with the most substantial change during the review period being the HS2017 implementation. Since that revision, the tariff has been updated two more times to implement the tariff liberalization for non-agricultural products and to amend certain dairy tariffs to align with the consumer price index movements since 1995.[109] Other changes to the tariff nomenclature during the review period were mainly for statistical purposes and due to changes in other taxes, i.e. recycling tax.

Iceland's WTO Schedule of tariff commitments is currently in the HS2002 nomenclature. The submissions of the HS2007, HS2012, and HS2017 changes to its schedule were outstanding as of May 2017.[110] Iceland is currently not covered by WTO waiver for these changes. Formal changes to Iceland's WTO schedule that were certified during the review period were the HS2002 changes and the expanded ITA product coverage.[111] These did not change the overall binding coverage or rates significantly, i.e. the additional ITA products lowered some of the bindings on these products and bindings were added to a few unbound lines.

Iceland maintains 95% binding coverage of its tariff, remaining statistically unchanged since 2012 (Table 3.1) . The unbound lines include certain fish, petroleum gas, fertilizer, tyres, paper, books, wool, yarn, fibre, motor vehicles, and airplane products. Iceland's bound rates offer considerable tariff protection, especially in agriculture and fisheries, where there are several *ad valorem* bound rates in excess of 200%, and more than 150 bound at over 100%. When examining the bindings of non-*ad valorem* rates, they offer considerably more tariff protection with an *ad valorem* component often exceeding 100%, and many over 500%, with a specific component that may allow the binding to go even higher, depending on which of the two components is higher.

APPLIED RATES

3As of 1 January 2017, Iceland removed the customs duties on all non-agricultural[112] products.[113] This measure was implemented in two phases, with tariffs eliminated on clothing and footwear products on 1 January 2016 and the remaining products on 1 January 2017. This initiative is expected to lead to a reduction in customs revenues of ISK 2.5 to 3.5 billion per year.[114]

3.34. As a result of this initiative, the simple average tariff rate has been reduced significantly from 8.3% in 2012 to 4.6% in 2017 (Table 3.1) . Agricultural products[115] have also seen some reductions since 2012, i.e. 28.6% to 20.2%, but they remain high and prohibitive in certain HS chapters, in particular, the meat, dairy, and plant and flower chapters (Table 3.2) . However, nearly 90% of all tariff lines are now duty-free, an increase from 70% in 2012 (Chart 3.1 and Table 3.1) .

Iceland continues to maintain a significant number (4.4%) of tariff lines with non-*ad valorem* rates, a slight decrease from 5% in 2012, and these constitute about 40% of all dutiable tariff lines. Non-*ad valorem* rates are mostly complex duties (3.7%), while 0.7% are specific duties (Chart 3.2) . For the purpose of tariff analysis, the *ad valorem* equivalents (AVEs) were calculated and these result in significantly high rates, averaging 75.8%, with more than one-fourth above 100%, thus offering significant tariff protection. In comparison, *ad valorem* applied rates averaged 21.6%. The highest rate of 429.6% was for meat of swine, and the next highest was 322.6% for milk and cream. Thus, non-*ad valorem* rates are concentrated in the sectors with highest tariff protection, i.e. meat and dairy (Table 3.2) . These two sectors are also the ones providing the most tariff peaks.

A comparison of Iceland's applied and bound rates was undertaken. While there were no cases of tariffs exceeding bindings when conducting a direct comparison of *ad valorem* rates, there may be some inconsistencies in a few instances when comparison was undertaken using *ad valorem* equivalents.[116] It is noted that the methodology was not precise and difficulties remain with obtaining adequate trade statistical information for more than one year for some tariff lines.

3.37. Iceland's submission to the Integrated Data Base for tariff and trade data was last notified in 2014, thus 2015 and 2016 submissions were outstanding as of March 2017.

Tariff structure of Iceland, 2012 and 2017

MFN applied

	2012	2017
Bound tariff lines (% of all tariff lines)	95.0	95.0
Simple average rate	8.3	4.6
WTO agricultural products	28.6	20.2
WTO non-agricultural products	2.5	0.2
HS01-24	22.1	15.5
HS25-97	2.5	0.0
Duty-free tariff lines (% of all tariff lines)	70.1	89.6
Simple average of dutiable lines only	27.8	44.3
Tariff quotas (% of all tariff lines)	..	1.6
Non-ad valorem tariffs (% of all tariff lines)	5.1	4.4
Domestic tariff "peaks" (% of all tariff lines)[b]	5.7	7.5
International tariff "peaks" (% of all tariff lines)[c]	8.5	7.5
Coefficient of variation	4.9	4.5
Nuisance applied rates (% of all tariff lines)[d]	0.1	0.1
Total number of tariff lines	8,513	8,971
Ad valorem rates	8,075	8,580
Duty-free rates	5,965	8,037
Specific rates	53	61
Compound rates	385	330

SPECIAL TARIFF TREATMENT AND DUTY SUSPENSIONS

Iceland maintains a number of exemptions to the customs tariff for various reasons; these include gifts, temporary import, designated investments, products of designated monopolies, special projects, etc. (Table 3.3) .

Iceland's Customs Law provides for duty suspensions on a few products. According to Article 7, duty suspensions apply to raw materials and certain grated cheeses, fresh potatoes, margarines, and rusks and similar toasted products where the products are used in domestic production.[117]

TARIFF EXEMPTIONS

Product/subject	Exemption	Law or reference
Exemption of import duty	Write-offs decided by the Committee	Committee on the write-off of public expenditure
Building material, plant equipment	Alcoa in Iceland import tax exemption	Law No. 12/2003
Alcohol	State Monopoly Board exemption	Regulation No. 505/1998

Tobacco	State Tobacco Monopoly	Letter 20/12/95 and 08/10/98
Building material, plant equipment	Duty exemptions for airport	Law No. 124/1999
Building materials machinery and equipment and other capital goods	Data centre exemption	Law No. 57/2010
Contracting expenses	EU contractors exemption	Law No. 53/2012
Construction and raw materials	Bakki Silicon exemption	Law No. 52/2013
Alloys	Icelandic railway exemption	Law No. 18/1977

TARIFF QUOTAS (TQS) AND ADMINISTRATION

Iceland maintains a number of TQs on agricultural products. There are essentially three different types of quotas – those pursuant to WTO multilateral rules (current and minimum access), those pursuant to FTAs (EU, EEA, and FTAs with third parties), and autonomous quotas. Determination of the quota amount, in-quota rate, and allocation is dependent upon the type of quota. WTO quotas are established by the statutes, whereas autonomous quotas are determined by the Minister who administers agricultural affairs on the basis of the provisions in the statutes.

WTO TQs are contained in Annexes IIIA and IIIB of the Customs Law. There are currently 141 tariff lines with WTO TQs covering products in the meat & edible offal, dairy, and preparations of meat sectors.[118] The Customs Law sets the in-quota tariffs at 32% and 30% of the base rate. In a few cases, the in-quota rates are higher than out-of-quota rates.[119] Quotas are allocated on a yearly basis based on the recommendation of a Committee established under the Minister in charge of agriculture. Allocation may be on the basis of drawing lots or based on the previous level of imports.

3.42. Autonomous quotas are contained in Annexes IVA and IVB and include meat, milk & milk products, butter, cheese, eggs, flowers & plants, potatoes, tomatoes, onion, cabbage, lettuce, carrots, cucumber, leguminous vegetables, and other vegetables. These quota levels and rates are determined by the Minister in charge of agriculture once domestic demand and pricing parameters have been determined. Annex V contains a subset of the Annex IV quotas for 23 tariff lines of TQs on products in HS chapters 2, 4, 6, and 7. These have preferential duty rates but the quota volumes are as stated in Annex IV.

Iceland also has a number of bilateral TQs pursuant to FTAs; the quota quantity and in-quota rates are set by the specific agreement. TQs for the European Union are on beef, pig meat, poultry, meat, cheese, sausages, and processed meat products. Iceland also has quotas on cheese and beef from EFTA States.[120]

PREFERENTIAL TARIFFS

Iceland's preferential agreements generally provide more market access for signatories through lower tariffs but this now only applies to agricultural goods as Iceland eliminated duties on industrial tariffs on an MFN basis. With the exception of the Faroe Islands,

Iceland only provides slight improvements in agricultural market access as most FTAs have tariff averages in agriculture near the MFN average of 20.2% (Table 3.4) . This indicates that Iceland continues to have sensitivities in certain agricultural products.

For GSP preferential imports, Iceland's Regulation on GSP provides for the product coverage.[121] As with the other preferential agreements, GSP benefits now only apply with respect to agriculture on 323 tariff lines, as other lines previously benefitting are now MFN duty-free. About 23% of agricultural product tariff lines are excluded from GSP, most being in the sensitive sectors of meat and dairy.

OTHER CHARGES AFFECTING IMPORTS

Iceland's Directorate of Customs charges certain customs fees for its processing and clearance of goods. A fee structure is set out for the customs clearance of freight, cargo, ships, etc. on the Customs website for services provided at certain times, e.g. after office hours.[122] Other fees are also set out for disposal of goods, temporary imports, cargo security seals, customs inspection, etc.

Since 1 January 2006, pursuant to Iceland's commitments under the EU Directive on packaging and packaging waste[123], Iceland has levied a recycling fee upon importation on all cardboard, paper, and plastic packaging waste.[124] Certain other categories of products (listed by HS code) are also subject to a recycling or disposal fee upon importation – oil products, organic solvents, halogenated compounds, isocyanates and polyurethanes, paint, printing inks, batteries and accumulators, photographic products, mercury products, pesticides, refrigerants, tyres, motor vehicles, synthetic fishing gear, and electrical and electronic equipment.[125] Importers, at the time of importation, should declare the net weight of all packaging imported into Iceland on the basis of which a fee is levied and collected by Customs. Exported packaging is exempt from the fee provided the exporter can demonstrate the packaging will be transported out of the country. The recycling fees on domestic packaging are collected by regional tax authorities in the same manner as the excise tax.

The recycling fee is collected in a recycling fund which is managed by a seven-member board. The fees are then channelled to cooperatives operated by local authorities to offset their costs of operating waste collection and disposal facilities. The fund has been running a surplus in recent years and has set aside the additional amounts for future liabilities.[126] The recycling fee varies depending on type of packaging or product concerned. The fees have been updated several times; as of January 2017, the recycling fee for paper/paperboard packaging was ISK 15/kg and for plastic packaging ISK 16/kg; fees for other products vary considerably, e.g. ISK 0.20/kg for certain oils, ISK 2,880/kg for certain photographic products, and ISK 707/piece for certain batteries for vehicles.[127]In 2015, the recycling fees levied on imported goods amounted to ISK 1,147.2 million.

In January 2014, Iceland's new stamp duty law came into force and replaced the previous 1978 law[129]; the new law only applies to the transfer of ownership of real estate and ships over 5 gross tons. The stamp duty on the documents for the transfer is now 0.8% of the value for an individual or 1.6% for a legal entity (company) . For individuals purchasing real estate for the first time, the rate is 0.4%. Historically, the stamp duty revenues were between 0.2 to 0.4% of GDP and mainly applied to the financial sector. With the new law, stamp duty is no longer applied to insurance contracts, loan agreements, or rental of real estate; and the overall rate has been lowered.

Since 2014, Iceland has launched reforms to simplify and improve efficiency in its VAT and excise tax systems. This has led to a reduction in the gap between the general and lower VAT rates, and also to its broader application and the elimination of the general excise duty. Since 2016, pursuant to the reforms, the tourism sector is now subject to VAT whereas previously it was exempt.[131]

VAT has undergone modernization and reform during the review period to lower the standard rate and increase the reduced rate, broaden the base, and increase the threshold. As of 1 January 2017, the VAT threshold was raised to ISK 2 million per year, the standard rate was 24% and the reduced rate was 11%.[132]

Following earlier reforms, in 2016 the Ministry of Finance and Economic Affairs launched a process for further reforms to the VAT. Draft legislation was circulated for comment on foreign enterprises selling electronically delivered services being able to opt for simple registration for the return of VAT.[133] This was still a draft and not a formal proposal as of May 2017. The Government was also examining the third phase of reforms and calling for proposals from the public to address these matters.[134] Further changes were envisioned but had not been further developed or approved as of May 2017.

The general excise duty was abolished as of 1 January 2015. However, a specific excise is still charged on certain motor vehicles (e.g. rental cars, taxis, etc.), based on CO_2 emissions. Further changes are due to take place in 2018 when the specific excise duty will be eliminated only on rental vehicles. This is expected to increase government revenues by ISK 2.5 billion.[135] Excise duty continues to be charged on imported and domestic alcohol and tobacco products.

There are a number of exemptions to the excise duty on vehicles, fuel, etc. for embassies and diplomatic missions, and for international organizations, and on tractors, snowmobiles, self-loading or self-unloading trailers and semi-trailers for agricultural purposes, vehicles owned by the Government used for fire-fighting and ambulances, vehicles owned by the Government or municipal authorities specially equipped for moving disabled people, vehicles owned by persons with disabilities specifically equipped with wheelchair lift, etc.[136]

Other fees are charged on certain fire and electrical safety, and electrical goods by the Iceland Construction Authority. The fee is collected by customs on imported goods' c.i.f. value at a rate of 0.15%; it is equally charged on domestic goods.[137] A carbon tax is also charged on domestic and imported carbon based fuels as a specific duty per litre which varies by product based on its emissions.[138] There is also a transport equalization fee applied on certain petroleum products such as gasoline, jet fuel, etc. to offset the transport costs within the country. A specific duty per litre is charged depending on the product concerned. According to the authorities, this is applied to imported products.[139]

IMPORT PROHIBITIONS, RESTRICTIONS, AND LICENSING

PROHIBITIONS AND RESTRICTIONS

Iceland maintains a number of measures that either prohibit or restrict imports. Many of these measures are long-standing, although there have been a few developments during the review period as outlined below. Eight categories of restrictions or prohibitions on imports are maintained and several relate to international agreements such as CITES, Montreal Protocol, etc. (Table 3.5) . Products prohibited due to sanctions or dual-use goods are not covered in this section (see Sections 3.1.8 and 3.2.3 respectively for the restrictions on these products) .

Other developments during the period include changes to the product coverage and the enumeration of certain exemptions in 2014 to CITES.[140] Certain sharks were added to the coverage, while certain whales, dolphins, porpoises, and sharks were excluded through the exemptions.

3.57. In its last notification of quantitative restrictions in 2004, Iceland notified the WTO Committee on Market Access that it did not maintain any quantitative restrictions.[141]

PROHIBITIONS OR RESTRICTIONS ON IMPORTS

Product	Measure	Legislation
Narcotic drugs	Prohibition	Act No. 65/1974 on Narcotics and Act No. 93/1994 on Medicinal Products; also Regulations Nos. 233/2001 and 232/2001 on habit-forming and narcotic substances and other controlled substances.
Certain animal and plant species pursuant to CITES	Restriction	Regulation No. 813/2014 amending Regulation No. 829/2005.
Asbestos and products containing asbestos	Prohibition	Act No. 61/2013, Chemicals Act, amending Act 52/1988 on toxic and dangerous substances.
Ozone-depleting substances	Prohibition	Act No. 61/2013, Chemicals Act, amending Act No. 52/1988 on toxic and dangerous substances; Act No. 7/1998 on public health and pollution control; and Regulation No. 586/2002 on substances that deplete the ozone layer
PCBs	Prohibition	Act No. 52/1988 on toxic and dangerous substances; Regulation No. 489/1988 on the import, use and disposal of PCBs
Weapons, firearms, ammunition	Prohibition	Act No. 16/1998 on Weapons; Regulations No. 16/1978 on firearms and ammunition, No. 174/1979, and No. 474/1988

		amendments to the regulation; and No. 536/1988 on the sale and handling of fireworks
Textile products treated with certain chemical substances	Prohibition	Regulation No. 448/1996
Batteries and accumulators containing above a certain percentage of mercury, cadmium, or lead	Prohibition	Regulation No. 571/1997

LICENSING

Iceland imposes import licences on twelve categories of goods (Table 3.6) . Most of these measures are non-automatic licences and imposed for security or safety reasons. There have not been many changes to the products subject to licensing requirements during the review period.

In 2013, Iceland was the first to ratify the new Arms Trade Treaty negotiated under the auspices of the United Nations to regulate international trade in conventional weapons; it subsequently entered into force in 2014. It creates a legally binding agreement to control the import, export, transit, trans-shipment, and brokering of these goods. While there are more requirements on exports, provisions on imports require each party to take measures for the regulation of imports which may include import systems. Iceland requires a licence for such products.

Amendments were made in 2013 to the Law on Radiation[142] , which clarified a number of provisions related to nuclear and radioactive material/equipment.[143] In particular, the amendments prohibited the importation of certain goods (food, feed, toys, jewellery and cosmetics) to which radioactive substances have been added.

Iceland last notified the products subject to import licence to the Committee on Import Licensing in 2004.[144]

PRODUCTS SUBJECT TO IMPORT LICENSING

Product	Regime	Automatic/non-automatic	Legislation
Agricultural products (animal products, fishery products, certain foodstuffs, live animals, fish, aquatic animals, insects, genes, feed, fertilizer, seeds, plants, soil, tree wood with bark, and used fishing equipment and clothing)	To control the import of certain agricultural products	Non-automatic	Act No. 54/1990, Act No. 25/1993, Regulation No. 189/1990, Regulation No. 448/2012
Used agricultural	Importation is prohibited,	Non-automatic	Act No.

machinery	except under certain conditions such as disinfection certified by an official veterinarian		25/1993, Act No. 87/1995, and Regulation No. 448/2012
Toxic and hazardous substances	To ensure the safe handling of the materials and to control the quantity of imported goods	Non-automatic	Act No. 52/1988
Conventional weapons	Pursuant to the Arms Trade Treaty	Non-automatic	
Machines for public works (mobile or construction machinery)	Prior declaration and approval needed from the Administration of Occupational Safety and Health	Non-automatic	Regulation No. 388/1989
Toys containing lead	Licences are required from the Food Agency for the import, production, and distribution of toys	Non-automatic	Act No. 52/1988 and Regulation No. 520/1991
Drugs and medicines	Importing, selling, or delivering complete medicines requires a licence for marketing authorization	Non-automatic	Regulation No. 462/2000
Telecommunications equipment	Import of certain telecommunications equipment requires prior approval or recognition	Non-automatic	Law No. 73/1984, Law No. 32/1993, Regulation No. 733/1983, Regulation No. 322/1985, Regulation No. 473/1989, Regulation No.71/1991
Ships, boats, and floating structures	Subject to prior approval of the Transport Authority	Non-automatic	Regulation No. 708/2000, Regulation No. 47/2003, Regulation No. 168/1997, and Regulation No. 708/2000
Weapons (including ammunition, fireworks, explosives)	Requires prior approval of the National Police Commissioner for the	Non-automatic	Act No. 16/1998, Regulation No.

	regulation and control of the importation of weapons		16/1978, Regulation Nos. 174/1979 and 474/1988, Regulation No. 536/1988, Regulation No. 684/1999
Nuclear and radioactive material/equipment	Requires prior approval and following the regulations of the Radiation Safety Authority	Non-automatic	Act No. 44/2002, Act No. 121/2013
Laser and IPL devices	Importation requires prior notification of the Radiation Safety Authority	Automatic	Regulation No. 1339/2015

ANTI-DUMPING, COUNTERVAILING, AND SAFEGUARD MEASURES

Iceland's regime on contingency measures has not undergone revision since the last review. The anti-dumping and countervailing duty legislation framework is contained in Articles 133-139 of the Customs Law and in Regulation No. 351/1994 on the preparation and application of the imposition and the collection of anti-dumping and countervailing duties, which remain applicable. Article 139 of the Customs Law provides for the WTO's special agricultural safeguard (SSG) mechanism. Anti-dumping and countervailing duties can be applied to goods, including goods assembled or produced in Iceland containing imported materials, and services.[145] There have been no anti-dumping or countervailing duty investigations by Iceland to date. Iceland last notified the Committee on Anti-Dumping Practices in 2012 that it had not taken any anti-dumping actions during the last six-month period. A similar notification was made to the Committee on Subsidies and Countervailing Measures in 2006.

The legislation and the regulations provide that the Minister of Finance and Economic Affairs can impose anti-dumping or countervailing duties following the advice of a seven-member Advisory Committee established to hear complaints. Temporary duties may be in place for a period of 12 months and final duties for a period not longer than five years. Duties may be invoked retroactively under certain conditions.

3.64. Pursuant to EEA provisions, anti-dumping and countervailing duties are not applied between EEA member States. In regard to FTAs, in particular EFTA FTAs, there is generally a provision to incorporate WTO anti-dumping and countervailing duty rules into the FTA, and in some of the more recent FTAs, the agreement goes further and often incorporates the "lesser duty" rule.

Iceland does not have global safeguard legislation. It notified the WTO to this effect in 1995.[146] It does however generally include safeguard provisions in free trade arrangements. Most EFTA FTAs, e.g. those with Ukraine, Central America, and the

Republic of Korea, have safeguard rules. These include provisions related to global safeguards and bilateral safeguards. The bilateral FTAs Iceland has concluded with China and the Faroe Islands also contain safeguard provisions similar to those of the EFTA Agreements. The global safeguard provisions in its FTAs generally reaffirm the rights of the parties pursuant to Article XIX of GATT 1994 and exclude imports of the parties when taking such safeguard measures if these imports are not a substantial cause of serious injury or threat thereof. The bilateral safeguard provisions provide a remedy in the case where an increase in imports causes serious injury or threat thereof, but generally only during the transition period or for a limited period of time.

3.66. Iceland's provisions on safeguards with the European Union emanate from their 1972 FTA and the EEA Agreement. Recently in 2015, the EU issued a new regulation on the safeguard measures between the EU and Iceland.[147] This revised regulation updates certain provisions pursuant to the EU's consolidation process and clarifies certain rules; it does not substantially alter the safeguard mechanism or procedures.[148]

IMPORTANT REGULATIONS

SANCTIONS

Iceland imposes a number of international sanctions on various countries or entities in order to maintain peace or security in the world or to uphold human rights and freedoms. The basis for Iceland's numerous sanction regulations is the 2008 Act on the Implementation of International Sanctions.[149] The Act provides for the enforcement of measures established by the UN Security Council or by other international organizations/groups of countries. The act lists the following types of enforcement measures that can be put in place by regulation:

ban on trade and investment;

ban on imports and exports;

freezing of funds and other assets; prohibition of communication, including telecommunications and other exchanges;

ban on movement of persons and vehicles;

ban on the provision of services and training;

ban on providing economic and technical assistance;

prohibition of activities and participation in the economy; and

other similar measures that are to maintain peace, security, or to ensure respect for human rights and fundamental freedoms.

3.68. Further to the Act, Iceland's Regulation on the Implementation of International Sanctions provides the general provisions and definitions for the legislation. Individual regulations are then issued for each measure which list the measure to be put in place and who they are to be levied against.

Thus, most of Iceland's sanctions are put in place through regulation. Many of them change or are amended frequently; the measures currently in place can be found on the Ministry of Foreign Affairs' website (https://www.mfa.is/foreign-policy/sanctions/) . As of March 2017, measures relating to trade were in place for 21 entities.[150] A majority of these were issued in respect of UN sanctions and concerned arms embargoes and bans on the provision of certain services. In practice, Iceland issues sanctions issued by the European Union based on their relationship through the EEA and EFTA, and by the Organization for Security and Co-operation in Europe (OSCE) .

Iceland also has in place export controls for goods, services, and investment relating to national security (Section 3.2.3) and takes measures to combat money laundering and terrorist financing pursuant to the recommendations of its Steering Committee to Combat Money Laundering and the Financial Action Task Force (FATF) .

MEASURES DIRECTLY AFFECTING EXPORTS

EXPORT PROCEDURES AND REQUIREMENTS

Iceland's Customs Law also provides for the procedures on exportation. Exporters are required to submit an export declaration through the EDI interface to the Directorate of Customs; this generally includes an invoice, bill of lading, freight bill, and other relevant documents such as a licence or certificate if necessary. The exporter is responsible for the accuracy of the information in the export declaration and for submitting the necessary information for special preferential tariff treatment if applicable.

There are simplified export procedures for postal trade exports on small consignments. These exporters can apply to the Directorate of Customs for a special licence to submit simplified export declarations for their shipments pursuant to the provisions in Article 40 of Regulation 1100/2006. Special export procedures for the fishing sector allow for the reporting of catch to occur after the ship has returned to Iceland from a foreign market. There have been no significant changes to the export procedures during the review period.

As of early 2017, the authorities had not made any decisions as to whether Iceland's single window would also be extended to apply to exports.

Icelandic Customs maintains lists for approved exporters that are allowed to provide proof of preferential origin pursuant to the provisions on origin in certain free trade agreements.

Since 2010, Iceland has provisions on cargo security measures to improve maritime safety and reduce terrorism or other illegal activities.[151] The Director of Customs has the role of certifying exporters, freight forwarders, cargo transporters and other companies as secure cargo handlers in respect of the cargo security measures. At each port of export there are restricted cargo security areas and a place for customs to inspect goods. Exported security containers and goods in bulk are required to have a cargo security declaration upon exportation. Depending on the type of cargo and container, they are generally then sealed for export.

EXPORT TAXES, CHARGES, AND LEVIES

Iceland does not have any export taxes, charges, or levies except for a fee on the export of horses (Section 3.2.3) and a 5% levy on the export of unprocessed fish.[152]

EXPORT PROHIBITIONS, RESTRICTIONS, AND LICENSING

3.77. Export restrictions, prohibitions, and licensing continue to apply in a number of cases; and most have remained in place for many years without change (Table 3.7) .

The Law on the Export of Horses[153] was adopted and entered into force in 2011, replacing the previous legislation on the exportation of horses.[154] The new law slightly amends the previous law by removing certain restrictions and increasing the export fee which has increased three-fold.

Iceland provides certain services for the exportation of meat, live animals, and wood packaging pursuant to import requirements in foreign markets.[155] For live animals, i.e. pet exports and live horses, Iceland provides an official veterinary certificate for exports destined for the EU, Norway, and Switzerland.[156] Iceland follows the FAO Guidelines for regulating wood packaging material in international trade, International Standards for Phytosanitary Measures No. 15, and thus provides certification for the export of wood packaging.[157]

As a member of the EEA, Iceland adopted EU legislation as it pertains to export controls of defence-related products and dual-use products. Through its Law on the Control of Services and Items that may have Strategic Significance, No. 58/2010, Iceland has implemented the relevant EU directives, regulations, and common position on the subject.[158] Thus, exportation of these products requires an export licence from the Minister of Foreign Affairs. In 2016 and 2017, Iceland issued new regulations pertaining to this legislation.[159] The new regulations amend the earlier regulations, updating them to align with the relevant EU directives on the matter.

Iceland ratified the Arms Trade Treaty in July 2013, which subsequently entered into force on 24 December 2014.[160] It focuses on the control of exports of conventional arms. The provisions of this agreement require parties to control exports, imports, transhipments, and dissemination of weapons, ammunition, and related components. Iceland implements these provisions through its regulation and licensing provisions for dual-use goods.

Iceland is a participant in the Australia Group, Missile Technology Control Regime, Nuclear Suppliers Group, and Chemical Weapons Convention, and follows the rules of the Wassenaar Arrangement but is not a member. Thus Iceland cooperates with these organizations on monitoring or controlling exports of products under their respective purview.

Transporting waste outside Iceland is not permitted. Iceland prohibits the export of wastes except under certain conditions.[161] For hazardous wastes and the removal of waste for recovery, an export licence is required from the Environment Agency of Iceland.

3.84. Other formalities or restrictions exist for the export of certain cultural objects or national treasures of significant cultural value. Pursuant to the Cultural Heritage Act, Iceland restricts or otherwise requires a licence from the Ministry of Education, Science, and Culture for the export of certain cultural objects such as identified in the Act.[162]

PROHIBITIONS OR RESTRICTIONS ON EXPORTS

Product	Measure/Rational	Legislation
Live horses	Requires prior inspection by the Chief Veterinary Officer of the export port;	Law No. 27/2011

	fee of ISK 1,500 to be paid to the protection fund; and a passport from the Farmer's association	
Narcotics	Export prohibition	Law No. 65/1974
Ozone-depleting substances	Export prohibition (with some exceptions, for example, export for the purposes of waste disposal or recycling; export to non-signatories of the Montreal Protocol (1987) is prohibited in all cases)	Regulation No. 586/2002 on Ozone Depleting Substances
Consumer goods that are a danger to health	Export prohibition	Act on Product Safety No. 134/1995
Wild animals and parts of wild animals, as well as eggs	Minister for the Environment shall in a regulation stipulate the requirements for the import and export of wild animals and their parts, as well as eggs	Act on Protection and Hunting of Wild Birds and Animals, No. 64/1994
Antiques and objects of historical value	Exports require a special licence to be granted by the Museum's Committee	Law on Export of Cultural Goods, No. 105/2001
Natural artefacts, micro-organisms and their DNA	Exports require a special licence from the Icelandic Institute for Natural History	Law on the National Institute for National History, No. 60/1992
Dual-use items and defence-related products	Applies Council Regulation (EC) No. 428/2009 for dual-use items, and Directive 2009/43/EC on defence-related products; licences from the Minister of Foreign Affairs are required	Act No. 58/2010 and Regulation 800/2011 on Control of Services and Items that May Have Strategic Significance
Plants and plant products	Exports require a special health certificate from the Agricultural Research Institute	Regulation No. 189/1990

EXPORT SUPPORT AND PROMOTION

Iceland's public-private partnership, Promote Iceland, also has a role in promoting Iceland's exports. It provides consulting, workshops, and information to help Icelandic companies obtain business in foreign markets. Its activities include providing information on export processes, customs, free trade agreements, exhibitions, IP rights, procurement, business culture, and key figures on markets.

Iceland does not have any export processing zones.

EXPORT FINANCE, INSURANCE, GUARANTEES

The New Business Venture Fund (NSA Ventures) is a state-owned venture capital fund that invests in new start-up companies. It was established by parliament and operates under Law No. 61/1997.[163] It provides finance for innovation and start-up businesses primarily through equity investments and small bridge loans. Funding for its operations was initially by the State but since 2005 it has been self-financed and not received any further support. It continues to have an Export Credit Guarantee Department to provide export credit insurance and guarantees to start-ups. According to the authorities, the export credit guarantee operation has been more or less dormant for the last 10 years, as there have not been any new credit guarantees since 2012.

MEASURES AFFECTING PRODUCTION AND TRADE

TAXATION

In 2016, total tax revenue in Iceland was ISK 794 billion and social contributions were ISK 87 billion compared to total government revenue of ISK 1,415 billion (ISK 1,031 after deducting ISK 384.3 billion in extraordinary revenue from the contribution from the estates of the failed banks) . Taxes payable by individuals are the main contributor to tax revenue, followed by taxes on sales and services. Over the past five years, several changes to the tax system have been implemented including simplification and broadening of the VAT system, and abolition of Act No. 97/1987 on Excise Tax. The increase in tax revenue in 2016 can be attributed to the changes to the VAT system as well as general economic growth

Corporations pay corporate income tax of 20% of net profits (including capital gains) plus a payroll tax. The payroll tax was increased from 5.34% of the wage bill to 8.65% following the financial crisis in 2008 but has since been reduced to 6.85%. Financial enterprises pay an additional payroll tax of 5.5%, plus a 6% charge on profits over ISK 1 billion and a tax of 0.376% on debts exceeding ISK 50 billion. Property taxes are collected by municipalities and, for corporations, averaged about 1.64% in 2016.

Income taxes on individuals are levied by the central and local governments as progressive taxes. As regards the central government rate, the first ISK 1.79 million of income is tax-free and the maximum rate for income over ISK 10.02 million is 31.8%. Local government income tax rates vary from one municipality to another and average 14.44% of total income. Income of individuals from dividends, rents, interest and capital gains are taxed separately at 20%.

Value added tax is the main component of general taxes on goods and services which is the second biggest source of tax revenue after taxes payable by individuals (Chart 3.3) . The principal legislation on VAT is Act No. 50/1988 on Value Added Tax which was last amended in 2016. The general rate for VAT is 24% with a reduced rate of 11% for food, accommodation, road tolls, books, newspaper and media subscriptions, audio recordings, indoor heating, and selected services. Enterprises with annual sales of taxable goods and services of ISK 2 million or less are exempt from VAT, meaning they do not charge VAT for sales but must pay VAT for inputs.

VAT on imports is assessed based on the import price plus customs duties and other charges. Exports of goods and services are zero-rated (i.e. VAT paid on inputs is refunded) as are some other goods and services including: transportation of goods between countries; design and planning of constructions based abroad; provisioning of inter-country vessels; sale and leasing of aircraft and ships; shipbuilding and maintenance of ships and aircraft; services to foreign fishing vessels related to landing and sale of fish in Iceland; direct payments to farmers; and telecommunications services.

The main legislative acts for excise duties are: Act No. 29/1993 on Excise Duties on Vehicles, Fuel, etc.; Act No. 96/1995 on Alcohol and Tobacco Tax; Act No. 129/2009 on Environmental and Resource Taxes; and Act No. 87/2004 on Oil Tax and Mileage Fee.

An exception from excise duties for rental vehicles under Act No. 29/1993 is to end with effect from 1 January 2018.[164]

Assessment for excise duties depends on the product and origin:

Excise duties on imports (except commercial imports of tobacco) are assessed and collected by the Customs Directorate and paid at the point of import;

Excise duties on domestic production and sales are assessed by the Internal Revenue Directorate at the point of leaving the factory; and

Excise duties on tobacco products and domestic production of alcoholic beverages are assessed when they leave the production centre.

3.95. In general, excise duties and other similar charges are applied to alcoholic beverages, mineral fuels, and vehicles as set out in Table 3.8.

EXCISE DUTIES AND RELATED TAXES

Product	Excise duty rate
Alcohol products	
Beer and ale containing more than 2.25% alcohol	ISK 117.25/cl of pure alcohol
Wine and fermented beverages up to 15% alcohol	ISK 106.80/cl of pure alcohol
Other alcohol	ISK 144.50/cl of pure alcohol
Tobacco	
Cigarettes	ISK 481.40/pack of 20 cigarettes
Snuff	ISK 26.75/g
Other tobacco	ISK 26.75/g
Excise duties on vehicle fuel	
Petrol	
General excise duty	ISK 26.80/litre
Special excise duty	ISK 43.25/litre (unleaded) ISK 45.85/litre (other)
Diesel	ISK 60.10/litre
Biofuels	Reduction based on the proportion of biofuel
Environment tax	
Petrol	ISK 5.50/litre
Diesel	ISK 6.30/litre
Mineral oils	ISK 6.90/kg

Fuel oil	ISK 7.75/kg

INCENTIVES

According to the EFTA Surveillance Authority, Iceland provided about €60 million in state aid in 2015, 81% of which was in the form of grants and 14% as tax concessions. About half the aid was for research, development and innovation (R&D&I), 23% for culture and heritage conservation, and 20% for regional development and cohesion. Most of the aid for R&D&I was provided through the Icelandic Centre for Research (Rannis) which provides public support for scientific research.[165]

Under Act No. 99/2010 on Incentives for Initial Investments in Iceland and accompanying regulations[166], a number of incentives were available for investment throughout Iceland and regional aids for investment outside of Reykjavik and surrounding municipalities. The Act expired on 31 December 2013. Six investment projects were approved under the Act and were eligible for grant aid, which was provided through reductions in various taxes and charges. In October 2014, the EFTA Surveillance Authority found that the aid provided under some of these projects was incompatible with the EEA Agreement and directed the Icelandic authorities to recover the aid.[167] At end-May 2017, recovery amounts had been calculated for the three companies concerned and recovery orders issued and put into formal procedures.

Under Act No. 41/2015 on Regional Incentives, which applies to Iceland outside the Reykjavik area, investment projects may qualify for tax incentives. These incentives include: an income tax rate ceiling of 15% for 10 years; accelerated depreciation allowances for real estate, equipment and moveable assets; reduction in property tax and the general social security charge by 50% for 10 years; and exemption from customs duties and excise duties for construction materials, machinery and equipment, and other capital goods. In addition, the State and municipalities may allow for leasing a site for the project at reduced rates. The Act expires on 1 July 2020.

To qualify for incentives under Act No. 41/2015, the investment project must meet criteria which include:

annual turnover of at least ISK 300 million or creation of at least 20 permanent jobs in the first two years;

commencement of the project after signing the investment contract;

minimum 20% equity from the investor; and

minimum operation period in Iceland of 10 years.

The incentives are not available for investments in financial services, airports or energy production. The general ceiling for aid is limited to 15% of the initial investment cost although this may be increased to 25% for medium-sized enterprises and 35% for small enterprises where: a small enterprise is defined as one employing less than 50 persons, with an annual turnover of €2 million or less, and total assets of €10 million or less; and a medium-sized enterprise is defined as employing 50-250 persons, with an annual turnover of €50 million or less, and total assets of €43 million or less.

In addition, under Act No. 152/2009 on Support for Innovation Companies, tax credits may be provided for 20% of the research and development expenses, up to a maximum total cost of ISK 300 million for internal research and development or ISK 450 million for R&D cooperation between two companies. Direct grants for R&D for up to 50% of the cost, up to ISK 45 million over three years, are available through the Technology Development Fund administered by Rannis, and Landsbanki provides innovation grants to companies of up to ISK 10 million per year.

TECHNICAL BARRIERS TO TRADE

As part of the EEA, Iceland applies EU legislation on technical regulations, standards, conformity assessment, certification, and accreditation, including harmonized technical regulations, and standards, and CE marking.[168] Under the EEA Agreement, Iceland is required to notify draft technical regulations, before they are adopted, to the EFTA Surveillance Authority, which publishes them on its website[169], and to DG GROW in the European Commission, which includes them in the TRIS database[170]. In March 2016, in a reasoned opinion, the EFTA Surveillance Authority stated that Iceland "still has not notified a number of the technical regulations in question, adopted in 2012, and is thus still in breach of its obligations under Directive 98/34[171] with respect to a number of these [...]. Furthermore, Iceland has not enacted a rule of non-enforceability concerning technical regulations adopted without following the due notification procedure in Directive 98/34 and the corresponding Icelandic implementing measures".[172] In July 2016, the Authority reiterated its assertion that non-enforceability rules should be implemented and the Government of Iceland again rejected this opinion in a letter dated 13 January 2017.

Several ministries are responsible for policy and legislation on technical regulations, standards, and related issues, including the Ministry of the Interior, the Ministry for the Environment and Natural Resources, the Ministry of Industries and Innovation, and the Ministry of Welfare.

Icelandic Standards (IST) is the national standards body. Under Act No. 36/2003 on Standards, all standards must be approved by IST before they become applicable in Iceland and IST is responsible for representing Iceland in international standards organizations. Four sector-specific committees operate under IST: BSTR in the building sector, FIF in the fishing sector, FUT in the information technology sector, and RST in the electrotechnical sector.[173]

IST is a member of the International Organization for Standardization (ISO), an associate member of the International Electrotechnical Commission (IEC), a member of the European Committee for Standardization (CEN) and the European Committee for Electrotechnical Standardization (CENELEC), and an associate member of the European Telecommunications Standards Institute (ETSI) .

The Icelandic Board for Technical Accreditation (ISAC), an independent department in the Icelandic Patent Office, is responsible for accreditation of inspection bodies, certification bodies, laboratories (testing and calibration) and notified bodies, in accordance with the relevant IST EN ISO/IEC 17000 series of standards and guides and the harmonized IST EN 45000 series of European standards. Additionally ISAC is the responsible body in Iceland for good laboratory practice (GLP) . The legal basis for ISAC's status and responsibilities is set out in Act No. 24/2006 on Accreditation, etc.[174] ISAC is a full member of the European co-operation for Accreditation (EA) . A list of accredited bodies in Iceland is available from ISAC.[175]

Under Act No. 91/2006 on Measurements, Measurement Standards and Weights, the Consumer Agency has legal responsibility for metrology and calibration services. The Agency was established under Act No. 62/2005 on the Consumer Agency and Consumer Spokesman, under the Ministry of the Interior, with responsibility for market surveillance of business operators, good functioning and transparency of the markets in respect to safety and consumers' legal rights, as well as enforcement of legislation for protection of consumers' health, legal and economic rights.[176]

The Icelandic Construction Authority, established under Act No. 160/2010 on Construction, is responsible for market surveillance for electrical equipment (except low-voltage consumer appliances), power plants and electrical installations, buildings and construction works.

Several other agencies, including the Icelandic Medicines Authority, the Environment Agency, and local health authorities, have specific responsibility for surveillance and enforcement for products for which they have competence, while the Customs Directorate is responsible for verifying conformity of imports with Icelandic legislation.

Under the TBT Agreement, Iceland's enquiry point for technical regulations is the Institute for Accreditation, Legal Metrology, Market Surveillance, Metrology and Electrical Safety and the enquiry point for standards is Icelandic Standards. The External Trade Department in the Ministry for Foreign Affairs has also been notified as an enquiry point. No specific trade concerns have been raised by other WTO Members about TBT measures taken by Iceland.[177] Iceland has made only two notifications to the WTO on TBT issues, the last in 2000.[178]

From 1 January 2012 to 30 April 2017, Iceland made 22 notifications to the EFTA Surveillance Authority and the DG GROW TRIS database of draft technical regulations.

As of 1 December 2010, almost 22,620 European standards (i.e. nearly all standards by CEN, CENELEC, and ETSI) had been transposed in Iceland.[179] Legislation on technical issues, often including conformity assessment, is generally found in the sector-specific law adopted by relevant ministries in order to transpose EU Directives, for example, Regulation Nos. 627/2013 and 1296/2013 on the entry into force of EU Regulations on medical devices and Regulation Nos. 424/2015, 385/2015, and 384/2015 on certain construction products. At end-November 2016, eight EU regulations and 19 EU directives relating to goods technical barriers had not yet been transposed by Iceland.[180]

As a member of the EEA, products placed on the market in accordance with harmonized technical regulations may circulate freely throughout the EEA and, when the EU negotiates mutual recognition agreements it does so on the basis that the third country will conclude a parallel MRA with the EEA. Through EFTA, Iceland has mutual recognition agreements with:

New Zealand (2000) covering pharmaceuticals (good manufacturing practices, GMP), medical devices, telecommunications terminal equipment, low voltage equipment, electromagnetic compatibility (EMC), machinery, and pressure equipment;

Australia (2000) covering electromagnetic compatibility (EMC), pharmaceuticals (good manufacturing practice, GMP), medical devices, telecommunications terminal equipment, automotive product, pressure equipment, machinery, and low voltage equipment;

Canada (2001) covering telecommunications terminal equipment, electromagnetic compatibility (EMC), electrical safety, recreational craft, pharmaceuticals (good manufacturing practices, GMP), and medical devices;

Switzerland (2002) covering machinery, personal protective equipment (PPE), safety of toys, medical devices, gas appliances and boilers, pressure equipment, telecommunications terminal equipment, equipment and protective systems intended for use in potentially explosive atmosphere (ATEX), electrical safety and electromagnetic compatibility, construction plant and equipment, measuring instruments and pre-packages, motor vehicles, agricultural and forestry tractors, good laboratory practice (GLP), good manufacturing practice (GMP) inspection and batch certification, construction products, lifts, biocidal products, cableway installations, and explosives for civil use;

United States, the first (2005) covering marine equipment, and the second (2006) covering telecommunications equipment, electromagnetic compatibility, and recreational craft; and

Turkey (2011) covering all sectors.[181]

SANITARY AND PHYTOSANITARY REQUIREMENTS

During the period under review, the legal and institutional framework for sanitary and phytosanitary (SPS) requirements in Iceland remained largely unchanged.[182] The Icelandic Food and Veterinary Authority (MAST), under the Ministry of Industries and Innovation,[183] is responsible for implementing legislation concerning food safety, animal health and welfare, control of feed, seed and fertilizers, plant health, and water for human consumption. According to the authorities, the Ministry of Industries and Innovation is the national notification authority and MAST is the enquiry point in the WTO for Iceland's SPS measures.

During the review period, a number of amendments were made to the legislation affecting SPS measures:

Act No. 54/1990 on the Importation of Animals was amended in 2013 through Act No. 60/2013 on the Protection of Nature requiring that before a certain species of animal or plant that is foreign to Iceland can be imported, a licence from the Environment Agency of Iceland must be obtained, as well as a licence from the Ministry of Industries and Innovation;

Act No. 54/1990 was further amended by Act No. 48/2015 authorizing MAST to grant licences for the importation of genetic material for beef cattle, if certain requirements are fulfilled. These requirements are related, for example, to the origin of the genetic material and to an investigation of the health standards of the animals born in the quarantine station. MAST was also granted powers to set standards for the farms receiving these animals. In the event that these requirements are not met, or if MAST considers there to be a risk of infectious diseases, MAST shall revoke the licence, destroy the genetic material and euthanize the animals; and

Act No. 25/1993 on Animal Diseases and their Prevention was amended by Act No. 71/2015 transferring the processing of applications for imports of raw products of animal origin from the Ministry of Industries and Innovation to MAST in order to simplify import procedures for these products.

Iceland notified two regular SPS measures to the WTO between 1 January 2012 and 30 April 2017.[184] The notifications covered the inspection procedures for imports of animal products originating outside of the European Economic Area (EEA), and measures on importation of animal products. Iceland did not notify any emergency measures during the review period.

3.117. Iceland is a member of the World Organisation for Animal Health (OIE) and the Codex Alimentarius Commission, and a contracting party to the International Plant Protection Convention (IPPC) .

SANITARY

Iceland, as a member of the EEA, has adopted EU legislation on SPS measures including foodstuffs, feed, and other food chain related issues, but maintains national rules on live terrestrial animals, germplasm (e.g. ova, embryo, and semen), and plant health. Measures on live aquatic animals follow EU legislation. MAST is the national European Food Safety Authority (EFSA) focal point and the contact point for the EU's Rapid Alert System for Food and Feed (RASFF) .

Most EU food safety rules are implemented in Iceland. All food business operators in the primary production of food and feed, irrespective of animal origin, must be registered with and approved by MAST.[185] Imported food must comply with the relevant requirements that are at least equivalent to those set forth in the EU food law and animal and plant health rules. EU legislation on novel foods[186] was adopted in Iceland through Regulation No. 990/2015 on novel foods.

Imports of live animals and animal products are subject to controls through an import permit system. Under Act No. 54/1990 on Importation of Animals, Act No. 25/1993 on Animal Disease Prevention, and related regulations (e.g. Regulation No. 448/2012 on the prevention of animal diseases and contaminated products), import prohibitions are maintained on live terrestrial animals, raw meat, raw eggs, and animal products not for human consumption[187] (e.g. meat and fat meal, raw skins and hides which have not been disinfected, and animal wastes) . However, the Minister for Fisheries and Agriculture may grant permits for imports, based on a positive recommendation from MAST.

Imports of used agricultural machinery, riding gear, and fishing gear are subject to similar import permit requirements provided they meet the cleaning and disinfection conditions set by MAST. However, some used riding equipment[188] and used fishing equipment[189] are strictly prohibited from importation.

3.122. Permit requests for first-time imports of live animals (i.e. new species) and products of animal origin (raw or unsterilized) must undergo a risk assessment by MAST. The authorities indicated that risk assessments follow international standards such as those laid down by the OIE, and are based on the information from exporting countries, OIE and other international institutions concerning animal and public health issues.

Import permits are applied to animal products. Imports of raw meat and meat products that have not been fully heat treated must be accompanied by certificates confirming that the meat was stored for at least one month at -18˚C or colder, and are free of salmonella and contaminants. Some products that have been treated with methods that are deemed equivalent to full heat treatment, including some cheeses and meat sausages and salted, dried or smoked meat, can be imported without the freezing requirements. Meat must be derived from animals that are slaughtered and processed in the establishments approved by the EU or authorized in the EEA. Products originating from outside the EEA must be accompanied by official certificates showing: origin and health, and that the animals from which the products were derived were not given growth-promoting substances.

When an application is submitted for the first time to import raw or unsterilized products, an importer must provide the MAST with the necessary information on the product for consideration and approval before the product is dispatched from the country of export. However, if the importer submits exactly the same application as previously, MAST can issue an import permit once the products have been stored for at least one month at -18˚C or less, and that storage can take place in Iceland. Live animals, including pets, cannot be dispatched from the exporting country until all requirements have been met and the import permit has been issued.

In addition to meeting health requirements such as vaccinations and testing, pets are subject to quarantine at the isolation station for four weeks upon arrival. Fur animals have been imported in recent years, but are subject to a longer quarantine period at a special isolation station. Iceland employs the EU's Trade Control and Expert System (TRACES)[191] for its sanitary measures. All imports of animal products from outside the EEA are subject to health check at an approved Border Inspection Post (BIP)

.[192]Importers must notify the BIP through TRACES at least 24 hours prior to the arrival of the imports. MAST is responsible for the control at the BIP.[193]

Feed imports may only be conducted by registered importers. Imported feed must be accompanied by documentation showing the ingredients, their chemical composition, and, if any ingredient is of animal origin, a health certificate stating the sanitary procedures used in production, packing, and handling (e.g. method of sterilization, autoclavation, etc.), and the absence of micro-organisms.

PHYTOSANITARY

The main legislation concerning phytosanitary measures is Act No. 51/1981 on Prevention of Diseases and Pests of Plants, and Regulation No. 189/1990 on Import and Export of Plants and Plant Products and its succeeding amendments.[194] MAST is the national plant protection organization of Iceland and is responsible for plant health and seed quality.

Entry into Iceland is prohibited for harmful organisms listed in Appendix I and plants listed in Appendix III of the Regulation; entry is permitted subject to specific requirements for plants listed in Annex IV; and Appendix II lists pests that may be present in a very small proportion of plants intended for future breeding. The Appendices were amended on 27 March 2015 and entered into force on 1 June with the addition of *Phytophthora ramorum* to Appendix I, firs (*Abies spp*) to Appendix III, and azaleas (*Rhododendron spp*) to Annex IV (except *Rhododendron simisii* and plants from areas where *Phytophthora ramorum* does not exist) .

Iceland maintains controls of quarantine organisms on potato and the export of wood packing materials. Iceland has implemented the EU legislation on seed.

All imported plants and plant parts are subject to phytosanitary checks and phytosanitary certificates are required.

With regard to genetically modified organisms (GMOs), Iceland has implemented the EU Directive 2001/18/EC on the deliberate release of GMOs into the environment. EU Regulations (EC) Nos. 1829/2003 and 1830/2003 on the marketing, labelling and traceability of genetically modified food and feed have not been incorporated into Icelandic legislation. Regulation No. 1237/2014 on traceability and labelling of GM food and GM feed applies to food and feed when more than 0.9% of each ingredient is produced from GMOs.

COMPETITION POLICY AND PRICE CONTROLS

During the period under review, there has been no substantive change to policy or legislation concerning competition in Iceland. The main legislation governing competition policy continues to be Competition Law No. 44/2005, as amended by Acts Nos. 52/2007, 94/2008, and 14/2011. The Law is administered by the Icelandic Competition Authority (ICA), which is an independent agency under the Ministry of Industries and

Innovation.[195] The Competition Authority reports to the Minister of Industry and Innovation.

The Law prohibits anti-competitive agreements and practices by businesses, abuse of a dominant position and agreements between businesses that restrict competition. Furthermore, the Competition Authority must be notified of mergers where the total turnover of the undertakings in question is ISK 1 billion or more. Under the provisions of the Law, the ICA may set conditions for mergers, prevent them from taking place or annul them after they have been concluded if it determines that they would obstruct effective competition.

As a member of the EEA, Iceland's competition policy is aligned with that of the European Union. Both national and EEA rules are applied in tandem. If restrictive practices affect trade between EEA countries, EEA rules apply. National decisions should not inhibit EEA rules. Furthermore, Iceland's membership of the EEA requires that the ICA enforce the prohibition rules (collusion and ban on abuse of a dominant position) of the EEA Agreement. This is done in close cooperation with the EFTA Surveillance Authority (ESA) . ESA ensures that the investigations and decisions of the ICA provide for an effective implementation of the EEA Agreement. Iceland has also subscribed to competition provisions within the context of the EFTA Convention and in each of EFTA's free trade agreements with third countries.

Additionally, the ICA cooperates with the authorities from other Nordic countries (Norway, Denmark, Sweden, Finland, the Faroe Islands, and Greenland) . There is also a formal agreement on exchange of confidential competition-related information between the authorities of Denmark, Iceland, Norway, and Sweden. According to the authorities, this formal agreement is under review and a new, fuller agreement is expected to be signed in 2017 or 2018 and is likely to also include Finland, Greenland and the Faroe Islands.

ICA's policy objectives are to contribute to increased competition in the domestic sector and public services. Based on these objectives, the ICA has prioritized important markets, such as the financial market, groceries and agriculture, construction, the public sector, as well as transportation. With respect to the public sector, the ICA advocates for competition incentives being used to increase efficiency and quality in public services, such as waste management, health care and education.

During the period under review, the ICA published 181 decisions and handled 36 appeals. Between 2008 and 2011, the number of pending cases had risen from around 100 to 170; this number has since been reduced and currently stands at around 80.[196] Since 2012, the ICA has prevented one merger and imposed conditions on a further 25 mergers, and has fined 17 companies a total of over €22 million for collusion or abuse of a dominant position.

Some of the important measures taken by the ICA during the review period have included reaching settlements with each of the three largest banks in Iceland and the two largest payment card companies in 2014. These settlements brought significant changes to the payment market, including reduced interchange fees. In March 2015, the ICA issued a report on competition in the groceries market. In the report, the ICA identified many obstacles to competition. The report summarized earlier recommendations and interpretations, concerning competition in the market and the conduct of companies. The compilation also addresses desirable changes in the agricultural sector, advocating for more competition. In 2014, the ICA fined two of the largest hardware store chains in Iceland for serious violations of the ban on collusion. In 2015, the ICA fined MS (dominant Icelandic dairy) for abusing its dominant position in the market. In 2015, the ICA also conducted a market investigation into the fossil fuel market in Iceland. According to the preliminary findings, there were signs of restrictions to competition in important sections of the market.

In 2015, the ICA issued an opinion, which found that due to the slot allocation arrangements at Keflavik Airport, the incumbent competitor, Icelandair, has enjoyed a *de facto* priority as concerns the most vital slot times. This also applies to the allocation of new slots that have become available. The arrangement has therefore limited the ability of other competitors to compete with Icelandair. The ICA has informed the Minister of the Interior and the Icelandic Transport Authority of these concerns and requested that this issue be addressed.

PRICE CONTROLS

According to the authorities, Iceland has no price controls except in the dairy market (Section 4.1.1.3.2.1) .

STATE TRADING, STATE-OWNED ENTERPRISES, AND PRIVATIZATION

STATE TRADING

As per the definition under GATT Article XVII, the only state trading enterprise notified by Iceland is the State Alcohol and Tobacco Company of Iceland (ÁTVR), which was established under Act No. 63/1969 on the Sale of Tobacco and Alcoholic Beverages.[197] Since June 2011, ÁTVR has operated in accordance with the provisions of Act No. 86/2011 on the Sale of Tobacco and Alcoholic Beverages. Act No. 86/2011 has however been amended twice, by law No. 126/2011 and No. 69/2014. Under the provision of the Act and its amendments, the ÁTVR, which is wholly state-owned, has the exclusive right to the retail sale and distribution of all alcoholic beverages with an alcohol content of more than 2.25%, as well as the exclusive right to the wholesale of tobacco to retailers.

The Act stipulates that the ÁTVR is required to sell alcohol products at the same prices in each of its 49 retail outlets. Under the Act, the mark-up above wholesale prices permitted for retail, is fixed at 18% for beverages with 22% alcohol by volume or less and 12% for beverages with more than 22% alcohol. Similarly, the mark-up for wholesale of tobacco is fixed at 18%.

Additionally, other regulations provide details on the terms of purchase and sale by the ÁTVR, such as Regulation No. 1106/2015 on ÁTVR Selection, Purchase and Distribution of Alcohol, and Regulation No. 496/2012 on ÁTVR Selection and Sale of Tobacco and Trade Terms with Suppliers.[198]

STATE-OWNED ENTERPRISES AND PRIVATIZATION

Due to the nature of the country and the economy, state involvement in the economy is quite prevalent and the near collapse of the financial sector in 2008 necessitated a state takeover of banks. At the start of 2016, the State had a majority stake in 34 enterprises. Furthermore, during the period under review, the Government's stake in the banks has increased, with the State having a 98% share in Landsbanki, 13% share in Arion Banki, and complete ownership of Islandsbanki. The increased shareholding has come about due to the signing of the "composition" agreements in late 2015, whereby the banks assigned most of their ISK assets to the State (17% of GDP), so that they could immediately distribute liquid foreign assets to foreign claimants (for details please see Section 4.3.1.1) . In a draft of an updated ownership policy for its financial services institutions, the Government has outlined plans to privatize Islandsbanki when the economic conditions are right, and the State will also sell a large stake in Landsbanki in due course. The Government's stake in Arion Banki will be sold as soon as possible, probably at the time the majority owner exits. The exact timeframe for the privatization has not been provided. The Government of Iceland had acquired a considerable stake in many companies through its shares in the banks, but these holdings have been exited for the most part as the banks have sold their stakes in these companies. The governance of SOEs is set out in the Government's ownership policy, which is modelled on the relevant OECD guidelines.

Under the policy, the ownership function is centralized within the Ministry of Finance and there is a clear separation of roles and responsibility between the State, as the owner, and the boards and management of the enterprises. According to the authorities, work is under way to update the ownership policy to better reflect the updated OECD guidelines.

The general policy concerning state involvement in the business sector has not changed during the review period. The central Government's current holdings include businesses involved in the production and distribution of electricity, postal services, the Housing Financing Fund, the Student Loan Fund, and some smaller financial institutions. In addition, Isavia, a wholly government-owned entity under the Ministry of the Interior, owns and operates all airports (see Section 4.3.3.1) . Local government holdings are mainly in geothermal production of heating and electricity, as the municipalities own almost all of the geothermal power companies, which supply heating to most homes in Iceland and, on an increasing scale, electricity to the aluminium industry.

There is free competition in the energy market, with consumers free to choose their supplier (Section 4.2) . However, FDI in critical sectors like energy is likely to be met with demands for Icelandic ownership, either formally or from overwhelming public opinion. For example, in 2008, Sudurnes Energy Company was split up into two separate companies, H.S Orka and H.S Veitur, with the former an energy production company and the latter a distribution company. In 2010, Canadian company Magma Energy acquired a 95% stake in the energy production company, H.S Orka, but sold a 33.4% stake to the Icelandic pension funds after considerable public pressure. In 2012, the company received an offer to buy out its stake, but negotiations were unsuccessful. In addition, several local governments own harbours and operating companies for harbours. The authorities also stated that the Government intends to add a special section to cover governance and ownership strategy in the energy sector in the update to the general ownership policy.

The authorities stated that private enterprises have the same access to financing as SOEs through the banking system. However, in exceptional circumstances, the State does provide financial guarantees or even direct loans to SOEs, but these have been mostly related to restructuring activities following the financial crisis, as well as situations where a limited liability company has been set up to conduct public policy initiatives, such as providing a loan to a special purpose vehicle for building a new state hospital. One exception would be financial guarantees on certain loans for Landsvirkjun (National Power Corp.), but these are being phased out.

Large SOEs

Company	Government stake (%)	EBIT (ISK billion)	Operating revenue (ISK billion)
ISAVIA*	100	4	26
Landsbanki	98	25	48
Arion Banki	13	27	53
Islandsbanki	100	22	53
Landsvirkjun	100	20	46
*Accounts for ISAVIA are for 2015			

GOVERNMENT PROCUREMENT

Iceland's legal framework underwent substantial revision during the review period with the adoption of the new Act on Public Procurement (PPA) .[199] There are a number of other laws and regulations that also came into force as a result of the new Act (Table 3.10) . It was implemented by Iceland to reflect new EEA rules on public procurement based on EU Directives Nos. 2014/23/EU, 2014/24/EU, and 2014/25/EU. Further, Iceland had fully implemented the Utilities (2014/23/EU) Directive and was in the process of implementing the Concessions (2014/25/EU) Directive through Regulations as of early 2017. Public procurement in Iceland amounted to ISK 167 billion (excluding municipalities) in 2015, and was estimated at ISK 250 billion when including municipalities.[200]

Responsibility for public procurement in Iceland is divided among a number of entities. The Ministry of Finance and Economic Affairs has the overall responsibility for the legal framework and policy, and the Central Purchasing Body (Ríkiskaup) is responsible for coordinating the procurement process. The Government Construction Contracting Agency, Icelandic Road and Coastal Administration, and Icelandic Maritime Administration have their own procurement functions for their particular areas, although their tenders are also often listed at the Central Purchasing Body. The Central Purchasing Body aims to promote maximum efficiency in procurement for state operations focusing on effective competition, equality and innovation. It provides guidance and expertise to government departments and agencies for the procurement process and prepares framework agreements on behalf of the State.

PUBLIC PROCUREMENT LEGAL FRAMEWORK

Law or regulation	Legal reference
Act on Public Procurement	Act No. 120/2016
Public procurement of clean and energy-efficient vehicles	Law No. 70/2012
Procurement covered by social services and other specialized services under the GPA	Regulation 1000/2016
The standard form for the single European qualification statement and standard forms for the publication of notices of public procurement above the EEA threshold	Regulation 971/2016
Public procurement requirements for information to be included in advertisements and other notices, supporting evidence for the economic and financial situation, and technical requirements for tools and the electronic receipt	Regulation 955/2016
Thresholds for public procurement in the EEA under the WTO GPA	Regulation 904/2016
Procurement agencies in the field of defence and security	Regulation 845/2014, updated by Regulation 221/2016
Procurement procedures of entities operating in the water, energy, transport and telecommunications sectors	Regulation 340/2017
Thresholds for public procurement in the EEA under the WTO GPA	Regulation 223/2016
Procurement procedures	Regulation 260/2016

Since 2014, Iceland has placed a priority on improving procurement.[201] In 2015, Iceland's Ministry of Finance and Economic Affairs created a special working group to examine and promote effective cooperation between the Government and the private sector on procurement. The working group suggested new ideas for public procurement and made the following recommendations:

Examine long-term needs for procurement and link to the budget;

Government to apply procurement procedures in a targeted manner, e.g. through joint purchases, mini-tendering, auctions, and contracting with fewer suppliers;

Include additional information so that the Government has a better overview of its purchases in order to further optimize procurement;

Create an incentive scheme for institutions and suppliers; and

Better incorporate market rent prices for institutions in order to optimize their office rents.[202]

The working group estimated that introducing these reforms would save the Government between ISK 2 to 4 billion a year in public procurement.[203] Thus, some of these have been incorporated in the new PPA by incorporating better framework contracts, i.e. by focusing on joint procurement and single supplier framework contracts.

The new Act on Public Procurement sets out to ensure the equal treatment of economic operators, encourage efficiency in public sector operations through active competition and to promote innovation and development in public procurement of supplies, works and services. It applies to the State, local authorities, their institutions and other public entities.

All public procurement, above domestic thresholds, is subject to the same general provisions regarding scope of applications, exceptions, general principles etc. Overall, the PPA is modelled on EEA Law. It incorporates developments in case law, interpretative communications, etc., that have a direct relevance for the interpretation of the Act.

The new thresholds for domestic public procurement went into effect as of 28 October 2016 and for the EEA as of 1 November 2016 (Table 3.11 and Table 3.12) . Article 23 of the PPA provides that procurement of goods and services over ISK 15.5 million and construction over ISK 49 million shall be awarded according to the procedures set out in Chapter IV. These apply to public bodies and agencies, including local governments. However, for local governments, implementation takes effect only from 31 May 2019, but local authorities will need to advertise tenders above these thresholds from 2017. Previously, local governments were only obliged to follow the public procurement law above EEA thresholds.

For procurement under the domestic thresholds, the PPA specifies that the procurer shall ensure efficiency and make comparisons among as many economic operators as possible, and this must be done electronically. Provisions on technical specifications and equality must also be respected. As set out in Chapter IV, when the threshold is exceeded, procurement is to be made on the basis of an open procedure (all economic operators may submit a tender following publication of a contract notice) or a restricted procedure (economic operators can apply for permission to participate in a procurement procedure following publication of a contract notice by submitting information for qualitative selection) . According to the authorities, the open procurement procedure is the most common procurement method. Almost 98% of procurement subject to the GPA carried out by the Central Purchasing Body on behalf of all state institutions was subject to open procedures during 2015 and 2016, according to the authorities.

Domestic thresholds: central Government (and sub-central Government from 2019)

	Threshold in GPA in SDR	Threshold in GPA in ISK	Applied threshold in domestic regulation in ISK
Supplies	102,650	15,500,000	15,500,000
Services	102,650	15,500,000	15,500,000
Construction Services	324,500	49,000,000	49,000,000

Source: Information provided by the authorities.

Iceland's PPA has provisions on electronic means of procurement. It allows for the use of electronic auctions but does not make it mandatory. However, a new rule to come into effect in 2018 would establish the use of electronic methods for all procurement. It also establishes an electronic dynamic purchasing system for making commonly used purchases; however, this is not widely used at present. For the communication and submission of documents, the PPA indicates that this will be conducted through electronic means. As of early 2017, the authorities confirmed that all tender documents are available electronically and are free of charge.

For procurement disputes, Iceland continues to use the Public Procurement Complaints Commission which operated under the old law and is also contained in the new PPA without change. It is established as an independent body under the Ministry of Finance and Economic Affairs to rule or decide on complaints of alleged violations of the PPA. The Commission has the right to impose administrative fines if violations are found. During the last three years, there have been between 25-30 complaints filed per year with the Complaints Commission; and the average procedure time for dealing with these complaints was between 100 and 125 days.[204] The process allows for the right to appeal.

Iceland has been a party to the WTO GPA since 2001 and has since also completed the procedures for becoming a party to the revised GPA, which entered into force for Iceland on 6 April 2014. Iceland's commitments under the new agreement provide the same or similar coverage with no significant changes according to the authorities.

GPA parties are required to notify the WTO of their laws and other relevant implementing legislation, including revisions thereof. Iceland had notified its original legislation in 2002, and most recently, in April 2017, notified its updated legislation.[205] Furthermore, pursuant to Article XVI:4, parties are to notify procurement statistics. As of early 2017, Iceland had notified such statistics for the years 2015 and 2016. Iceland's FTAs generally have provisions on government procurement.

INTELLECTUAL PROPERTY RIGHTS

There were several developments in the field of intellectual property (IP) in Iceland during the review period. These developments include new legislation on geographical indications (GIs), amendments to trademark law,[207] and a new fee structure. Intellectual property is covered by the EEA, thus Iceland has implemented relevant EU regulations and directives in the field of IP. However, further changes are foreseen in the near future to incorporate recently added EEA legislation, in the areas of patents, trademarks, and trade secrets.

Iceland's Patent Office (Einkaleyfastofan – ELS/IPO)[208] is the main agency involved in intellectual property issues; it covers patents, trademarks, design, related rights and accreditation.[209] Also, since September 2012, the Ministry of Industries and Innovation has general oversight of the Patent Office and is responsible for overall policy matters on industrial intellectual property rights.[210] Copyright matters are under the responsibility of the Ministry of Education, Science and Culture.

3.161. Iceland adheres to the key IP international agreements, e.g. Paris Convention for the Protection of Industrial Property, Protocol Relating to the Madrid Agreement Concerning the International Registration of Marks, and Patent Cooperation Treaty, etc.[211] During the last five years, Iceland ratified two new treaties that entered into force: Singapore Treaty on the Law of Trademarks and Convention on the Rights of Persons with Disabilities.[212]

MAIN INTELLECTUAL PROPERTY LAWS AND REGULATIONS

	Law	Reference
Patents	Patents Act	Act No. 17/1991
	Act respecting Employees' Inventions	Act No. 72/2004
	Fees for Patents	Regulation No. 818/2016
	Patent applications	Regulation No. 477/2012 amended with Regulation No. 938/2013
	Compulsory licence for the export of drugs to developing countries and countries plagued by severe health problems	Regulation No. 1011/2006
	Copyright Act	Act No. 73/1972
Copyright	Trademark Act	Act No. 45/1997
Trademarks	Trademark Amendment Act	Act No. 44/2012
	Trademark Amendment	Article 42 of Act No. 130/2014
	Trademark Regulation	Regulation No. 310/1997
	Trademark Amendment Regulation	Regulation No. 511/2012
	Collective Marks	Act No. 155/2002
	Fees for trademarks and collective marks	Regulation No. 818/2016
	Classification of goods and services for trademarks	Announcement No. 130/2017
	Registration of trademarks and certification marks owned by the employer in certain foreign countries	Announcement No. 228/1990
	Design Act	Act No. 46/2001
Designs	Design Regulation	Regulation No. 706/2001
	Fees for Designs	Regulation No. 818/2016
	Protection of topographies for semiconductors	Act No. 78/1993
GIs	Act on the protection of product names as designations of origin, geographical indications or traditional specialties	Act No. 130/2014
	Regulation on the registration of product names	Regulation No. 596/2016
Other	Collection of Evidence Relating to	Act No. 53/2006

	Alleged Violations of Intellectual Property Rights	
	Provisions for hallmarks	Act No. 138/2011
	Board of Appeal of Industrial Intellectual Property Rights	Regulation No. 275/2008

Source: Icelandic Patent Office. Viewed at: www.els.is.

Intellectual property activity in Iceland trended slightly upward during the period 2012-16 (Table 3.14) . There has been a steady rise in European patent (EP) validations of patents. Regarding trademarks, there has been a slight increase in national applications and registrations, but a slight decrease in Madrid system applications in recent years. For patents, during 2012-14 there was a backlog of patent applications and since that time, a balance has been reached. Thus, in Iceland there are 52,000 registered trademarks owned by foreigners and 7,300 owned by Icelanders as of the end of 2016.[213]Furthermore, a report that examined intellectual property trends in Iceland states that the number of trademark listings in Iceland is comparable to other Western countries taking into account the size of the country and market, but patent and design applications by Icelanders has generally trended downward in recent years and this has created some concerns.

The policy acknowledges that intellectual property creates a strong competitive environment, increases value creation, drives economic growth, and that innovation plays a key role in the betterment of society. The policy made the following proposals:

Establish a Technology Transfer Office (TTO);

Public research grants to take into account IP potential;

Strengthen patent technology development grants to cover costs of the patent process;

Assist SMEs to protect IPR;

Explore the adoption of utility models;

Increase awareness of IP in the business community;

Promote education and training in IPR;

Improve the Patent Office appeals procedure;

Review the provisions on corporate names;

Review the rules on inventions by employees; and

Increase emphasis on monitoring IP infringement.

While no annual status report has been issued at this time, the authorities have reported that work has begun to establish a TTO, and also with respect to increasing awareness of IP with the cooperation of government agencies and changing the name of the IPO.[216]

Patents

Iceland's main patent law dates from 1991 and there have been no amendments or changes to it during the review period. However, in 2012 and 2013 there were changes to the Patent Regulation. Iceland also introduced new fee schedules for patents in 2014 and 2016 (also applicable to trademarks, designs and appeal procedures) .[217] The 2014 regulation raised the fees for Patent Office applications and related fees and simplified the overall fee structure, whereas a slight increase was introduced in 2016.

The changes made in 2012 were outlined in the last trade policy review.[218] The new patent regulation that entered into force in May 2012 introduced several changes, but mostly clarified the established patent application procedures and requirements. The changes from 2013 were minor changes only correcting misspellings and wording, and one correcting the period of validity of Supplementary Protection Certificates as well.

3.167. Iceland cooperates with other Nordic countries on patent matters through the Nordic Patent Institute which coordinates matters between Nordic States and offers patent search and analysis services to businesses.

Copyright

3.168. There have been several changes to the legal framework on copyright during the review period; thus the 1972 Copyright Law remains applicable with these amendments. The Copyright Law was amended four times in 2016 in relation to: authors' exclusive rights and collective agreements, implementation of a directive regarding orphan works, prolongation of the protection period for sound recordings, and copying for personal use.[219] Pursuant to the copyright reform initiative, the Copyright Act continues to be amended and updated in stages as the different sections are prepared and incorporated in legal texts. There is no registration of copyright in Iceland.

TRADEMARKS

Iceland's trademark law underwent amendment in 2012 and 2014 for minor changes.[220] The 2012 changes were outlined in the last trade policy review; they mainly resulted from the ratification of the Singapore Treaty but, in addition, invalidation procedures were introduced and the Icelandic procedures were aligned with Nordic legislation.

In 2014, a new Act No. 130/2014 on the protection of product names as designations of origin, geographical indications or traditional specialties entered into force. In addition to providing for registration of product names (usually referred to as GIs) by the Food and Veterinary Authority, it introduced a new Article 14(1)(10) in the Trademark Act. According to the provision, the IPO is responsible for verifying if there is a registered GI or if a prior GI application has been filed when examining the registration possibilities for trademarks.

In 2017, Iceland introduced revised rules on the classification of goods and services for trademarks.[222] These rules follow the changes made in the 11th edition of the Nice Agreement and make other corrections. Previously, Iceland had incorporated changes from the 10th edition of the Nice Agreement in 2016, but these were superseded, and the 2017 rules are currently applicable.

Designs

There were no amendments to the Act on Designs during the review period; therefore designs continue to follow the provision in the 2001 Design Act, as last amended in 2011.

GEOGRAPHICAL INDICATIONS (GIS)

During the review period, Iceland enacted its first Act specific to GIs, Act No. 130/2014 on the protection of product names as designations of origin, geographical indications or traditional specialties;[223]it also has an accompanying Regulation No. 596/2016.[224] The Act and Regulation apply to food, wine, spirit drinks, and other products (i.e. wool, feathers, skin/fur, leather, horns and bones, cotton, cork, hemp, wicker, natural rubber and resins, natural pigments, flowers, essential oils, tobacco, and mixtures for animal feed) listed in Annex I of the regulation.[225] The product name may be protected if the product is originating in a specific region, place or country; it has qualities or characteristics of the geographical area; and the production, processing and preparation of the product takes place in the defined geographical area. A name referring to a territory may also be protected. The law provides that the name will be protected against any misuse, imitation, and misleading associations or any other activity that could mislead consumers. In order to protect a GI, a registration process must be followed as outlined in the law and regulation, accompanied by a fee of ISK 75,000. GIs are registered by the Icelandic Food and Veterinary Authority (MAST), with fees regulated by Regulation 596/2016.

As part of the agreements reached with the European Union on agriculture in 2015, Iceland also concluded an agreement on geographical indications (Section 2.3.2.2) . As a result of this agreement, a list of 1,150 protected agricultural products and foodstuffs of the European Union will receive the same level of protection in Iceland as in the EU market. As of the first quarter 2017, the agreement had not yet entered into force.[226]

Appeals and enforcement

Iceland has provisions for appeals in several of its intellectual property laws. For example, the laws on patents, trademarks and designs have articles that pertain to the settling of disputes. Furthermore, the Regulation on the Board of Appeal of Industrial Intellectual Property Rights, No. 275/2008, provides that appeals must be filed with the Ministry of Industries and Innovation within the statutory time limit, which is two months from the date of the decision of the IPO. Then the matter is referred to the Board of

Appeal to examine the matter through submissions and hearings. A ruling is then taken by the Board and sent to the parties of the dispute. Following the appeals procedure, parties may bring the disputed matters to national courts.

Provisions relating to IP infringement are to some extent provided for in Icelandic laws on IP rights. Furthermore, Act No. 31/1990 relating to Attachment of Property, Restraining Orders etc.; Article 132 of the Customs Law; and Act No. 53/2006 on Collection of Evidence Relating to Alleged Violations of Intellectual Property Rights provide for the procedures in relation to IP infringement. Apart from the right holder's initiative in such matters, IP infringement matters in Iceland can in general first be addressed by a district magistrate/sheriff to invoke an injunction. In general, IP infringement matters are heard before the Reykjavik District Court. For copyright infringement, Article 59a provides that copyright collecting societies may file for an injunction against intermediaries such as internet service providers to block users' access to web sites containing infringing material. There were no available statistics on IP enforcement.

Iceland accepted the amendment to the TRIPS Agreement on patents and public health on 12 October 2015; it subsequently entered into force in January 2017.[227] Upon accepting the amendment, Iceland reviewed the relevant provisions of the Patents Act and since the provisions were already considered to be in line with the TRIPS amendments it was not considered necessary to make any legislative changes. Iceland did not make any notifications to the WTO on IP during the review period.

TRADE POLICIES BY SECTOR

AGRICULTURE

FEATURES

Agriculture is a relatively small part of the economy in Iceland. Agriculture, hunting, and related services contributed 1.1-1.2% to GDP in 2013-16, and it remains small compared to fishing and aquaculture (Section 4.1.2) . The manufacture of food products, beverages and tobacco products (less fish processing) contributed a further 1.7% to GDP. In employment terms, in 2014, agriculture employed about 3,900 people or 2.2% of employed persons, a decline from 5,000 people in 2011.[228]

After several years of steady increases, the value of agricultural output (in producer prices) was relatively stable from 2014 to 2016 at ISK 50 to ISK 52 billion. Production of animals and animal products dominates total production with milk representing about 21% of the total value of all agricultural products, and sheep and goats about 12%. Crop output represents about one-third of total output, but most of this is forage production linked to livestock (Table 4.1) .

Only about 1% of Iceland's land area of 103,022 km^2 is suitable for cultivation and about 25% is suitable for grazing, some of which can also be used to grow fodder crops. In 2010, there were about 2,592 farms, practically all family owned and operated. Most farms tend to be small in business terms: in 2013, there were about 43 cows on the average dairy farm.[229]

4.4. In addition to the harsh climate and lack of suitable land, the scope for increasing productivity in Iceland is limited to some extent by the narrow genetic base: there is only one dairy breed, one sheep breed, and one horse breed. These breeds have developed in isolation from the rest of the world and are vulnerable to transmittable diseases, making it difficult to safely introduce new genetic material.[230]

TRADE

4.5. Iceland is a net importer of agricultural products (WTO definition[231]) with, in 2016, exports of US$95 million and imports of US$492 million. The main exports are water, sheep meat products, and pure-bred horses. Exports of mink skins declined by nearly three-quarters in 2014 compared to 2013 but recovered in 2016 – although still less than in 2013. According to the authorities, the fluctuations in export values for furskins were linked to prices on the Copenhagen Fur market where the majority of skins are sold. Imports are more broadly based than exports and increased from US$402 million in 2012 to US$492 in 2016. The increase in the US dollar value of imports of animal feed preparations was linked to increased production of milk, poultry and pigs and the stronger króna (Table 4.2) .

4.1.1.3 Agriculture policies

4.6. Agriculture policy is the responsibility of the Ministry of Industries and Innovation, which was formed in September 2012 by the amalgamation of the Ministry of Fisheries and Agriculture, the Ministry of Industry, Energy and Tourism and part of the Ministry of Economic Affairs. In January 2008, the Icelandic Food and Veterinary Authority (*Matvælastofnun* - MAST) was established as an inspection and administrative body with responsibilities that include: food safety; plant and livestock quality, and health-related matters; feed, seed, and fertilizer services; administration of organic production; and monitoring of animal welfare.[232]

4.7. The Farmers' Association of Iceland (BI) represents farmers in discussions and negotiations with the Government in developing general and sectoral policies as well as providing extension and advisory services to farmers through the Agricultural Consultation Centres (RML) . BI's members are agricultural associations representing farmers in different regions and farming companies most of which represent specific agricultural sectors, such as the Association of Egg Producers, the Association of Poultry Farmers, the Association of Sheep Farmers, and the Federation of Dairy Farmers.[233]

4.8. The overall objective of agriculture policy is to maintain and strengthen a diverse agricultural sector, as far as natural and marketing conditions allow. The main emphases of policy are: to meet domestic demand to the extent that this goal is realistic; to maintain sustainable production of high quality and healthy products; to improve efficiency and competitiveness; to improve farmers' incomes; to improve creativity and create job opportunities; and to sustain livelihoods in rural areas.

4.9. The legal basis for agriculture policy is set out in several legislative acts, including:

Act No. 99/1993 (last amended in 2016) on Agricultural Produce, which sets out the policy framework, the legal basis for production controls, and provisions for slaughter and processing, pricing and support measures; and

Act No. 70/1998 (last amended in 2016) on Agriculture, which provides the legal basis for development projects, extension services, and livestock improvements.[234]

4.10. Under Act No. 99/1993, the Government and the Farmers' Association of Iceland (BI) negotiate multiannual agreements on agricultural policy and support for agriculture. Following the expiration of the previous agreements between the Government and the Farmers' Association, new agreements were concluded for the ten year period from 2017 to 2026 with extensive reviews in 2019 and 2023. These agreements called for a revision of Act No. 99/1993, which entered into force on 1 January 2017. The agreements are implemented with regulations which include a general regulation on support for agriculture and three sector-specific regulations:

Regulation No. 1240/2016 on horizontal support for agriculture;

Regulation No. 1150/2016 on support for cattle;

Regulation No. 1234/2016 on support for horticulture; and

Regulation No. 1151/2016 on support for sheep.[235]

TRADE POLICIES

Tariffs on agricultural products (WTO definition) vary considerably within and among product groups averaging 20%, varying from zero to nearly 430%, and with a standard deviation of 41. Nearly 41% of the 1,990 tariff lines for agricultural products, and nearly all under HS headings 02 (meat and edible meat offal) and 04 (dairy products, eggs, etc.) are non-*ad valorem*, mostly with *ad valorem* and specific duty components

Iceland reserved the right to use the special agricultural safeguard on 390 tariff lines but it has never applied it to any tariff line.[236]

According to a notification by Iceland to the WTO on imports under tariff quotas, Iceland has nine minimum access quotas and 78 current access quotas. Out of the total of 87 tariff quotas, 57 had imports greater than 100% of the tariff quota quantity in the year ending 30 June 2016 and 59 in the year ending 30 June 2015. However, the notification also notes that, for a range of products under tariff quota commitments, the applied tariff for all imports is equal to, or less than the in-quota tariff although the notification lists all bound tariff quotas and the import level. Therefore, these quotas do not have a specific administration or allocation system.[237]

For other quotas, including quotas applicable under agreements with the European Union, Norway and Switzerland, the Ministry of Industries and Innovation posts invitations for applications for TQ allocations and the results of the allocations on its website.[238]

In June 2016, the Ministry of Industries and Innovation amended the system for administering the WTO tariff quotas for meat, butter, cheese, eggs and their products, and meat preparations by requesting applications for allocations for the six month period ending 31 December 2016 instead of a twelve month period. Once awarded, an allocation is not transferrable.[239]

In September 2015, Iceland and the EU reached an agreement on trade in agricultural products, and the protection of geographical indications. Under the agreement, Iceland:

granted duty-free access for a range of agricultural products (mostly processed products but also live animals, and some fresh fruits and vegetables);

expanded existing tariff quotas for beef, pig meat, poultry, cheese, and certain meat products;

reduced tariffs on imports of meat, some vegetables, and some other products; and provides protection for EU-listed GIs.

In return, under the Agreement, the EU grants duty-free access for a range of products and opens or expands tariff quotas, including an expansion of the existing quota for skyr from 380 to 4,000 tonnes over four years.

According to the European Commission, the agreement will mean that 99% of the value of trade in EU processed agricultural products and 91% of basic agricultural products will be duty free and Iceland will afford the same level of protection to the 1,150 agricultural products and foodstuffs on the GI list.[240]

4.19. According to the notifications by Iceland to the WTO, export subsidies for agricultural goods have not been provided since the year ending 31 August 1998.[241]

DOMESTIC POLICIES

DAIRY AND BEEF

A quota system for milk production was first introduced in 1980 based on individual non-transferrable quotas for milk producers and went through a number of reforms until, in 1992, the current system of freely transferable quotas was introduced and production subsidies were linked to the quota and paid directly to the farmer. The introduction of freely transferable quotas resulted in a considerable level of trade in quotas and concentration of production: between 1995 and 2005 the number of dairy farmers fell by 50% and average production per farm increased by 100%.[242]

Regulation No. 1150/2016 and the Agreement on the operating environment for the cattle sector represent a change in policy for dairy and cattle farming in Iceland.[243] The Agreement states that the 2019 revision will consider the feasibility of abolishing production quotas, based on a vote by milk producers. Furthermore, the system of "support entitlements" (basic payments to all active dairy and cattle farmers) is to be phased out over the duration of the Agreement while payments per litre of milk produced are to be de-linked from support entitlements and increased while a new system for supporting beef production is introduced.

The total production quota for milk for 2017 was set at 144 million litres which is divided among the individual quota holders. Production in excess of the quota must be exported (Article 11 of Regulation No. 1150/2016) . Payments to farmers are made in equal monthly payments of one-twelfth of annual quota.

Minimum prices paid by dairies for milk delivered within the production quota are decided by the government-chaired Agricultural Pricing Committee (Verdlagsnefnd buvara) which includes representatives of the Farmers' Association and, on behalf of consumers, the labour union. Since 1 January 2017, the minimum price has been ISK 87.40 per litre.

In addition to payments for milk delivered to dairies, headage payments are provided for dairy and beef cows, initially for a total of 25,000 dairy and 3,000 beef cows with the number revised annually. The payment per cow is subject to a reduction factor depending on the number of cows on the farm.

Other programmes covered by the Regulation and Agreement include a breeding programme, investment aids, measures to help balance production and demand, and support for beef production. The measures to balance production and demand are discretionary and are to be allocated when there is a need to respond to changes in supply and demand. These measures could include improved marketing of cattle products, support for diversification, temporary farm support, and compensation for slaughtering. The measures for beef production include a slaughter premium and ISK 100 million in 2017 for a quarantine facility for imports of genetic material (Table 4.3) .

The 2016 amendments to Act No. 99/1993 included a provision to change the specific duties for certain cheese and milk powder products[244] based on changes to the SDR/ISK exchange rate from 1995 to 2016 effective from 1 March 2017 and annually thereafter based on the annual change in the exchange rate.[245] This resulted in a reduction in the specific duty component of the tariff on these products as the ISK had appreciated relative to the SDR, for example, the tariff on HS 0406 2000 (grated or powdered cheese) was 30% + 715 ISK/kg which was reduced to 30% + 635 ISK/kg.

SHEEP

4.27. Programmes relating to sheep production are set out in the Agreement on the operating environment for the sheep sector and Regulation No. 1151/2016 on support for sheep.

As for dairy farming, the support entitlements for sheep farming are to be phased out by end-2025 and replaced by quality assurance premiums for farmers for sheep meat meeting requirements relating to,*inter alia*, animal welfare, sustainable land use, and quality.

4.29. Headage payments for winter-fed sheep will be introduced from 1 January 2020 with higher payments for new entrants. In addition, starting in 2018, farm support payments, also based on the number of winter-fed sheep, will be paid to producers keeping over 100 winter-fed sheep. The farm support payments range from ISK 20,000 for farms with 101-120 sheep up to a maximum of ISK 320,000 for farms with more than 800 sheep.

In addition, support under the Agreement is also available for wool production, regional support for some regions, investment aid, and promotion of higher value sheep products

HORTICULTURE

The programmes relating to horticulture are set out in the Agreement on the operating environment for the horticulture sector and Regulation No. 1234/2016 on support for horticulture.

Under the Agreement, producers of tomatoes, cucumbers and bell peppers are supported by direct payments based on estimates of production which may be adjusted depending on actual production. In addition, electricity subsidies are available for illumination of greenhouses (which are heated by geothermal energy) of up to 95% of the cost of the transfer and distribution of electricity

OTHER POLICIES AND SECTORS

In addition to support under sector-specific agreements and regulations for dairy, beef, sheep, and horticulture, there is a separate Agreement on the general operating environment for the agricultural sector and Regulation No. 1240/2016 on public support for agriculture.

In addition to several programmes for agriculture in general, the Agreement and Regulation include sector-specific programmes for pig and goat farming, and forestry. The general programmes include advisory services, breeding projects, the Genetic Resource Council, vegetation resources, new entrants (recruitment), and rural employment under the Agricultural Productivity Fund. In addition, the programme for land cultivation provides subsidies for cultivated land, including cultivation of forage crops.

Under Regulation No. 1240/2016, support for goat farming is divided among headage payments (up to 60% of the total), slaughter premiums (up to 17% of the total), goat-milk subsidies (up to 8% of the total), and support for breeding (up to 15% of the total) . Support for pig farming includes subsidies to improve pig housing including investment support for new construction and the demolition of existing buildings.

DOMESTIC SUPPORT LEVELS

WTO notifications

In September 2014, Iceland provided a notification to the WTO on domestic support for the calendar years 2004 to 2012[246] and in May 2017, a notification on domestic support for calendar years 2013 to 2015.[247] For this Report, the Ministry of Industries and Innovation also provided estimates for 2016. In current Icelandic króna terms, support under the Amber Box increased steadily from 2004 to 2016, apart from a decline in 2015 before growth resumed in 2016 when it reached ISK 21,265 million. Throughout 2004-16, most Amber Box support was to dairy farmers from direct payments (ISK 5,622 million in 2016) and market price support (valued at ISK 12,874 million in 2016) . The market price support element is based on the difference between the 2016 applied administered price of ISK 103.2 per kg and the external reference price of ISK 6.30 per kg (from supporting tables to Iceland's Uruguay Round commitments[248]) . In comparison, the external reference price used in the OECD's estimates of support was ISK 36.95/kg in 2015.

Total support under the Green Box in 2016 was ISK 5,807 million, most of which was for general services and decoupled income support. Since 2004, Green Box support has fluctuated although, after a fall in 2011 compared to 2010, it followed an upward trend to

2016. Blue Box support started in 2006 and, after an initial peak in 2007, increased steadily to ISK 670 million in 2016. All Blue Box payments are for bovine animals

OECD monitoring and evaluation of agricultural policies

Compared to the methodology used to calculate the level of support provided under the Amber, Blue, and Green Boxes in the WTO, the OECD's annual monitoring and evaluation reports on agricultural policies in OECD countries use a different methodology to calculate the value of support which is expressed in a number of indicators, including: the Producer Support Estimate (PSE) for gross transfers from consumers and tax payers to agricultural producers; the Total Support Estimate (TSE) for transfers to the agricultural sector in general; and the Single Commodity Transfers (SCT) for transfers to specific commodities. As previously noted, the PSE represents the value of transfers to producers, unlike support under the Amber Box, Blue Box and Green Box which measure compliance with WTO commitments. Therefore, the value of support as notified to the WTO is neither compatible nor comparable with the values calculated by the OECD.[249]

According to the OECD, the TSE had been relatively stable from 2006 to 2013, but then increased in the following two years reaching nearly ISK 27 billion in 2015, compared to a total value of production of ISK 34 billion. While the TSE represents total transfers to producers, including government support for research, the PSE represents total transfers to producers resulting from government policies, and the PSE, at nearly ISK 26 billion in 2015, accounted for most of the TSE. At 56% of gross farm receipts, the PSE for Iceland was the third highest among OECD countries.[250] Market price support, which is largely the result of high tariffs and high domestic prices, was the main element of support

The degree of support to producers from high domestic prices is reflected in the Producer Nominal Protection Coefficient (NPC), where a coefficient greater than one indicates the degree to which domestic prices exceed the reference price. In Iceland, the Producer NPC varies from one commodity to another and averages 2.02 overall – indicating that, on average, domestic prices of supported commodities are twice the external price.

Most support for agriculture is provided to specific commodities, as shown by the Specific Commodity Transfers (SCT) to producers (Chart 4.2) . In terms of gross farm receipts, the SCT varies from 73% for poultry meat to 28% for beef (Table 4.7) .

Producer support estimate (PSE) is the annual monetary value of gross transfers from consumers and taxpayers to agricultural producers, measured at the farm-gate level, arising from policy measures that support agriculture, regardless of their nature, objectives or impacts on farm production or income.

Single commodity transfers (SCT) is the annual monetary value of gross transfers from consumers and taxpayers to agricultural producers, measured at the farm-gate level, arising from policy measures directly linked to the production of a single commodity such that the producer must produce the designated commodity in order to receive the transfer.

Market price support (MPS) is an indicator of the annual monetary value of gross transfers from consumers and taxpayers to agricultural producers arising from policy measures creating a gap between domestic producer prices and reference prices of a specific agricultural commodity measured at the farm-gate level.

The Producer Nominal Protection Co-efficient (Producer NPC) is an indicator of the nominal rate of protection for producers measuring the ratio between the average price received by producers (at farm-gate), including payments per tonne of current output, and the border price (measured at farm-gate level) .

Source: Icelandic authorities and OECD Producer and Consumer Support Estimates database. Viewed at:http://www.oecd.org/chile/producerandconsumersupportestimatesdatabase.htm [March 2017].

FISHERIES

FEATURES

Fisheries are an important part of the economy of Iceland contributing over 5% to GDP in 2015, with fish processing contributing an additional 3.1%. In 2014, 4,400 people were employed in fishing and 4,700 in fish processing.

The value of the total catch was ISK 133 billion in 2016, down from a peak of ISK 159 billion in 2012. Cod remains the most important species in terms of value, representing nearly 44% of total value of catch in 2016, while mackerel has increased in importance, from negligible levels in 2005 to ISK 18 billion in 2011 and ISK 11 billion in 2016 Of the total value of catch of ISK 151 billion in 2015, ISK 137 billion was caught in Iceland's 200 mile EEZ.[251]

After several years of decline up to 2008, the fishing fleet increased and has remained relatively stable since 2012. However, most of the increase between 2008 and 2012 was in small undecked vessels which account for a small portion of the total catch. The numbers in other size categories have declined or remained stable (Chart 4.3 and Chart 4.4) . In addition there are two registered whaling vessels although neither was active in 2016.

Although the majority of vessels are less than 10 GT or undecked, these categories account for a relatively small amount of the value and volume of catch, while the 45 vessels (including trawlers) of over 1,000 GT account for two-thirds of the volume of catch. In terms of value, vessels under 1,000 GT account for over half the value of total catch as they specialize in higher-value-per-kilogram fish (Chart 4.4) . This reflects that the largest vessels hold most of the quotas in small pelagics, i.e. capelin, herring and mackerel, while the higher-value species are mostly demersal, including cod.

In terms of fish processing, several long-term trends appear to have come to an end in the 2010-17 period. The quantity of fish for oil and fishmeal production, which had been in steady decline since the early 2000s when it accounted for about two-thirds of total fish processing, has fluctuated since 2010 reflecting reductions in capelin catch which had been mostly used for meal and oil production. On the other hand, the quantity of frozen fish had increased steadily to over half of the total by 2010, but has since declined to 40% in 2015 (Chart 4.5) . According to the authorities, the change from long-term trends in the mid-2000s is due to climate change and mackerel and capelin stocks moving further north.

Aquaculture is much smaller than the capture subsector but it has been growing significantly in recent years. In 2016, about 15,000 tonnes of farmed fish were produced – an increase of 80% compared to 2015. Salmon are the main species produced (8,000 tonnes) followed by Arctic char (4,200 tonnes) .

TRADE

According to UN Comtrade, total exports of fish and fish products were US$ 1,925 million in 2016, representing 43% of exports of goods, while imports were US$ 134 million.[252] Furthermore, imports of some products, such as shrimp, are processed in Iceland and the processed products exported. Thus, in 2016, US$ 44 million in frozen shrimp (HS 030616) were imported and US$ 78 million of prepared shrimp (HS 160521) were exported. The applied tariff on imports of all fish and fisheries products is zero, except for imports of meat of whales and other cetaceans, which are subject to an applied tariff of 30% plus ISK 363/kg.

According to Statistics Iceland, total exports of fish and fish products were ISK 265 million in 2015. Exports of cod and products of cod have traditionally been greatest, at ISK 100 million in 2015, followed by capelin, redfish, and haddock. Changes in the value of exports have been driven by changes in prices more than changes in quantities, for example, the value of shrimp exports more than doubled from 2007 to 2015, while the quantity exported fell by nearly one-third (Table 4.10) .

The main destination for exports is the United Kingdom (18.3% of total exports of fish), followed by Spain (8.8%), France (8.8%), Norway (7.6%), and the United States (6.9%) . However, the authorities noted that some of the larger fish exporters export to large cold stores and the fish products may then be re-exported to other countries, but they do not have data on these re-exports.

POLICIES

The Department of Fisheries and Innovation in the Ministry of Industries and Innovation is responsible for developing policies and preparing legislation. The Directorate of Fisheries, which is run as a separate entity within the Ministry, is responsible for implementing government policy, running the management system, monitoring and controlling fishing activities, collecting data, and imposing penalties for illegal catches. The Icelandic Coast Guard's responsibilities include inspection, control, and enforcement of the laws at sea. T he Marine and Freshwater Research Institute (MRFI) in the Ministry is responsible for research and advising the Government on sustainable use of marine resources. Both the directorate and the MRFI provide information on fisheries to the authorities, the fishing sector, and the public in their respective fields.[253] The main stakeholders in the industry include Fisheries Iceland (which was formed in 2014 from the merger of the Federation of Icelandic Fishing Vessel Owners and the Federation of Icelandic Fish Processing Plants), and the National Association of Small Boat Owners. These stakeholders represent the fisheries and processing industries in policy discussions with the Ministry.

The principal legislation regulating fishing in Iceland includes:

Act No. 116/2006 (last amended 2016) on Fisheries Management;

Act No. 71/2008 (last amended 2015) on Aquaculture;

Act No. 151/1996 (last amended 2012) on Fishing Outside Icelandic Jurisdiction;

Act No. 57/1996 (last amended 2015) on the Treatment of Commercial Marine Stocks; and

Act No. 74/2012 (last amended 2015) on Fishing Fees.

4.53. Under these acts, the Ministry issues numerous regulations (58 in 2016) which provide details for many of these laws including setting catch quotas.

The Fisheries Management Act consolidated most of the existing legislation on fisheries management, including Act No. 38/1990 on Fisheries Management. The Act states that fish resources are the property of the nation and that the policy objective is to promote conservation and efficient utilization of these resources to ensure stable employment and settlement. The Act provides the legal basis for the Minister to establish, through regulations, total allowable catches (TACs) for individual marine stocks which are allocated to individual vessels under the individual transferable quota (ITQ) systems. There are two quota systems: the general system; and a system that applies to small boats (less than 15 GRT) which may only fish with hand lines or longlines. The Ministry reserves part of the TACs for fishing companies that have been affected by significant shocks due to a fall in catches or quotas and for vessels from disfavoured areas that are heavily dependent on fishing.[255]

The MRFI is responsible for assessing marine stocks and these assessments are reviewed by the International Council for the Exploration of the Sea (ICES) . Based on these assessments, the Ministry establishes a TAC for each species.

For some fish stocks that are shared with other countries, international and/or bilateral agreements may apply and under them Iceland has a quota share:

Iceland is a contracting party to the Northeast Atlantic Fisheries Commission (NEAFC) that administers stocks in the international area in the Northeast

Atlantic. Icelandic vessels fish blue whiting, Northeast Atlantic mackerel, Atlanto-Scandian (Norwegian spring-spawning) herring, and deep-sea redfish in the NEAFC convention area;

Iceland has an agreement with the Russian Federation and Norway for fishing cod in the Barents Sea, subject to a TAC;

Iceland is a contracting party to the International Commission for the Conservation of Atlantic Tuna (ICCAT) and has a quota share for East Atlantic blue fin tuna; and

Iceland is a contracting party to the Northwest Atlantic Fisheries Organization (NAFO) and has a share in the northern shrimp catch.

The TACs established by the Ministry and the international/bilateral arrangements are distributed among ITQ holders and assigned to specific vessels. The system covers all economically important species, about 95-97% of total catch in value terms.

In addition to the TAC and ITQ system, a number of other effort and gear restrictions apply including permanent closure of nursery areas; closure of spawning areas for cod during the spawning period; temporary closure of areas with excess juveniles; a 12-mile exclusion limit for large trawlers; and mesh-size limits and other equipment-related measures to reduce by-catch and catch of juveniles.

After the TAC for the fishing year is decided, 5.3% of the allowable catches of all species is deducted and reserved, *inter alia*: for support for rural communities deemed to be in a "vulnerable" position regarding population development; for coastal fisheries; and for areas that experience a sudden or drastic decline in fishing opportunities.

With a stated aim of reinforcing regional settlement, a coastal fisheries option was initiated within the fisheries management system in 2008. The coastal fisheries operate in the summer months (May to August) with a common pool quota. The total pool quota is allocated for each month for four geographical regions. The vessels that can apply for a coastal licence are small vessels using hand lines only, fishing mostly cod, haddock and saithe. Coastal fishing boats are not allowed to take part in the general commercial part of the management system during the coastal operational season. In 2016, the total quota for the coastal fisheries amounted to 8,600 tonnes of demersal species.

Discards of commercial species are prohibited and all catches of commercial species must be retained and landed.[256] Furthermore, vessel owners may not leave port to fish unless they have an adequate quota for the trip.

Each landing must be registered and information on the catch sent to the Directorate of Fisheries, with about 85,000 landings registered each year. There are several flexibility options within the system to support the landing obligation including provisions for transferring quota to the following year (up to 15%), and for catching in excess of quota (5%, which is taken from the following year's quota) .

Under the ITQ system, up to 50% of a quota may be transferred to (an)other vessel(s) in any year, and the quota is lost if the vessel catches less than 50% of total quota for two successive years. There are limits to the amount of quota which any single fishing company, or group of companies linked by ownership may own: 12% of the quota share for cod; 20% for haddock, saithe and Greenland halibut; 35% for redfish; 20% for herring and capelin; and 20% for offshore shrimp. Furthermore, a fishing company or a group of linked companies is not permitted to hold more than 12% of the value of the combined quota shares for the stocks utilized by TAC allocations.[257] However, consolidation of quotas has continued, with the ten largest quota holders responsible for 50% of the total of all TACs (measured in cod equivalents) and the twenty largest responsible for 71%.[258]

Under Act No. 74/2012, vessel operators must pay a fishing fee to offset the cost of services provided by the State and as a tax on the exploitation of marine resources. The fee is based on total earnings before tax (EBT) plus a portion of EBT for processing operations under a methodology set out in the Act. The fees for each fishing season in ISK per kilogram of ungutted catch are set out in regulations by the Ministry of Industries and Innovation.[259] In quota year 2016/17, the total fee was estimated to be ISK 5.2 billion, or about 3% of the 2015 catch value.

In addition to the regular fees applicable to all vessels using a harbour, fishing vessels pay harbour fees which vary from 0.7% to 2.3% of landed value, the lower rates applying to sea products that are frozen or processed at sea. Fishing vessels also pay fees for registration of landing weights and species by harbour employees. This information is sent to the Directorate's online database and the fees are intended to cover the costs of registration. Under Act No. 116/2006 an export levy of 5% is applied to exports of unprocessed fish by the Directorate of Fisheries.

There are no direct government financial transfers to the fisheries sector, including fishing processing and, with tariffs on nearly all fishing products at zero, no consumer transfer to the sector either. A tax concession for the crew of fishing vessels was phased out in 2013.[260] Government support to the fishing sector is through research, management, and regulation. According to the OECD, the fisheries support estimate (FSE) for Iceland was negative for 2012-14, indicating a net average annual contribution of ISK 4.4 billion from the fisheries sector as fees were greater than the estimates of support. In 2015, there was a net contribution to the sector of ISK 0.8 billion as general services support was ISK 4.2 billion while cost recovery charges (fees) were ISK 3.4 billion (from ISK 8.1 billion the previous year) .[261]

As noted in the previous review, foreign ownership of fishing operations and primary fish processing (defined as salting, freezing, drying, and other processing to protect from decay, and the production of fish oil or fishmeal) is limited to no more than 25% direct and 49% combined direct and indirect ownership. In certain circumstances, direct foreign ownership of up to 33% may be permitted.[262]

MINING AND ENERGY

The unique geography and natural terrain provide Iceland with an unusual energy profile. Iceland is the world's largest green energy producer per capita and also has the world's highest share of renewable energy in any national total energy budget. Currently, hydro and geothermal sources supply almost all of Iceland's electricity and 85% of Iceland's total consumption of primary energy (Chart 4.6); the remainder comprises fossil fuels (refined oil), which are used entirely for transport and fisheries.

Hydropower is responsible for nearly three quarters of electricity generation, while the rest is produced through geothermal means. Around 80% of the electricity generated is consumed by the industrial sector (mainly aluminium); residential consumption is around 5%. Around 90% of space heating is through direct geothermal energy.

Electricity prices for industrial consumers are low compared to other European countries: in the second half of 2015 the average price for industrial consumers was €0.029 per kWh, the lowest in the EEA, while electricity prices for households were €0.127 per kWh which was fo 4.71. Companies in the energy sector in Iceland are vertically integrated. Under the law, a single power company can function as generator, distributor and supplier. However, accounting separation is required between concession (transfer of electricity in a certain area) and competitive activities.

Companies owned by the State or municipalities dominate the electricity sector. Landsvirkjun, which is wholly state-owned, is the largest energy company in Iceland, providing approximately 75% of all the electricity produced in Iceland.[264] Furthermore, Landsvirkjun is responsible for more than 96% of all hydro generation in Iceland, and its share in total geothermal electricity generation is around 11%.

Landsvirkjun has US Dollar denominated long-term contracts with foreign-owned energy intensive companies (aluminium smelters); as such it sells 80% of the electricity it generates to these companies. The remaining 20% is bought by public utilities and the Icelandic Transmission System Operator (Landsnet) .

Currently Landsvirkjun's core debt programme is run under its Euro Medium Term Note (EMTN) master agreements. They consist of two agreements, an EMTN programme, which is guaranteed by the State and another without a state guarantee.[265] The Minister of Finance manages the ownership of Landsvirkjun and appoints all five board members and five alternate members. Lansdvirkjun is also the main owner of Landsnet, with a share of 65%.

Orkuveita Reykjavíkur (OR) is a public utility company, which is owned by the City of Reykjavík and adjacent municipalities. It is the largest local provider of electricity and heating to end-users. The main service area of the company is the larger Reykjavik Metropolitan Area, covering two-thirds of the Icelandic population. HS Orka is the third main electricity-generating firm in Iceland. It was privatized in 2007. Its largest shareholder is the Canadian Alterra Power, which owns two-thirds of the company. The rest is owned by a group of Icelandic pension funds. There are several other small electricity firms and utilities in Iceland; these are owned by the Icelandic State and/or municipalities.

REGULATION

The energy sector in Iceland is governed by Act No. 57/1998 on Survey and Utilization of Ground Resources, Act No. 65/2003 on Electricity, Act No. 13/2001 on Prospecting, Exploration and Production of Hydrocarbons and accompanying regulations and amendments[266], and Act No. 109/2011 on the Taxation of Hydrocarbon Extraction. All the above Acts are administered by the National Energy Authority (Orkustofun) .

The National Energy Authority (NEA) is a government agency under the Ministry of Industries and Innovation. The NEA's main responsibilities include advising the Government on energy issues and related topics, licensing and monitoring the development and exploitation of energy and mineral resources, regulating the operation of the electrical transmission and distribution system, and promoting energy research. Furthermore, administrative decisions made by the NEA with respect to the above-mentioned Acts can be appealed to the Appeals Committee for Environmental and Resource Matters as per Act No. 130/2011. Since the establishment of the committee in 2012, appeals have averaged 120 annually, while in 2016 there were 175 appeals. Complainants have recourse to the courts after the non-judicial appeals process has been exhausted.

Under the provisions of these laws, investment and/or ownership of energy exploitation rights and the production and distribution of energy are limited to EEA and EFTA residents. Act No. 57/1998 stipulates that resources within the ground belong to the owner of the land. However, a licence from the National Energy Authority is required to survey or prospect on the land[267]; additionally a compensation agreement with the landowner is required. Recent changes to Act No. 57/1998 on Survey and Utilization of Ground Resources and Act No. 65/2003 on Electricity stipulate that:

> The State or municipalities can no longer sell the ownership of resources; however, utilization rights can be leased to a developer for up to 65 years with a possibility of extension. Royalties for the utilization are determined by the Prime Minister.
>
> Producers of electricity compete in an open market in Iceland. Therefore CHP power plants are obliged to keep separate accounts for heat and power production to prevent cross subsidization of electricity.

The energy market in Iceland is open, with foreign companies operating in the sector. As part of its accession process to the EU, which was suspended in September 2013, Iceland implemented the first and second electricity directives of the EU. The generation and distribution segments of the market are open to competition from companies in the EEA. The Electricity Act allows third-party access for transmission and distribution networks. Under the provisions of the Electricity Act, only Landsnet (IceGrid), a private company may provide electricity transmission services in the country and it also has the exclusive right to construct new transmission infrastructure. Landsnet operates under a concession arrangement and is subject to regulation by the National Energy Authority (NEA) .

The NEA determines the revenue framework on which Landsnet's tariff is based. The law stipulates that a single power company can function as generator, distributor and supplier. However, accounting separation is required between concession (transfer of electricity in a certain area) and competitive activities. While consumers must use the distributor holding the concession for their respective area, the distributor need not be the same company as the supplier, thus consumers are able to choose their supplier.

Power companies determine the price of electricity that they sell, while transmission and distribution fees are set by the NEA.[268] The NEA sets an upper limit on Landsnet's income, and Landsnet's profits are also bound by an upper limit under the Act. These measures indirectly control the tariff that Landsnet may charge. Iceland also operates a policy of equalization of energy prices. Under this policy, homes that are heated by oil and electricity (where no other means of heating are available) are subsidized by the State. The annual subsidy amount is approved by the Parliament in the Budget each year; in 2015 it was over ISK 1.2 billion. With a view to promoting a more efficient market for electricity trading, Landsnet has been working on establishing an electronic market for electricity trading (ISBAS) . However, it is unclear when it would be operational.

At the time of the last review, the authorities were in the process of preparing a comprehensive energy strategy for 2020 that was to be released in 2012. The salient features of the strategy were: replacing fossil fuels with renewable energy; following an environmentally protective and precautionary approach in hydroelectric and geothermal energy production; supporting diversified industry with an emphasis on ecologically beneficial high-tech industry; sustainable utilization of all energy sources; and encouraging better energy utilization. The strategy was not concluded in 2012 as planned. The authorities stated that they are currently in the process of preparing a new comprehensive energy strategy, which they aim to publish in 2018.

FINANCIAL SECTOR

BANKING

Iceland was one of the countries' worst affected by the 2008 financial crisis: the financial system was on the verge of collapse; equity prices fell by over 90%; money market rates rose to 18%; and the Icelandic króna depreciated by around 40% in real terms. As a result of lower asset prices, debt to collateral ratios increased and, along with higher inflation and a currency depreciation, resulted in a spike in non-performing loans. The Government intervened through several emergency measures, including: liquidation of the three largest commercial banks and the establishment of three new commercial banks, which took over their domestic operations; the introduction of capital controls; and putting in place an international financial aid package.[269]

STRUCTURE AND PERFORMANCE

Since the crisis, the banking system has stabilized and recovered. Currently the banking sector in Iceland is comprised of four commercial banks and four savings banks (compared with nine in 2012) . Two of the commercial banks are wholly state-owned, while a third has a minority government stake. The activities of the banks are focused mainly on serving the domestic economy.

The assets of the financial system rose from ISK 7,715 billion in 2010, to nearly ISK 10,034 billion in 2016, while over the same period the assets of the commercial banks rose from ISK 2,627 billion to ISK 3,199 billion. The restructuring of the banks has also resulted in the ratio of non-performing loans[270] to total loans declining from a peak of 20% in 2010 to 2.1% in 2016 (Chart 4.7) .[271]

Furthermore, during the period under review, Icelandic banks have been profitable, with return on assets being 1.8% and return on equity 9% in 2016. In 2016, income from equity securities and upward loan value adjustments contracted significantly from 2015 and operating expenses rose. On the other hand, net interest income rose markedly. Additionally, the banks' capital position is robust, with capital adequacy ratios of 28%; including 27% in Tier 1 capital. Both ratios are well in excess of the statutory minimum

With regard to the banking sector, a lingering issue had been the resolution of the estates of the failed banks. In June 2015, the authorities announced a plan to unwind both the estates of the failed banks and the remaining offshore ISK holdings, comprising mainly bank deposits, treasury securities and equity interests, which involved a combination of incentives so as to motivate the boards responsible for winding up the insolvent banks to reach voluntary agreements with the claimholders to allocate outstanding assets in a way that ensured financial stability. These included:

Measures to neutralize the threat from distributing króna-denominated assets[272], such as making an offsetting "stability contribution" to the Icelandic treasury;

extending the maturity of foreign-currency denominated domestic assets; and

refinancing or otherwise ensuring the repayment of foreign-exchange denominated loans granted by the authorities to the new banks following the crisis.

The "composition" agreements were signed in late 2015; these discounted further bank claims in default since 2008–09 as a *quid pro quo* for lifting capital controls on the estates. The estates assigned most of their ISK assets to the State (17% of GDP), distributed recoveries to the Central Bank of Iceland (CBI) as a claimant (about 4%), termed out their domestic foreign currency deposits for seven years (4%), and drew from their external assets so as to refinance certain CBI and Government claims on the banks (2.5% of GDP) . They agreed to these actions so they could immediately distribute liquid foreign assets worth around 35% of GDP to their mainly foreign claimants, with more to follow over time.

With respect to the offshore ISK holders, the CBI held a euro auction in June 2016. All accepted bids were offered to investors at the same price. The auction exchange rate was based on a sliding scale according to the size of the total bid, with a best rate of ISK

190:€1, implying a euro premium of roughly 27% over the onshore market rate. Participation was voluntary. Settlement took place on 29 June 2016. Since then, a further two auctions have taken place (Section 1.1) .

Direct state assistance to the financial sector amounted to around 34% of GDP. Both the CBI and the banks had to be recapitalized. To cover this, the Government gave the CBI a bond equivalent to 17% of GDP in 2009. In 2009 to 2012, it provided the banks a separate bond equivalent to 15% of GDP. According to the IMF, recoveries are estimated at 43% of GDP. These consist of: bank equity and subordinated debt taken in 2009 as consideration for recapitalizations, the estimated value of which was 15% of GDP at end-2015; dividends and coupons on those claims, cumulating to around 3% of GDP in 2010-15; the stability contributions from the failed bank estates in the context of the compositions, valued on an accruals basis at 17% of GDP; and profits and interest payments to the CBI by the asset management subsidiary it established in 2009 to hold its seized collateral, cumulating to an expected 8% of GDP over 2010-16. Thus the State is estimated to have made a net gain in excess of 9% of GDP.

REGULATION

During the period under review, significant regulatory changes have included the establishment of the Financial Stability Council (FSC) and the Systemic Risk Committee (SRC) in 2014 as the official fora for collaboration on financial stability.[273] The FSC is a three member Council (Minister of Finance (chair), CBI Governor, and Director General (DG) of the Financial Supervisory Authority), which is responsible for formulating public policy on financial stability; assessing economic imbalances, financial system risks, undesirable incentives and other circumstances liable to jeopardize financial stability; defining actions, other than implementing the CBI's monetary policy management tools, which are considered necessary to influence the financial system with the objective of reinforcing and safeguarding financial stability; and confirming definitions of systemically important regulated entities, infrastructure and markets of such nature that their activities can impact financial stability. The FSC draws from recommendations and assessments from the SRC and other available data and submits recommendations to the relevant authorities.

The SRC is a five voting member Committee (CBI Governor (chair); DG of the Financial Supervisory Authority (Deputy Chair); CBI Deputy Governor; Deputy DG of the Financial Supervisory Authority; an outside expert in financial markets appointed by the Finance Minister; and the Permanent Secretary of the Finance Ministry in a non-voting capacity) . The SRC evaluates the current situation and outlook for the financial system, systemic risk, and financial stability. The SRC is mandated to take account of the FSC's official policy and intermediate objectives on financial stability. Its assessments are based on analysis carried out by the CBI and the Financial Supervisory Authority's joint risk assessment groups. Assessments and recommendations are submitted to the FSC.

Additionally, new liquidity rules issued by the Central Bank of Iceland took effect in December 2013, based on the liquidity coverage ratio (LCR) issued by the Basel Committee, and set minimum liquidity under stress scenarios.[274] Banks must fulfil requirements for both foreign-denominated and overall liquidity. Furthermore, a net stable funding ratio (NSFR) on foreign currency funding was put in place in December

2014. This was based on the Basel Committee's rules on NSFRs. The funding ratio is intended to ensure a minimum level of stable one-year funding in foreign currencies and therefore restrict the degree to which the commercial banks can rely on unstable short-term funding to finance long-term foreign-denominated lending. The rules on funding ratios reduce maturity mismatches and limit the extent to which the banks can depend on unstable short-term funding to finance long-term assets that could prove difficult to sell.

In early 2016, the Financial Stability Council (FSC) recommended that the Icelandic Financial Supervisory Authority (FME) impose three capital buffers[275]: a 2% capital buffer on systemically important financial institutions as of 1 April 2016; a systemic risk buffer amounting to 3% of risk-weighted domestic assets on systemically important deposit-taking institutions as of 1 April 2016; and a 1% countercyclical capital buffer on all financial institutions, effective 12 months after the date of the FME's decision. In addition, a capital conservation buffer was put in place at the beginning of 2016; it will rise in increments to 2.5% by the beginning of 2017. In October of 2016, the Financial Stability Council recommended that the Systemic Risk Buffer be increased by 1.25%, effective 12 months after the date of the FME's decision. Capital buffers may only include Tier 1 capital. When fully implemented, in November 2018, the combined capital buffers imposed on the three largest banks will be 8.75%.

From 1 April 2017, the Icelandic Financial Supervisory Authority (FME) can set ceilings on loan-to-value (LTV) and debt-service-to-income (DSTI) ratios of consumer mortgage credit. Before the FME can do this, the Financial Stability Council is required to give its opinion on the matter. The FME has yet to use this authorization.[276] There is a bill under discussion in the Icelandic Parliament that will, if passed, grant the Central Bank of Iceland authorization to limit the lending of financial undertakings to unhedged parties. Before the CBI can do this, the Financial Stability Council is required to give its opinion on the matter.[277]

Currently there is one stock exchange in Iceland, which is operated by Nasdaq Iceland hf., a part of the Nasdaq Group. Trading at the Nasdaq Iceland is governed by the Issuer Rules, the Member Rules and the Warrant Rulebook. The market is supervised by the Financial Supervisory Authority of Iceland. As of end of April 2017, there were 17 companies listed on the exchange with a market capitalization of €8.7 billion, compared with €2.2 billion in 2013. The OMX18 index has risen from 1,144 points in July 2014 to 1,822 points in April 2017.

To operate in Iceland, Insurance companies need an operating licence from the Financial Supervisory Authority of Iceland. Restriction on investment in the sector depends on the insurance company's risk profile. Currently there are 12 insurance companies operating in Iceland. Four companies operate in the non-life insurance segment, five operate in the life insurance segment, there are two reinsurance companies, and there is the Iceland Natural Catastrophe Insurance, which operates under special legislation (Act No. 100/2016 on Insurance Activity and Act No. 55/1992 on Iceland Catastrophe Insurance) . At the end of 2015, the assets of all insurance companies stood at approximately ISK 165 billion compared with over ISK 140 billion in 2011.

The solvency ratio of the three largest companies was within the range of 125% and 156%. Both segments of the insurance market continue to be profitable, with non-insurance companies registering a profit of over ISK 4 billion in 2015, a decline from around ISK 8 billion in 2012, while over the same period the profits of life insurance companies grew from about ISK 1.2 billion to over 1.7 billion.

TELECOMMUNICATIONS

The review period has seen the share of the information and communications sector in GDP steadily increasing to 5.1% in 2016 compared with 3.6% in 2010. This is in contrast to the previous review period where the share of the sector declined. Total income rose from ISK 43.4 billion in 2010 to nearly ISK 55 billion in 2015; during the same period, investment in the sector rose from around ISK 5.3 billion to ISK 8.6 billion. The fixed-line segment has been the major recipient of the investment due to fibre optic roll-out replacing copper. With regard to income generated, the largest amount is derived from the mobile networks followed by data transfer and internet services. During the review period, total telecommunication subscriptions continued to rise, resulting in the telecommunications penetration rate rising from 163% in 2010 to over 176% in 2016. The growth has come about almost entirely due to increased mobile subscriptions.

FIXED-LINE TELEPHONY

During the period under review, the fixed-line segment has continued to decline as it did during the previous review period. Total subscribers declined from nearly 142,500 in 2010 to around 136,000 in 2016, while total traffic declined from about 620 million minutes to about 330 million minutes. Fixed-line services accounted for around 25% of total revenue in the telecommunications industry in 2016, a fall from over 30% in 2010. Currently there are three main service providers in the fixed-line segment: Siminn, Vodafone, and 365. Although it has been losing market share, Siminn continues to dominate, with over 56% market share followed by Vodafone, which has a 30% share of the market. Both providers are classified as having "significant market power" in certain service markets and hence may be subject to various obligations, imposed by the Post and Telecom Administration (PTA) with respect to access to infrastructure, interconnection, and carrier selection and pre-selection.

MOBILE TELEPHONY

The mobile communications market has continued to grow steadily. Total subscriptions rose from 375,430 in 2010 to over 451,000 in 2016. Over the same period, traffic has also increased from around 750 million minutes to around 827 million minutes. Growth was driven by increased subscriptions and usage by the younger segment of the population. The mobile sector is the largest revenue generator in the telecommunications sector, accounting for nearly 30% of total revenue in electronic communications in 2015. Currently there are four main companies operating in the mobile communications sector (Nova, Siminn, Vodafone, and 365) . Siminn has continued to lose market share and is no longer the main supplier. Nova has the largest market share with nearly 35% of the market followed by Siminn (32.6%) and Vodafone (27.8%) .

INTERNET

As is the global trend, the internet sector has been the fastest growing subsector within the electronic communications industry. Total subscriptions rose from around 110,000 in 2010 to nearly 128,000 in 2016. Furthermore, in 2015, the internet sector accounted for nearly 18% of total revenue in the electronic communications sector compared with 16.4% in 2010. At present, four companies operate in the market, with Siminn controlling nearly 48% of the market in 2016; its market share has fallen from over 52% in 2010. Vodafone, the other major internet service provider, controlled nearly 28% of the market in 2016.

REGULATIONS

During the period under review, there have been no significant changes to the legislation governing the telecommunications sector in Iceland except for Act No. 62 of 25 June 2012 amending the Electronic Communications Act and the Act on the Post and Telecom Administration, which addresses cyber security. The legal framework for electronic communications and postal services is influenced by Directives of the European Union. Having signed the Agreement on the European Economic Area, Iceland made a commitment to adopt all of the Directives of the European Union in the fields of electronic communications and postal services.

The main laws governing the sector continue to be the Act on the Post and Telecom Administration No. 69/2003 and Electronic Communications Act No. 81/2003. The Acts implement the major provisions of the EU Communications Directive package of 2002. The Acts are administered by the Postal and Telecom Administration (PTA) which is part of the Ministry of the Interior. The PTA is also the regulator for the sector.

The PTA's responsibilities include *inter alia*: implementing the Electronic Communications Act and supervising electronic communications as provided for in the Act; encouraging competition in postal and electronic communications services and preventing unfair business practices; participating in developing the market for electronic communications and information technology; safeguarding public interest; advising the authorities and ministries and ensuring that Iceland fulfils its international obligations as well as making recommendations, if necessary, for amendments to acts and regulations; and participating in cooperation resulting from international obligations.

The Electronic Communications Act provides for a general authorization for natural persons and legal entities established within the EEA and within WTO Member states to start operations, implying that they do not need a licence, unless specific frequencies are involved. Registration with the PTA is required for all operators. An individual licence is required for all frequencies except open spectrum. In most cases the procedure is simple and frequencies are assigned by the PTA within six weeks of receipt of application.

The Act also addresses transparency and non-discrimination; rules on number portability, and on carrier selection and pre-selection; and provisions relating to competition within the sector. Furthermore, under Chapter VII of the Act, the PTA is expected to "ensure access and interconnection and interoperability of services in a satisfactory and efficient manner" (Article 25) and may, *inter alia*, impose obligations with respect to open and non-discriminatory access and price control. The Act also ensures that all users are entitled to universal service at the same tariff rate throughout the country. To ensure this obligation is met, the PTA may place obligations on electronic communications providers and set minimum quality requirements. The PTA also operates the equalization fund, which subsidises universal service operations that are unprofitable or loss making.

Violations of the provisions of the Electronic Communications Act or the Act on the Post and Telecom Administration must be rectified within a month of their notification by the PTA. If operators fail to remedy the violations, the PTA has the authority to impose daily fines, or to cancel the right to use numbers or the general authorization to operate. Serious or repeated violations may result in imprisonment. Rulings by the PTA may be referred to the Rulings Committee for Electronic Communications and Postal Affairs, and to the courts.

TRANSPORT

AIR TRANSPORT

The air transport sector in Iceland comprises passenger and cargo airlines, airports, and associated services. The sector has continued to grow during the review period, with the sector's contribution to GDP rising from 6.6% in 2010 to approximately 15% in 2016; however, the authorities stated that the contribution to GDP is hard to estimate due to an annual growth of 30-40% over the past few years.

Since 2011, total passenger traffic has grown significantly and was over 7.6 million (including transit/transfer passengers) in 2016 compared with 3.3 million in 2011, of which 6.8 million were international passengers (Chart 4.10) . The growth was due almost entirely to the increase in international passenger traffic, while domestic passenger traffic fluctuated slightly during the review period. Growth of international traffic is due to Iceland attracting more tourists as well as Icelandic airlines becoming a more financially viable option for transatlantic passengers and the promotion of Iceland as a transatlantic hub. The total number of passengers through Keflavik airport in 2017 is estimated to be in the region of 9 million.

After declining during the previous review period, total mail and cargo also increased during the current review period from about 40 thousand tonnes in 2011 to over 52 thousand tonnes in 2016. The increase is due to strong growth in online shopping (mainly from China), as well as an increase in the export of fresh fish.

There are 24 foreign passenger transport operators in Iceland which operate scheduled air services. Currently, there are four international and nine domestic airports operating scheduled flights in Iceland. In 2016, Reykjavik airport accounted for nearly 50% of domestic traffic, while nearly all international air traffic was through Keflavik airport. All airports in Iceland are state-owned. Since its establishment in 2010, Isavia, a government-owned company with the Ministry of Finance as a sole shareholder, has been responsible for all operations, development, assets, and obligations of all airports, based on an annual service agreement with the Ministry of Transport. Furthermore, Isavia manages air traffic in the Icelandic air traffic control area. It is also the owner and operator of Fríhöfnin ehf (The Duty-free store), Tern Systems ehf, Domavia ehf and Suluk ApS. Ground handling at Keflavik airport is provided by four independent service providers: Ace Handling, Airport Associates, IGS Ground Services and SouthAir. Airline operators are also allowed to undertake ground handling services themselves; this is the most common method at the domestic airports.

With regards to procedures and fees, Iceland accords national treatment to both domestic and international airline companies. Scheduled air services to certain domestic destinations that are not economically viable, but fall within given criteria of public service obligation, are subsidized by the Government. Such contracts are awarded to airlines via an open tender.[278]

Act No. 60/1998 as amended on Aviation is the main legislation governing the air transport sector. The Act is administered by the Icelandic Transport Authority, which is under the Ministry of the Interior.[279]The authorities stated that the Aviation Act follows European legislation, thus making Iceland compliant with European rules on licensing, access to aircrafts and ground handling, competition, slot allocation, airport charges, and aviation safety and security. Furthermore, under the provisions of the Act, EEA operators are allowed to engage in cabotage, while non-EEA operators are only allowed to engage in cabotage if specified in a bilateral agreement.[280]

The Icelandic Transport Authority was established in accordance with Act No. 119/2012 on the Icelandic Transport Authority (ICETRA), Administrative Institution for Transport Affairs. Under the provisions of the ICETRA Act, all tasks that were the responsibility of the Icelandic Civil Aviation Administration have been taken over by ICETRA. As such, ICETRA is responsible for *inter alia*: overseeing general aviation; overseeing commercial aviation of Icelandic parties, procedural rules of air operators, flight crew members, as well as the financial status of air operators; ensuring the issuance of air operator licences in accordance with Council Regulation No. 1008/2008 and Commission Regulation No. 965/2012 on air transport flights with subsequent amendments; issuing air operator certificates which attest that the air operator is in control of flight safety aspects in its operations.

Furthermore, all licences for flight operations are subject to ICETRA's approval and control. ICETRA is also responsible for overseeing flights of foreign carriers to and from Iceland and issues permits to fly through Icelandic airspace. Assessments of air operators' management of flight operations are also carried out by ICETRA.

As per EU regulations, Iceland operates under a "Single European Sky". In addition, Iceland has bilateral aviation agreements with Armenia; Azerbaijan; Bahrain; Barbados; Brazil; Canada; Chile; China; Columbia; Croatia; Denmark; Dominican Republic; Egypt; Finland; Germany; Ghana; Hong Kong, China; India; Indonesia; Jamaica; Jordan; Kuwait; Laos; Lebanon; Luxembourg; Macau, China; Malaysia; Mongolia; Netherlands; Norway; Oman; Paraguay; Qatar; Russian Federation; Rwanda; Saudi Arabia; Singapore; South Africa; Spain; Sweden; Syria; Thailand; Turkey; Turkmenistan; United Kingdom; Viet Nam; and Zambia. Iceland is also party to the EU-USA Open Skies

Agreement, which is the only open skies agreement that Iceland has in place other than the "Single European Sky".[281]

Under the provisions of Act No. 34/1991 on Foreign Investment in Companies, foreign ownership in Icelandic companies involved in airline operations may not exceed 49%. This limitation does not apply to nationals of the EEA, who are treated as Icelandic nationals. Additionally, no entity may be granted an operating licence unless it is effectively controlled by EEA nationals. There are no limitations on foreign participation in auxiliary services.

MARITIME TRANSPORT

As an island nation with a high dependence on international trade, maritime transport is very important for Iceland. Nearly all of Iceland's merchandise trade is conducted by sea. There are around 1,200 open boats, 1,100 decked vessels, a petroleum tanker, a container ship and a chemical tanker registered in Iceland.

At the time of the last review, there were approximately 60 harbours in Iceland, of these 15 had appreciable cargo activities, with four of these ports having the capability to handle ships of up to 40,000 DWT. The rest were essentially fishing ports but were able to accommodate larger merchant vessels for fish-based products. Faxafloahafnir Associated Icelandic Ports was the largest port in the country, accounting for nearly 50% of total cargo in Iceland. Harbours and coastal protection structures are owned and operated by the municipalities where they are located.

In 2013, the Icelandic Maritime Administration Act of 1996 was repealed and the Iceland Maritime Authority (IMA) dissolved. Currently, the sector is governed by two agencies, the ICETRA and the Icelandic Road and Coastal Administration (IRCA) . The ICETRA has regulatory and oversight responsibilities, while infrastructure project procurement and operational tasks are the responsibility of the IRCA.

ICETRA's responsibilities include *inter alia*: port state control of foreign merchant vessels in Icelandic ports; seamen's certification and crew issues; implementation of the International Convention on Standards of Training, Certification and Watchkeeping for Seafarers (STCW); issuing professional diving and pilots' certificates; and maritime traffic services and security. Preparing new maritime legislation, publishing marine-safety training materials and training are also the responsibility of ICETRA. Iceland's maritime legislation is fully aligned with EU regulations on freedom to provide services, transfer of cargo and passenger ships between registers, action to safeguard free access to cargoes in ocean trades, and maritime cabotage. With respect to cabotage, Iceland is the only WTO Member that has scheduled a binding commitment on cabotage.

With respect to harbour administration, the IRCA is responsible for coastal protection and harbour projects, research, and planning for the development of coastal protections and harbours. The State is responsible for conducting basic research pertaining to harbour projects as well as provision of financial support for new harbour projects.

The Director General of IRCA is a member of the National Transport Plan Committee, which is responsible for developing proposals for a 4-year and a 12-year transport policy plan for the Minister. Furthermore, most harbour funds are owned by municipalities but most harbour development projects are eligible for state grants and in the transport plan there is a list of approved harbour development projects that have been approved for state grants.

The port state control system implemented in 2011 continues to be in use. It follows the EU Directive on port state control. Under this system, termed the New Inspection Regime (NIR), inspections are targeted according to a Ship Risk Profile so that "risky" ships are inspected frequently, while "good" ships are inspected less frequently. A ship's risk profile is determined according to, *inter alia,* age, flag, type, and company.

Iceland has ratified and incorporated into its laws and regulations most of the conventions and instruments adopted by the International Maritime Organisation (IMO), such as: the International Convention for the Safety of Life at Sea (SOLAS); International Convention on Standards of Training, Certification and Watchkeeping for Seafarers (STCW); International Convention on Standards of Training, Certification and Watchkeeping for Fishing Vessel Personnel (STCW-F); International Convention on Load Lines; International Convention for the Prevention of Pollution from Ships (MARPOL); Convention on the International Regulations for Preventing Collisions at Sea (COLREG); International Convention on Maritime Search and Rescue (SAR); and Convention for the Suppression of Unlawful Acts against the Safety of Maritime Navigation (SUA) .

TOURISM

Since 2010, the tourism sector's importance in Iceland's economy has increased significantly. Tourisms' contribution to GDP nearly doubled from 5.6% in 2010 to around 10% in 2016. Between 2010 and 2015, the number of visitors to Iceland has grown at an average annual rate of around 22%, to reach nearly 1.3 million visitors in 2015.

The tourism sector has overtaken fisheries and aluminium as the largest export sector responsible for nearly 40% of Iceland's export receipts of goods and services in 2016. Employment in the sector also rose during the review period from 15,700 in 2010 to 24,200 in 2016.

Total spending on tourism-related activities has also increased steadily from 2009 to 2015: from ISK 93 billion to ISK 222 billion, about half of which is from air passenger transportation and accommodation

The tourism industry tends to be cyclical and income elastic. As such, the recent growth can be attributed in part to the ongoing economic recovery in key source markets (Europe and North America) after the global economic crisis of 2008; as well as Iceland becoming a more affordable destination due to the exchange rate depreciation. As a result, the average spend per person rose from ISK 140,300 in 2010 to ISK 161,600 in 2015. Additionally, better and more frequent flight connections and improved and more specifically targeted marketing campaigns have also had a positive impact. Another positive impact of the marketing campaigns has been the increased share of visitors in winter months.

Although tourism remains very cyclical, and the number of summer visitors is much greater than the number who come in winter, both have increased significantly, as indicated by the number of arrivals to Keflavik airport (although this also reflects the growing number of transit passengers) (Chart 4.10) . In 2011, nearly half the tourists came in the summer months, while around 20% came in the winter season; in 2015, the share of visitors in winter had risen to nearly 30%, while the share of those coming in the summer had fallen to around 40%.

REGULATION

The main legislation governing the tourism sector is the Tourism Administration Act (Act No. 73/2005) . The Act is administered by the Icelandic Tourist Board.

The objective of the Act is to promote the development of tourism as an economic sector and an important facet of Icelandic economic and societal activity. The guiding principles are economic efficiency, Icelandic culture, environmental protection, professionalism, and the safeguarding of consumer interests.

The Icelandic Tourist Board is an independent authority under the Ministry of Industries and Innovation. Under the provisions of the Act, the Icelandic Tourist Board is responsible for: (i) issuance of licences, registration of operations, and monitoring in order to ensure that requirements for operations are met; (ii) development, quality control, and organizational issues related to tourism; that is, the implementation of a defined tourism strategy, the co-ordination of environmental and educational affairs, the dissemination of information, regional and local development, and international collaboration; and (iii) marketing and promotion of tourism services.

Furthermore, Act No. 41/2015 on Regional Incentives, which applies to the whole of Iceland outside the capital area, is also applicable to the tourism sector. Incentives under the Act include the authorization to: fix an income tax rate ceiling of only 15% for 10 years; depreciate real estate, equipment and moveable assets fully; reduce the rate of property tax and the general social security charge by 50%; grant exemption from customs and excise duties for construction materials, machinery and equipment, and other capital goods; and the State and municipalities are allowed to lease a site for projects at reduced rates. Additionally, under Commission Regulation (EC) No. 651/2014, on General Block Exemptions, state aid is permissible for certain categories; these include: incentives as training aid of up to a maximum of €2 million; incentives as aid to SMEs, which includes up to 10% of investment cost in medium-sized enterprises or 20% of investment cost in small enterprises, up to a ceiling of €7.5 million; and incentives as aid to environmental protection investment projects with a ceiling of €15 million. According to the authorities, the Regulation falls under the Agreement on the European Economic Area and is currently being incorporated into Icelandic legislation.

STRATEGY

Under the Government's growth plan (Iceland 2020), the tourism sector was specifically identified as a main growth sector.[282] In this regard, parliament approved the Tourism Strategy 2011-2020, in 2011. Salient aims of the strategy are:

to increase the profitability of the sector, through *inter alia* off-season product development and marketing;

to engage in systematic development of tourist destinations, effective product development, and promotion and advertising work so as to create the opportunity to lengthen the tourist season, reduce seasonal fluctuations, and contribute to better distribution of tourists throughout the country[283];

to enhance quality, professionalism, safety, and environment-awareness in the tourism sector[284]; and

to define and maintain Iceland's uniqueness as a tourist destination, in part through effective analysis and research.

BUSINESS TRAVEL TO THE COUNTRY

STATE DEPARTMENT SUGGESTION

COUNTRY DESCRIPTION: Iceland is a highly developed stable democracy with a modern economy.

ENTRY REQUIREMENTS: A passport is required, but no visa is needed for tourist or business stays of up to three months. U.S. citizens should be aware, however, that because of Iceland's participation in the Nordic Passport Union, the three-month period begins as soon as they enter the Nordic area (i.e., Denmark, Greenland, Faeroe Islands, Finland, Norway, Sweden or Iceland.) For further information concerning entry requirements for Iceland, contact the Embassy of Iceland at 1156 15th Street N.W., Suite 1200, Washington, D.C. 20005, tel (202) 265-6653, or the Icelandic Consulate General in New York at 800 Third Avenue, 36th Floor, New York, NY 10022, tel (212) 593-2700. See also the Embassy's web site at http://www.iceland.org.

CRIME INFORMATION: Iceland has a relatively low crime rate, but minor assaults and other street crimes have become more common, especially in the capital city of Reykjavik. Tourists should be aware that downtown Reykjavik can become especially disorderly on weekend evenings. The loss or theft abroad of a U.S. passport should be reported immediately to the local police and the nearest U.S. Embassy at Laufasvegur 21 in Reykjavik, tel. (354) 562-9100. U.S. citizens may refer to the Department of State's pamphlet *A Safe Trip Abroad* for ways to promote a more trouble-free journey. The pamphlet is available by mail from the Superintendent of Documents, U.S. Government Printing Office, Washington, D.C. 20402, via the Internet at http://www.access.gpo.gov/su_docs, or via the Bureau of Consular Affairs home page at http://travel.state.gov.

MEDICAL FACILITIES AND INSURANCE: Excellent medical facilities are available. To obtain emergency medical assistance anywhere in the country, dial 112. U.S. medical insurance is not always valid outside the United States. U.S. Medicare and Medicaid programs do not provide payment for medical services outside the United States. Doctors and hospitals often expect immediate cash payment for health services. Uninsured travelers who require medical care overseas may face extreme difficulties.

Check with your own insurance company to confirm whether your policy applies overseas, including provision for medical evacuation, and for adequacy of coverage. Serious medical problems requiring hospitalization and/or medical evacuation to the United States can cost tens of thousands of dollars. Ascertain whether payment will be made to the overseas hospital or doctor or whether you will be reimbursed later for expenses you incur. Some insurance policies also include coverage for psychiatric treatment and for disposition of remains in the event of death.

Useful information on medical emergencies abroad, including overseas insurance programs, is provided in the Department of State's Bureau of Consular Affairs brochure

Medical Information for Americans Traveling Abroad, available via the Bureau of Consular Affairs home page or autofax: (202) 647-3000.

OTHER HEALTH INFORMATION: Information on vaccinations and other health precautions may be obtained from the Centers for Disease Control and Prevention's hotline for international travelers at 1-877-FYI-TRIP (1-877-394-8747); fax 1-888-CDC-FAXX (1-888-232-3299), or via CDC's Internet site at http://www.cdc.gov.

TRAFFIC SAFETY AND ROAD CONDITIONS: While in a foreign country, U.S. citizens may encounter road conditions that differ significantly from those in the United States. The information below concerning Iceland is provided for general reference only, and may not be totally accurate in a particular location or circumstance.

Safety of Public Transportation: Excellent
Urban Road Conditions/Maintenance: Excellent
Rural Road Conditions/Maintenance: Fair to Good
Availability of Roadside Assistance: Good

Less than a third of the country's total road network was paved (2,262 miles of paved road versus 5774 miles of gravel or dirt road). Most of the 900-mile ring road (Highway 1) that encircles the country is paved, but many other roads outside the capital, especially those that run through the center of the country, are dirt or gravel tracks. Even those roads that are paved tend to be narrow and lack a shoulder or margin. Most bridges are only one lane wide, requiring drivers to be cognizant of oncoming traffic.

Extreme care should be taken when driving in rural areas during the winter (October through April), when daylight hours are limited and the weather and road conditions can change quickly. Many routes in the interior of the country are impassible until July due to muddy conditions caused by snowmelt. When driving in the interior, consider traveling with a second vehicle and always inform someone of your travel plans. For information on current road conditions throughout the country, call the Public Roads Administration (Vegagerdin) at 1777 or consult its web site at http://www.vegag.is. For recorded weather information in English, call the Icelandic weather office (Vedurstofa Islands) at 902-0600, ext. 44.

The law requires drivers to keep headlights on at all times. Unless otherwise posted, the speed limit in urban areas is 50 km per hour (31 mph). In rural areas, the speed limit is 80 km per hour (50 mph) on dirt and gravel roads, and 90 km per hour (56 mph) on paved highways. There is no provision for turning right on red in Iceland. Use of seatbelts is mandatory in both the front and rear seats, and children under the age of six must be secured in a special car seat designed for their size and weight. Drivers are held responsible for any passenger under the age of fifteen who is not wearing a seatbelt. No one who is less than 140 cm (approximately 54 inches) tall or weighs less than 40 kilograms (88 lbs.) is allowed to ride in a front seat equipped with an airbag.

Driving under the influence of alcohol is considered a serious offense in Iceland. Drivers can be charged with drunk driving with a blood alcohol level as low as 0.05. The minimum punishment for a first offense is a ISK 30,000 (about $380) fine and the loss of driving privileges for two months.

Hikers and backpackers are well advised to stay on marked trails, travel with someone, let someone else know their travel plans, and check weather reports.

For additional general information about road safety, see the Department of State, Bureau of Consular Affairs home page road safety overseas feature at http://travel.state.gov/road_safety.html. U.S. citizens staying for less than 90 days can drive in Iceland on their U.S. licenses. For specific information concerning Icelandic driver's permits, vehicle inspection, road tax and mandatory insurance, contact the Iceland National Tourist Organization offices in New York via the Internet at http://www.iceland.org/oeku.htm.

AVIATION SAFETY OVERSIGHT: The U.S. Federal Aviation Administration (FAA) has assessed Iceland's Civil Aviation Authority as Category One -- in compliance with international aviation safety standards for the oversight of Icelandic air carrier operations. For further information, travelers may contact the Department of Transportation at 1 (800) 322-7873, or visit the FAA Internet home page at http://www.faa.gov/avr/iasa/. The U.S. Department of Defense (DOD) separately assesses some foreign air carriers for suitability as official providers of air services. For information regarding the DOD policy on specific carriers, travelers may contact DOD at (618) 229-4801.

CUSTOMS REGULATIONS: Icelandic customs authorities encourage the use of an ATA (Admission Temporaire/Temporary Admission) Carnet for the temporary admission of professional equipment, commercial samples, and/or goods for exhibitions and fair purposes. ATA Carnet Headquarters, located at the U.S. Council for International Business, 1212 Avenue of the Americas, New York. NY 10036, issues and guarantees the ATA Carnet in the United States. For additional information call (212) 354-4480, send e-mail to atacarnet@uscib.org, or visit http://www.uscib.org for details.

CRIMINAL PENALTIES: While in a foreign country, a U.S. citizen is subject to that country's laws and regulations, which sometimes differ significantly from those in the United States and may not afford the protections available to the individual under U.S. law. Penalties for breaking the law can be more severe than in the United States for similar offenses. Persons violating Iceland's laws, even unknowingly, may be expelled, arrested or imprisoned. Penalties for possession, use, or trafficking in illegal drugs in Iceland are strict and convicted offenders can expect jail sentences and heavy fines.

SPECIAL CIRCUMSTANCES: Extreme care should be exercised when touring Iceland's numerous nature attractions, which include glaciers, volcanic craters, lava fields, ice caves, hot springs, boiling mud pots, geysers, waterfalls and glacial rivers. There are few warning signs or barriers to alert travelers to the potential hazards. For example, several tourists are scalded each year because they get too close to an erupting geyser, or because they fall or step into a hot spring or boiling mud pot. High winds and icy conditions can exacerbate the dangers of visiting these nature areas.

DISASTER PREPAREDNESS: Also be aware that Iceland is occasionally subject to natural disasters in the form of earthquakes, volcanic eruptions, avalanches, and violent storms. Learn how to prepare for and react to such events by consulting the web site of Iceland's National Civil Defense Agency at http://www.avrik.is. General information about natural disaster preparedness is available via the Internet from the U.S. Federal Emergency Management Agency (FEMA) at http://www.fema.gov.

CHILDREN'S ISSUES: For information on international adoption of children and international child support enforcement issues, please refer to our Internet site at http://travel.state.gov/children's_issues.html or telephone (202) 736-7000.

REGISTRATION/EMBASSY AND CONSULATE LOCATION: Americans living in or visiting Iceland may register at the Consular Section of the U.S. Embassy in Reykjavik and obtain updated information on travel and security within Iceland. The U.S. Embassy is located at Laufasvegur 21, tel (354) 562-9100; fax (354) 562-9118.

AIR TRAVEL TO ICELAND

Icelandair operates regular schedules to and from Amsterdam, Baltimore/Washington, Barcelona, Boston, Copenhagen, Frankfurt, Glasgow, Halifax, Hamburg, Helsinki, London, Milan, Minneapolis, Munich, Narsarssuaq (Greenland), New York, Orlando, Oslo, Paris, Stockholm and Zurich.

SAS also flies between Iceland and Copenhagen, and GO between Iceland and the UK. Air Atlanta runs charter flights on behalf of Icelandic travel agencies, and airlines from other countries have operated intermittent international services.
Airport: Keflavík International Airport is located 50 km (31 miles) from Reykjavík. Coach shuttle services to major hotels in Reykjavík are synchronized with incoming and outgoing flights, fare ISK 600/USD 8. Taxis are also available to and from the airport, fare about ISK 5,000/USD 75.

Booking in advance is not only a way of being sure of finding a taxi for the airport, but can also prove cheaper. Taxis offer discount fares of ISK 4,900/USD 74 for larger cabs, if bookings are made with a day's notice. Limousines are available, but should be booked in advance; fares are in the range ISK 5,100-12,750/USD 77-192.

Travellers should allow 2 hours and 15 minutes' connection time between Reykjavík and Keflavík Airport for transportation, check-in, etc. "City check-in" is also possible by phone and the night before departure. The duty-free store at Keflavík Airport is open for incoming as well as outgoing passengers.

AIR TRAVEL IN ICELAND

Íslandsflug and Flugfélag Íslands (Air Iceland) operate regular schedules between Reykjavík and major towns all around the country, often several times a day. Regional carriers also operate in some places.
Reykjavík Airport (for domestic flights) is located five minutes' drive from the city centre. Greenland and the Faroe Islands: Day trips and longer tours to Greenland are offered on a regular basis in summer by Íslandsflug and Air Iceland. Air Iceland also operates two or three schedules a week to the Faroe Islands.

Travelling in Reykjavík
Taxis are readily available. The only time they may be difficult to find is late at night. For evening and weekend services, a surcharge is made. Fares within Reykjavík are likely to be in the region ISK 500-1,000 (USD 7-15).

There are no railways in Iceland.

The bus system is very efficient and runs from 7 am to midnight on weekdays and 10 am to midnight at weekends. Tickets may be purchased from the driver or the main bus station. Bus stops are marked SVR. The main terminal is at Hlemmur at the junction of Laugavegur and Rauðarárstígur.

Travel Formalities
Travel documentation requirements: Nationals of the Scandinavian countries do not need a valid passport to visit Iceland.
Nationals from the following countries require only valid identification (although a passport is the standard) for a tourist visit: Austria, Belgium, France, Germany, Greece, Italy, Liechtenstein, Luxembourg, Netherlands, Portugal, Spain, Switzerland and the United Kingdom.

For visits of less than three months, nationals of many countries (including the USA and Canada) do not require a visa.

DUTY-FREE ALLOWANCE

Incoming passengers may bring in 1 litre of spirits (up to 47% alcohol content); 1 litre of wine (up to 21% alcohol) or 6 litres of beer; and 200 cigarettes or 250 g of other tobacco products.

TAX-FREE SHOPPING

Visitors can reclaim value-added tax (VAT) on purchases exceeding ISK 4,000 in each shop. Look for the "Tax-Free Shopping" logo and ask the shop assistant for a refund. You will be given a refund cheque or coupon which you can cash in at the airport on leaving the country. The refund amounts to approximately 15% of the purchase price.

MONEY

Currency:
The unit of currency in Iceland is the Króna, plural Krónur, local abbreviation kr., international abbreviation ISK.

Prices:
The general level of prices in Iceland is similar to that in the other Nordic countries and quite high. Alcohol is very expensive, especially at bars and restaurants.

Cash and Exchange:
Banks and some post offices will advance cash against the main debit and credit cards.

Travellers cheques and exchange:
Travellers cheques and foreign currency can be exchanged at banks and most hotels. Notes can be exchanged after normal banking hours. Some shops accept payment in foreign currency. ATMs are found outside almost all banks and in main shopping centres.

COMMUNICATIONS

All phone numbers in Iceland are seven-digit with no regional code prefixes. For international dialling to Iceland, dial the international code, then 354 and the full number in Iceland.

TELEPHONE/FAX/TELEGRAMS

Direct dialling and fax transmission are available to most countries. Overseas rates are discounted at night. Cables and telegrams can also be sent 24 hours a day, dial 146.

OPERATOR SERVICES	
119	Trunk Calls. Domestic operator-connected calls. Information and connections for conference lines. 24 hr. service.
118	Directory inquiries. Telephone, fax and cellphone numbers; name and address of subscribers. Open 8 am-10 pm daily.
147	Telex. Telex transmission and reception. 24 hr. service.
114	International directory inquiries. International telephone and fax numbers. 24 hr. service.
115	International operator connections. International operator-connected calls and conference lines. 24 hr. service.

The telephone and telegraph office on Austurvöllur in the centre of Reykjavík is open 9 am to 7 pm on weekdays, and 11 am to 6 pm on Saturdays and Sundays.
The business traveller should consider placing long-distance calls at the telephone and telegraph office. Calling from a hotel is expensive in Iceland, just as in other countries. Many hotels allow guests to send faxes; these can also be sent from the main post office on Pósthússtræti in the centre of Reykjavík. Major hotels also allow guests to use e-mail and the Internet.

POST OFFICES

Post offices are generally open from 8:30 am to 4.30 pm, Mondays to Fridays; those at Ármúli 25 and Kringlan shopping mall in Reykjavík stay open until 6 pm.

POSTAL RATES			

WEIGHT GR.	ICELAND	EUROPE (A)	ELSEWHERE (A)
20 g	35	50	75
50 g	45	95	135
100 g	55	125	220
250 g	105	245	465
500 g	145	435	900
750 g	185	585	1200
1000 g	200	715	1500
1250 g	215	835	1800
1500 g	235	955	2100
1750 g	250	1085	2400
2000 g	265	1190	2700
Further information is given at the Iceland Post headquarters, telephone 580 1000.			

Post codes

To be doubly sure that mail sent from other countries reaches its destination in Iceland, it is recommended to use the prefix IS before the post code. Example: IS-101 Reykjavík.

RADIO/TV/NEWS

A short news broadcast in English is made daily for travellers during the summer, from the end of May to the beginning of September, on Radio 1 at 8.55 am. A recording of the broadcast can be heard by telephone, dial 515 3690.

State TV and the commercial Channel 2 and Sýn stations screen large amounts of foreign material in the original languages with subtitles. A range of satellite transmissions are also relayed direct without subtitles.

Major newspapers from several countries are imported daily and are on sale in bookstores and certain other shops.

USEFUL NUMBERS

Emergency phone numbers:	Tel.
Ambulance	112
Fire	112
Police	112

Dentist, Emergency (Sat. & Sun. 10 am-12 am)	568-1041
Doctor, Emergency (Mon.-Fri. 8 am-5 pm)	525-1000
Night Doctor (Mon.-Fri. 5 pm-8 am. Sat. & Sun. 24 hrs.)	552-1230
Emergency Ward, City Hospital tel. 525 1000	525-1000
Pharmacies (at least one is open 24 hrs.), for information call:	551-8888
Information:	
Icelandic Tourist Board, Lækjargata 3, 101 Reykjavík	552-7488
Information desk at the City Hall of Reykjavík	563-2005
Information Service of the University of Iceland	525-4666
Tourist Information Centre, Bankastræti 2, 101 Reykjavík	562-3045

SUPPLEMENTS

ICELANDIC ECONOMIC AND FISCAL SITUATION

KEY POINTS

•The economy has continued its strong rebound (GDP growth exceeded 7 % in 2016)

•Two major contributors – terms of trade and tourism
•Solid internal and external balance
•Inflation under the 2½% target for over three years - inflation expectations also at the target
•Responsible fiscal consolidation and fiscal framework
•Steep decline in debt ratio
•Credit ratings rising - Return to an A-rating category in Sept 2016
•Well capitalized banking system - capital ratios remain above 25%
•Successful removal of capital controls
•Continued favorable economic prospects

STRONG GROWTH

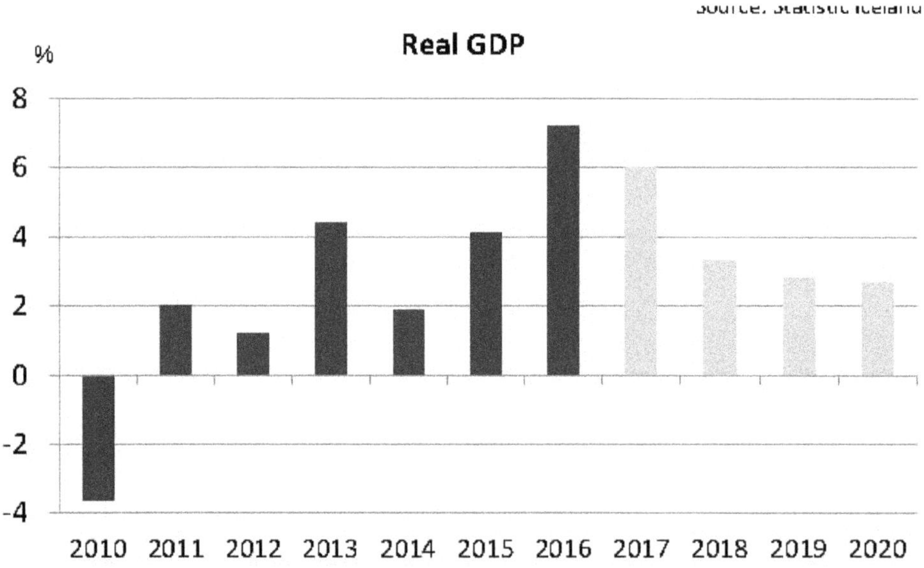

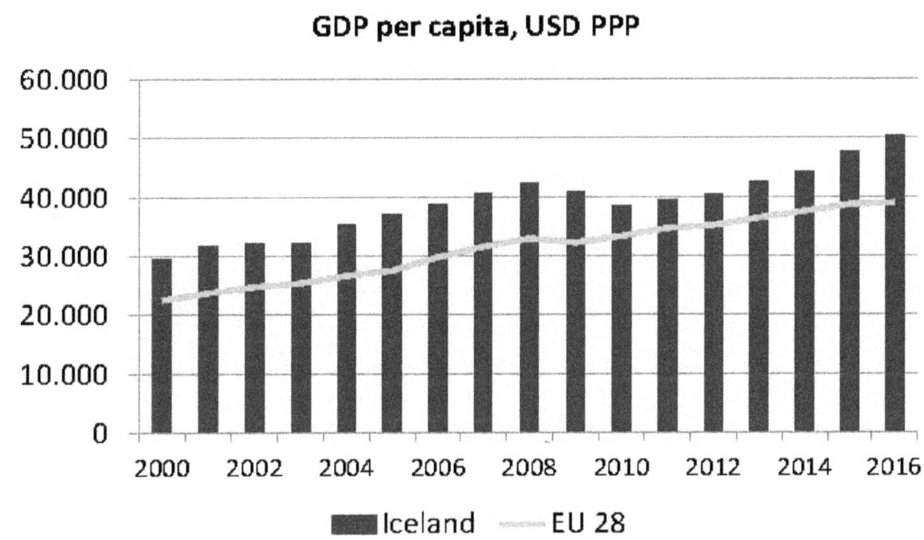

•GPD growth (2016) 7.2%

•Unemployment (May) 5.3%

•Inflation, CPI in July 2017: 1.8%,

•HPI in June 2017: -2.6

•Positive current account balance

•1,8 million foreign visitors to Iceland in 2016

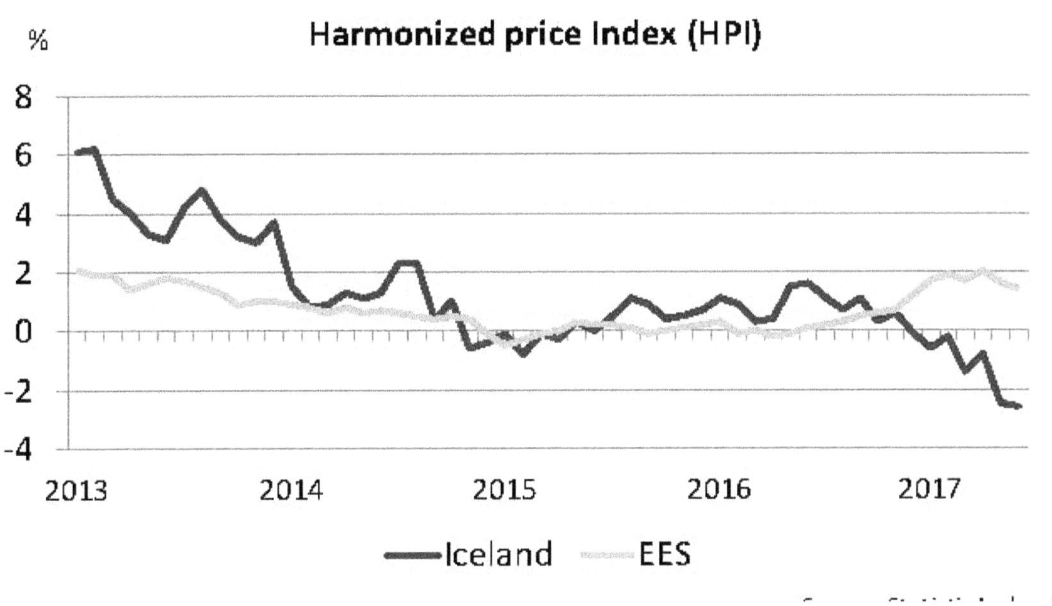

Source: Statistic Iceland

RECENT DEVELOPMENTS, YEAR OVER YEAR

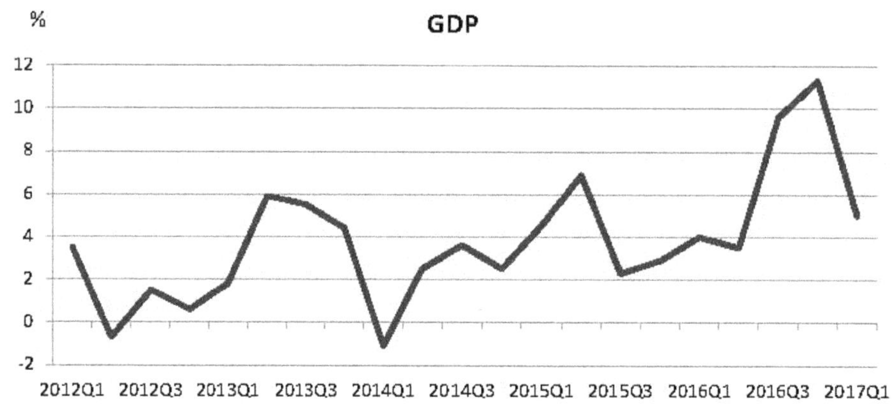

1

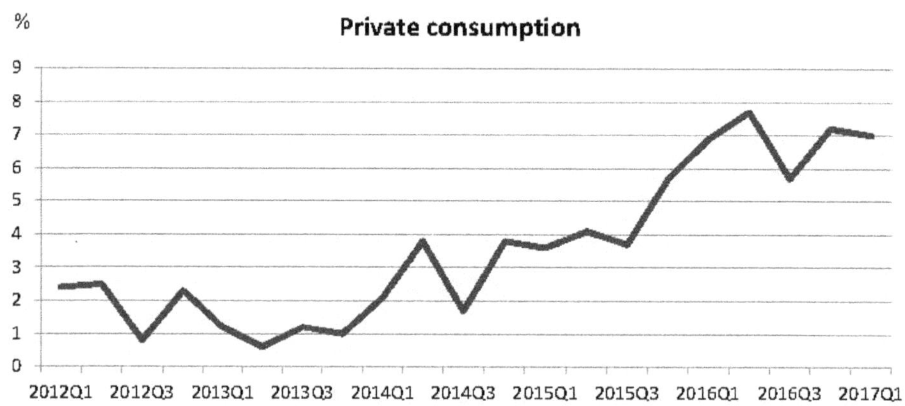

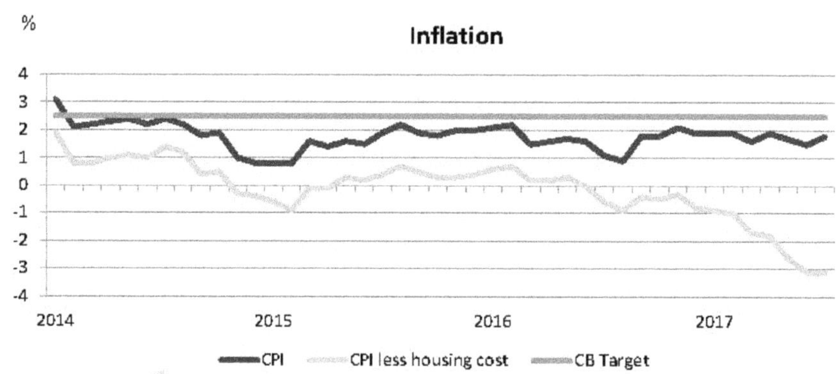

Source: Statistic Iceland

FORECASTS

•IMF and OECD published new forecasts for Iceland in June 2017

•Statistic Iceland assumes the real GDP growth to be 6.0% in 2017 and 3.3% next year

•Inflation is expected to exceed the inflation target in 2018 but inflation is expected to stay low

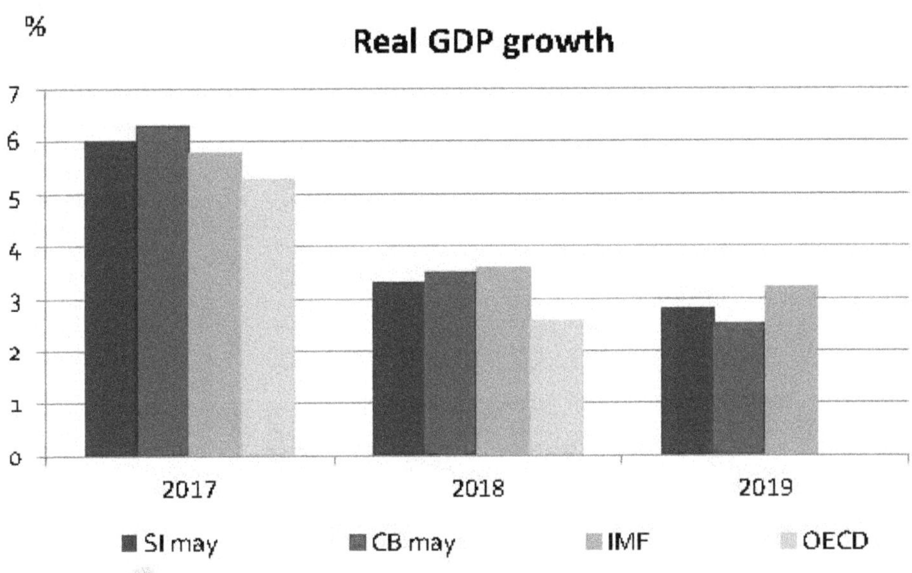

Source: Statistic Iceland, Central Bank, IMF, OECD

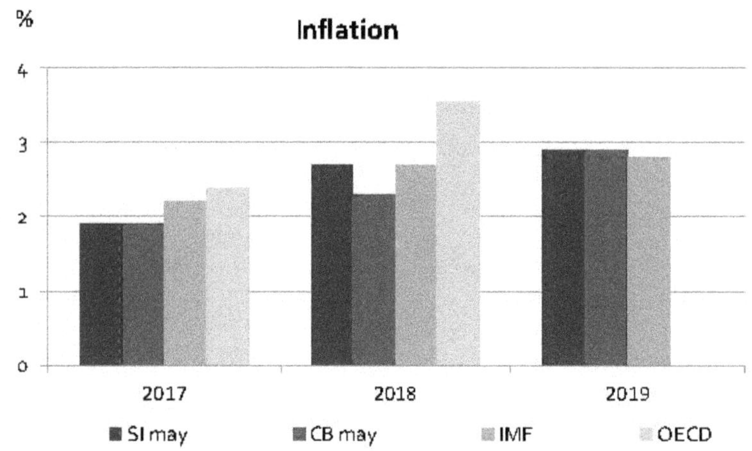

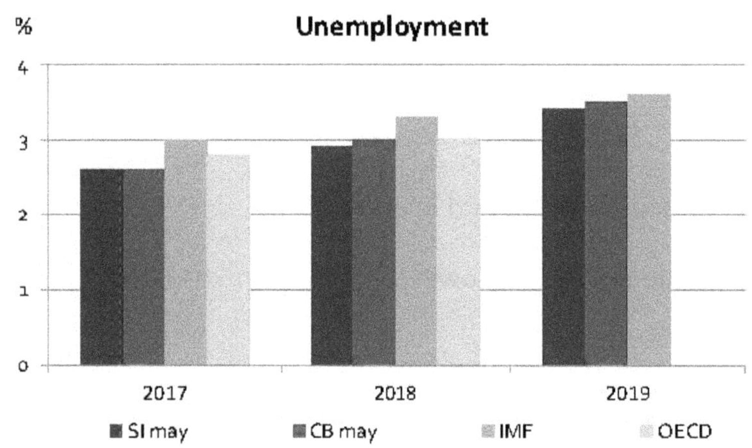

INTERNATIONAL COMPARISON

Ministry of Finance and Economic Affairs

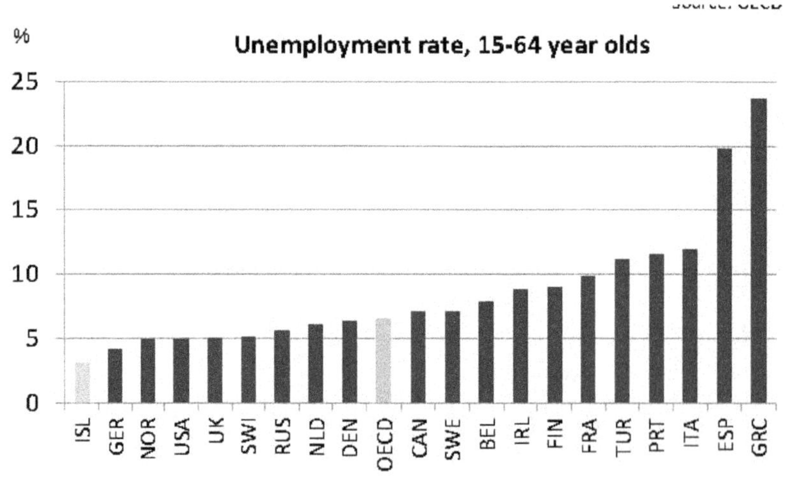

In 2016 Iceland was the fasted growing economy among the OECD countries

•Iceland has the highest participation rate in the labour market, both among men and women

•Unemployment rate was around 3% in 2016 and is expected to stay low

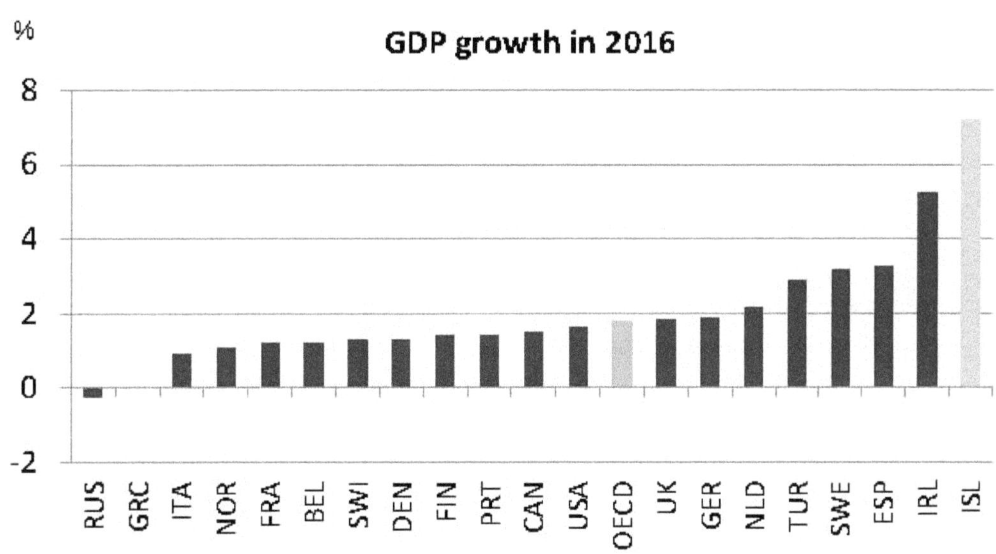

Source: OECD

POPULATION

•Total population January 1, 2017: 338,349
•Life expectancy (2016): Men: 80.7, women: 83.7
•In 2017 there are 30.275 foreign citizens in Iceland, thereof 13,795 from Poland
•In 2016, 2,873 people with Polish citizenship immigrated to Iceland, Polish citizens were also the largest group of foreign nationals to emigrate from Iceland in 2016, or 1,117.

•In the 1st quarter of 2017, 1,790 foreign citizens immigrated to Iceland and 620 emigrated

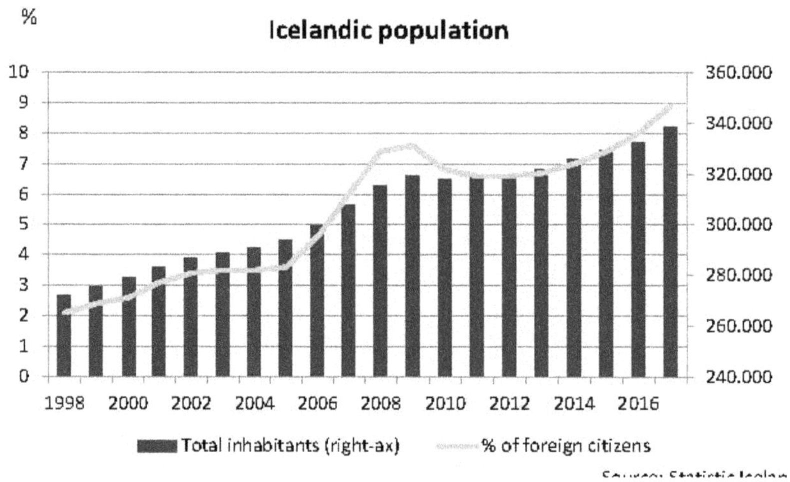

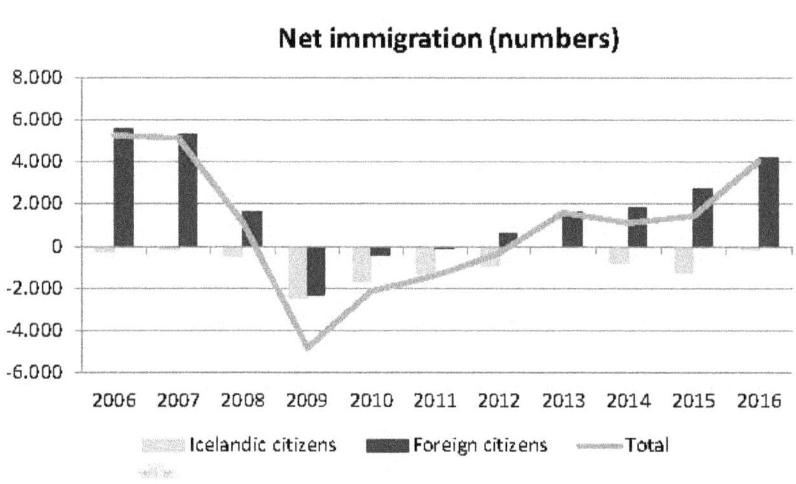

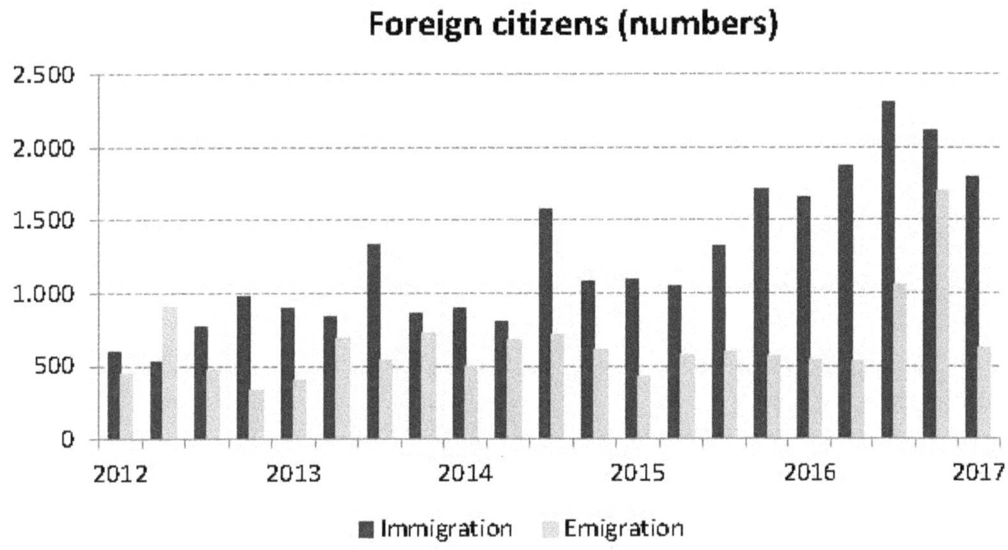

PRIVATE CONSUMPTION

- Substantial private consumption growth since 2013
  - As a share of GDP, private consumption is still well below its long term average
  - Number of Icelanders traveling abroad has increased, especially since 2015
  - Robust growth in domestic debit- and credit card usage so far in 2017

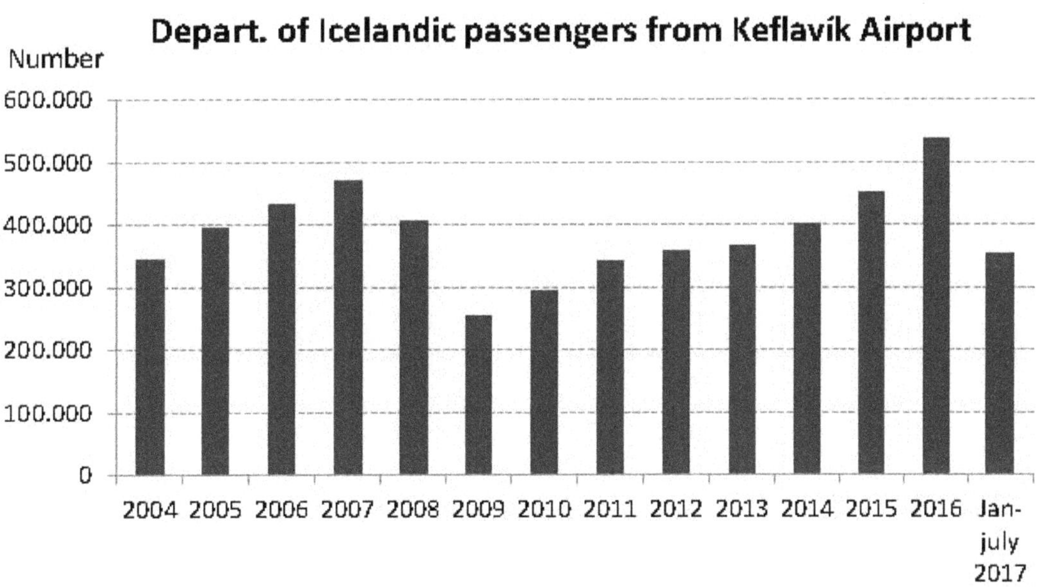

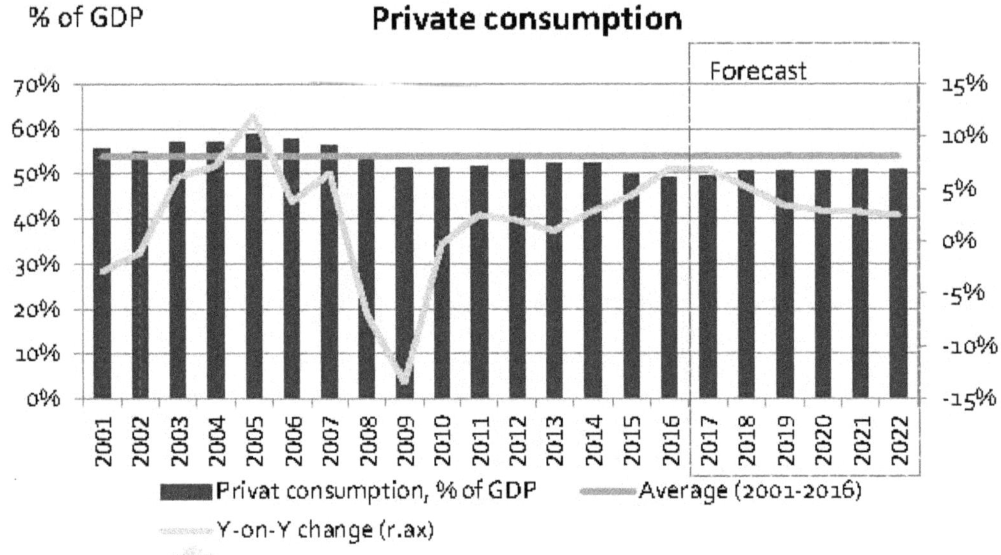

% of GDP

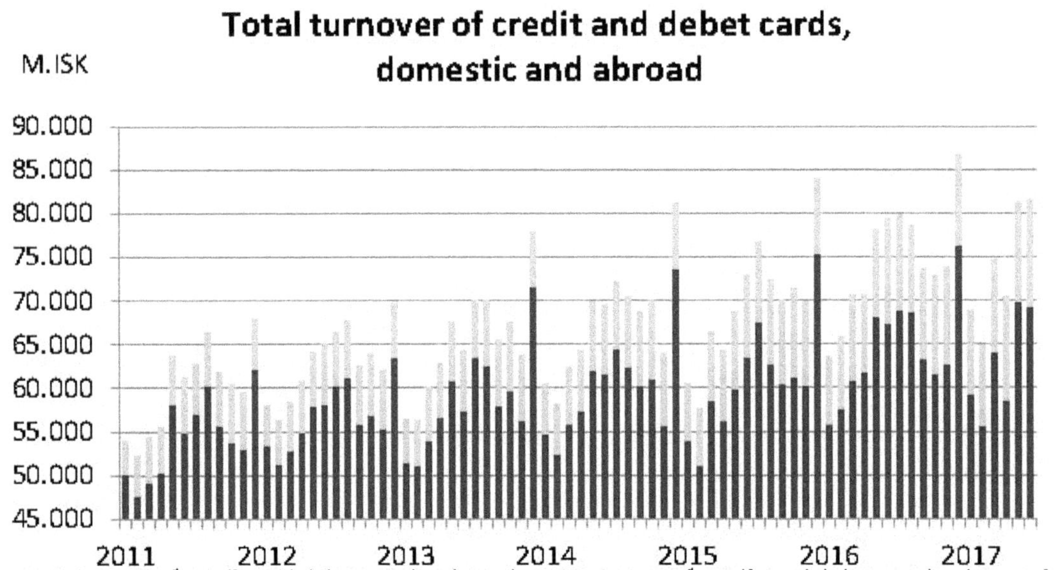

HOUSING MARKET

•Turnover in the real estate market has risen, and residential housing prices have increased far in excess of the general price level.

•Prices have risen sharply in the recent term because new construction has been unable to keep pace with demand stemming from population growth and the tourism boom.

•Prices are now high in historical context and appear to have risen in excess of wage growth in the past few months.

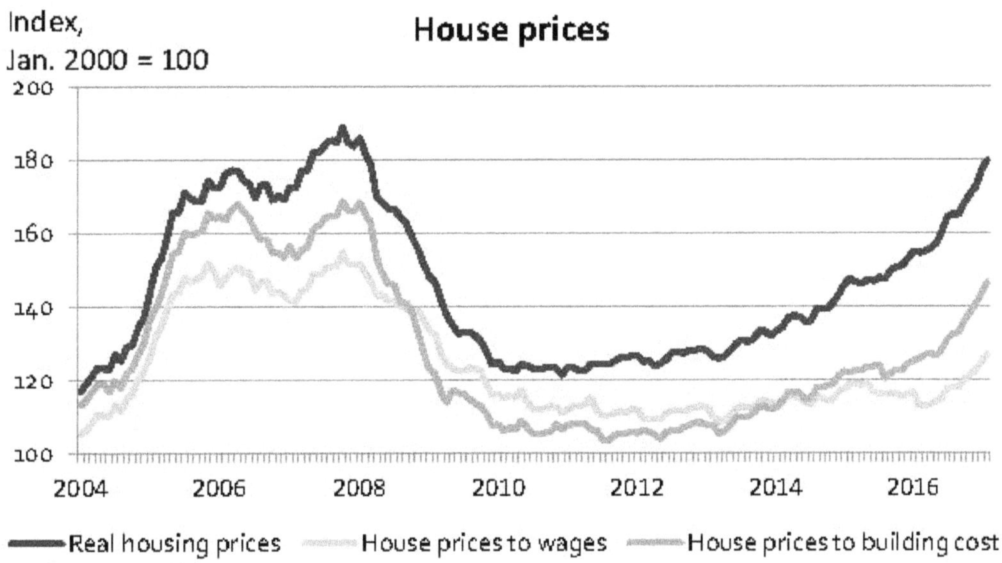

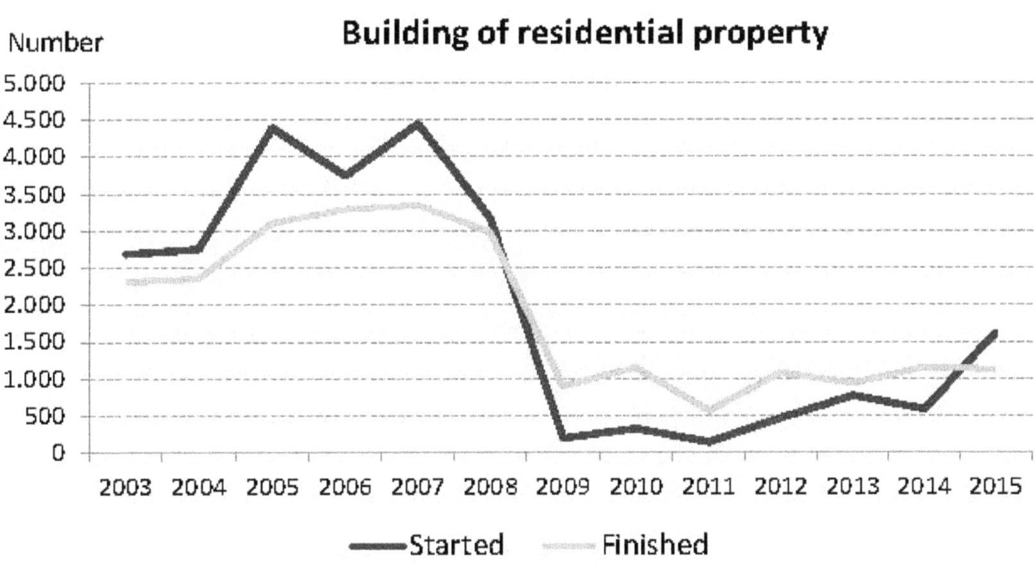

Index, Jan. 2000 = 100

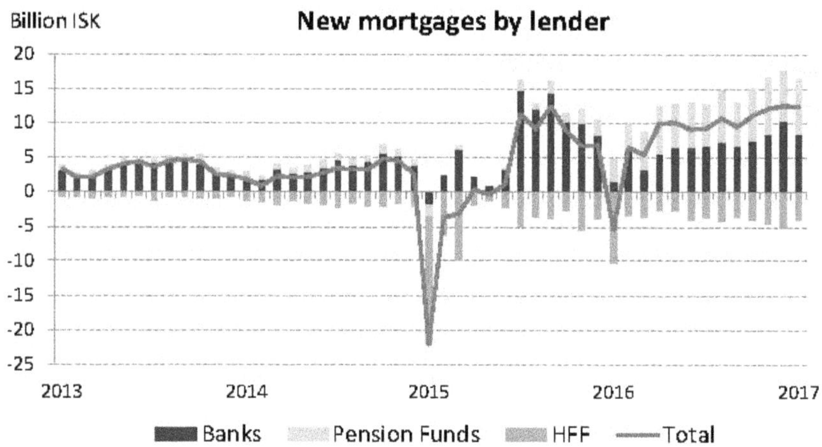

Source: Federation of Icelandic Industries

INVESTMENT

•Business sector investment has risen as a share of GDP in the last two years

•Lending to tourism companies has increased markedly in the recent past, in line with increased investment in the sector.

•At the end of 2016, lending to the tourism industry accounted for 8.5% of loans granted to the private sector.

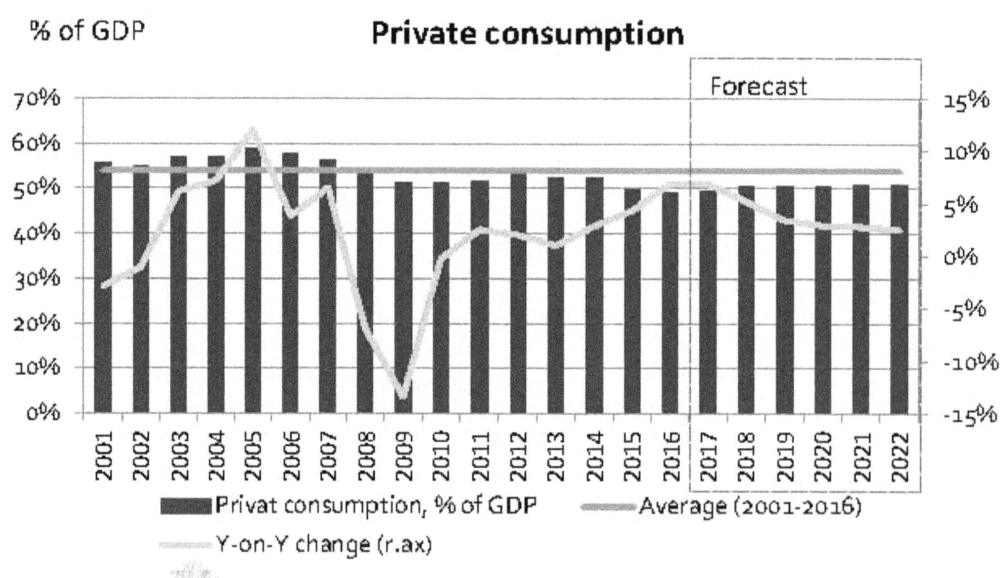

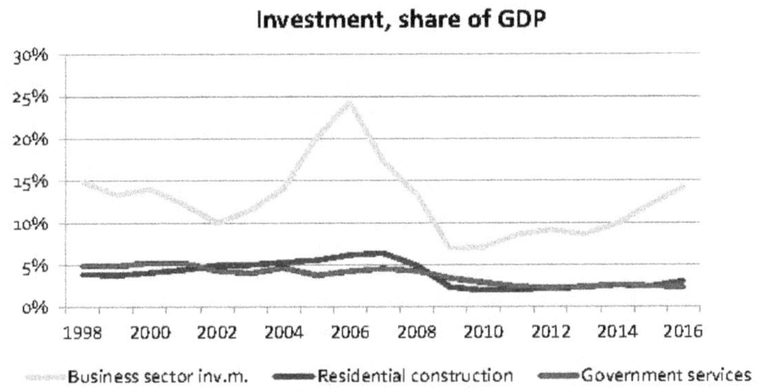

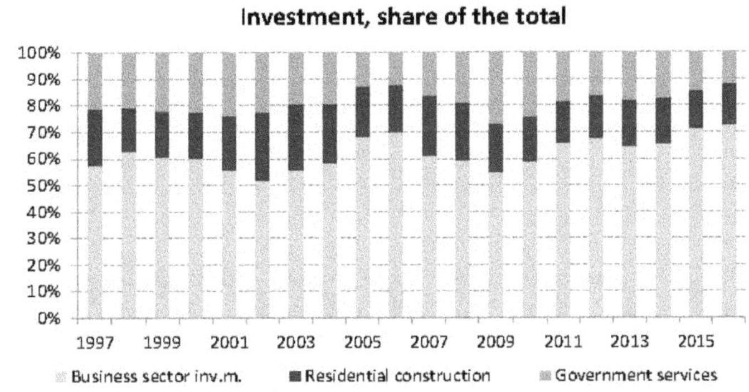

Source: Central Bank

EXTERNAL POSITION

The real exchange rate in terms of relative consumer prices has risen sharply from the autumn 2009. The increase has continued so far in 2017, with the real exchange rate about a fifth above its twenty-five year average in Q1.

•The rise is due for the most part to the nominal appreciation of the króna

•Iceland's net international investment position (NIIP) has improved substantially in the recent term and is now positive by 1.1% of GDP.

•1

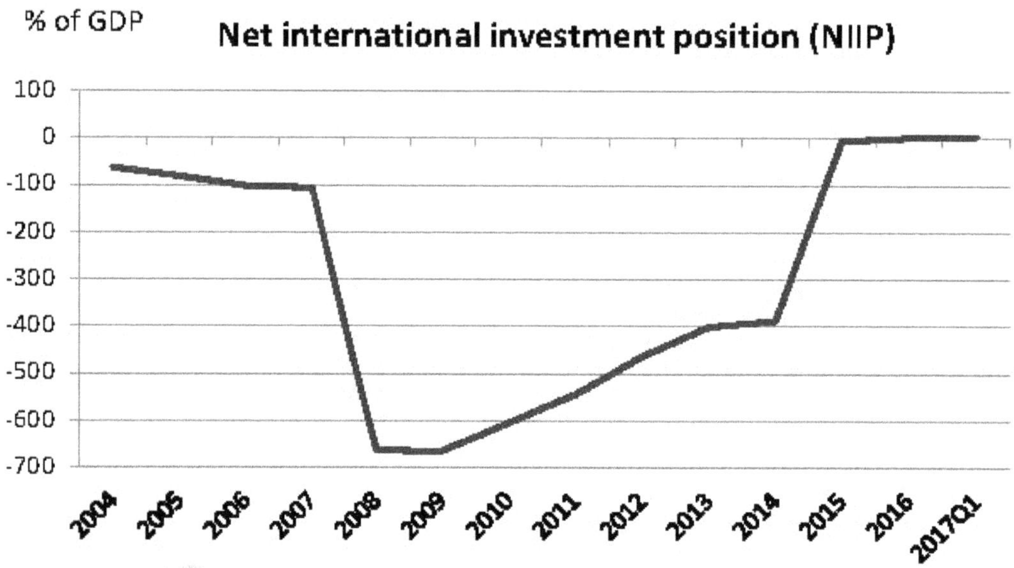

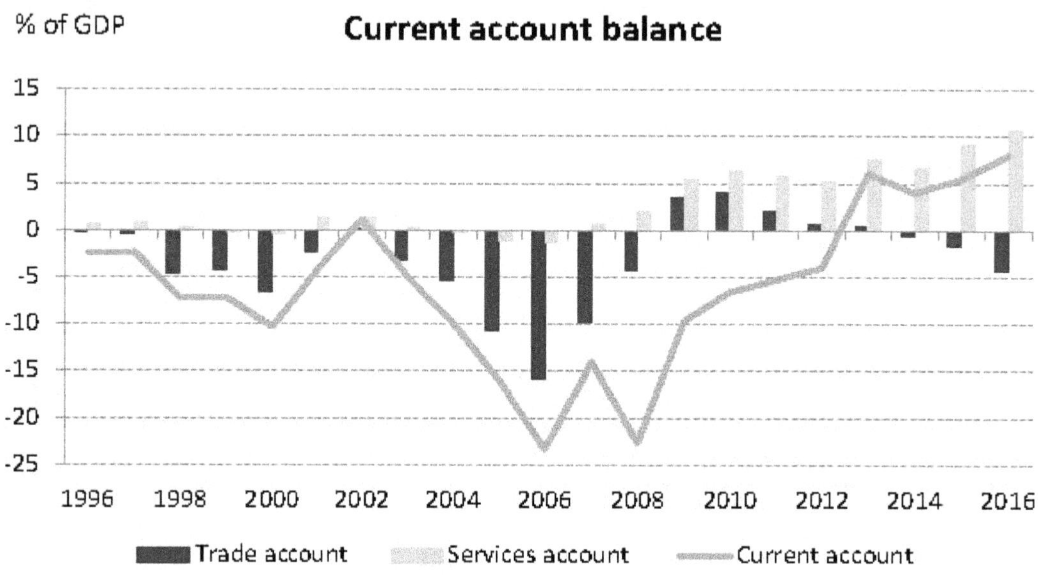

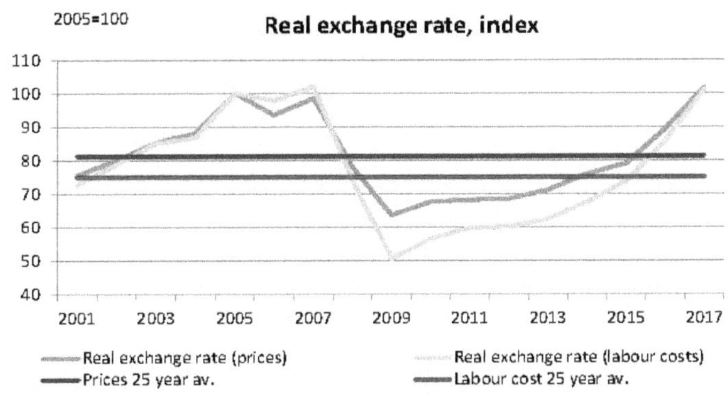

TRADE

•Terms of trade have improved markedly, and exports have grown rapidly

•The rise in the exchange rate is due largely to growth in tourism, considerably better terms of trade, and a substantial improvement in Iceland's external position.

•Exports of goods and services combined rose by over 11% in 2016

•The surplus of balance of trade in goods and services in 2016 was 158,836 million ISK

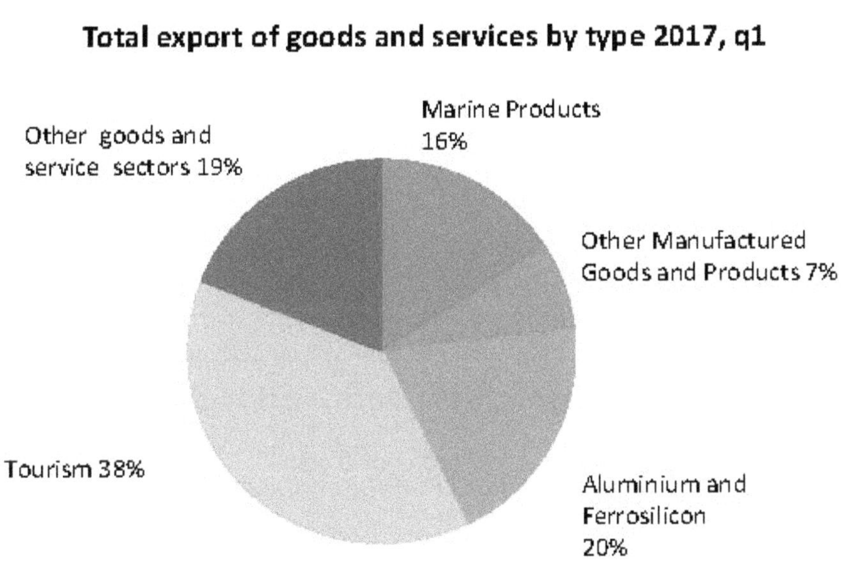

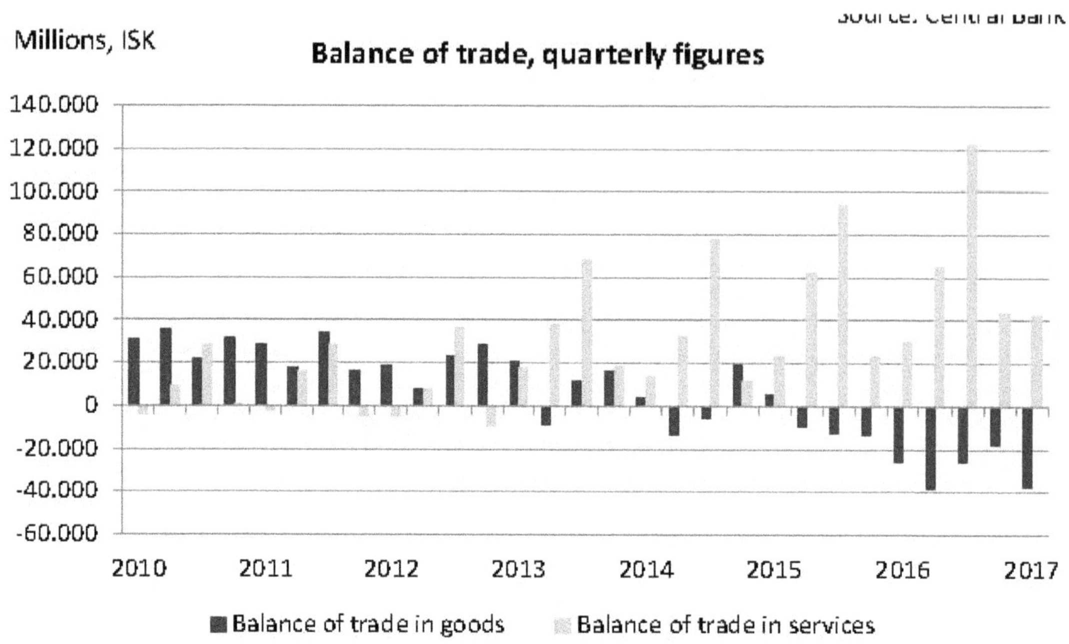

Source: Statistic Iceland

Source: Central Bank

DEBT LEVELS

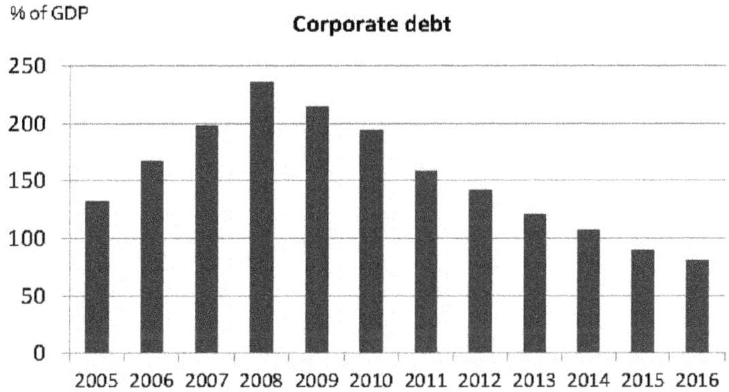

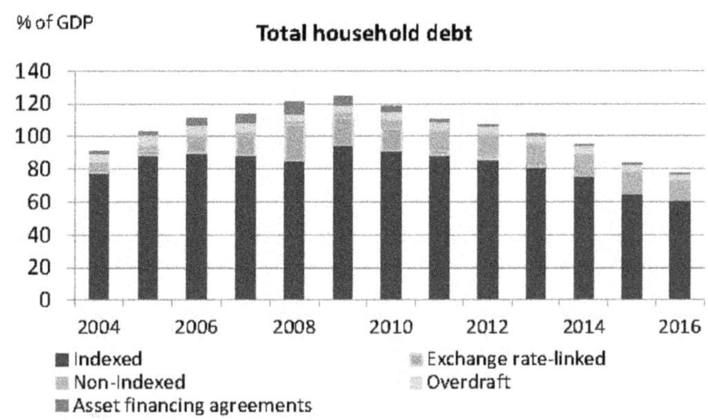

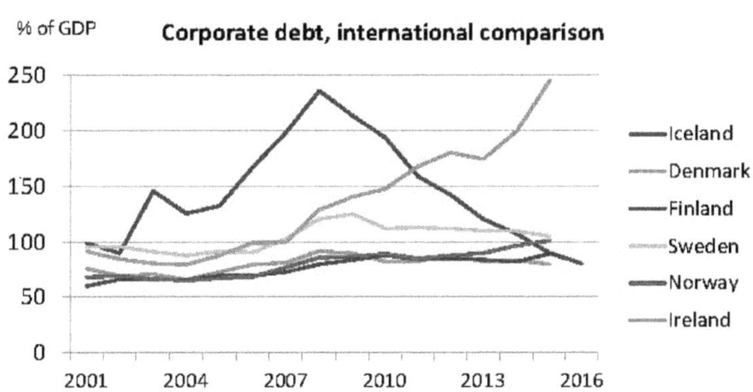

•Total household debt continues to decrease, debt has not grown in line with increases in housing prices

•Household debt was reduced by 33 b.kr. in 2016 in connection with the Government's debt relief measures

•Loans to tourism companies account for around 14% of the commercial banks' total corporate lending.

Source: Central Bank

LABOUR MARKET – FOREIGN LABOUR

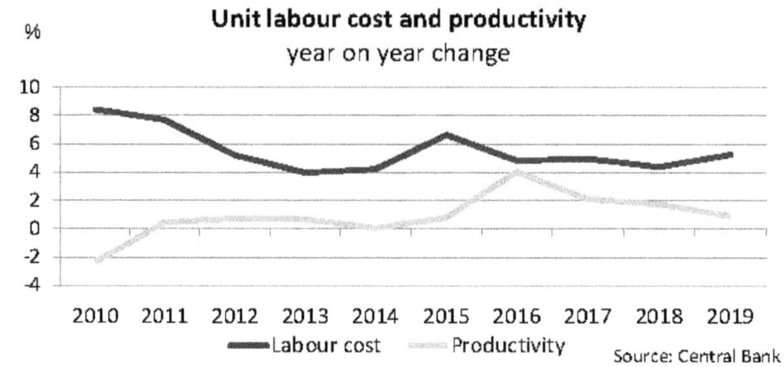

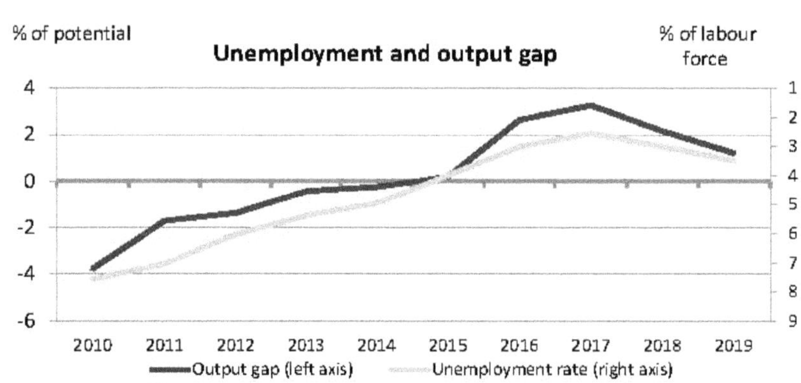

LABOUR MARKET – FOREIGN LABOUR

Ministry of Finance and Economic Affairs

Source: Directorate of Labour

•From the year 1996, the highest numbers of foreign immigrants to Iceland were Polish citizens, with the exception of 2004, when Portuguese citizens were most numerous.

•At the end of 2016 there were 20.273 foreigners in the workforce, 10,3% of the labour market

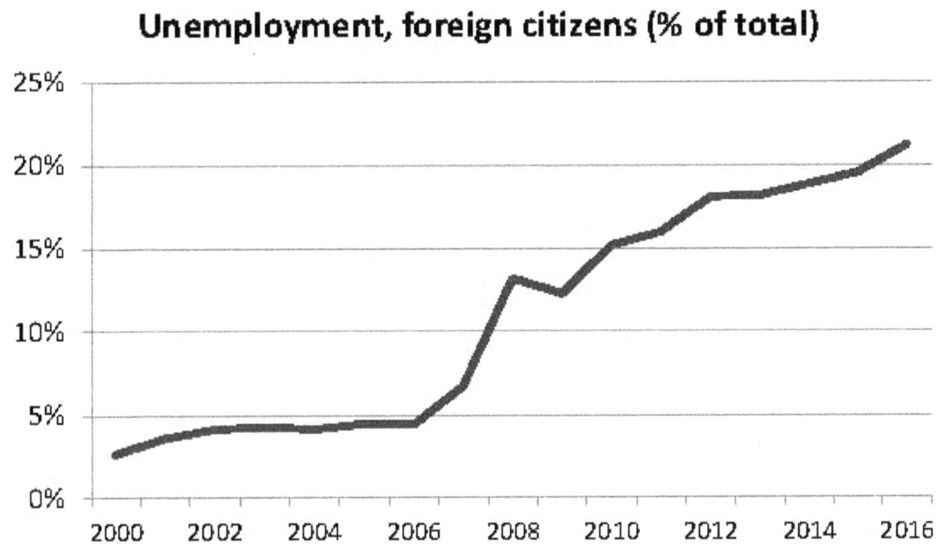

Source: Directorate of Labour

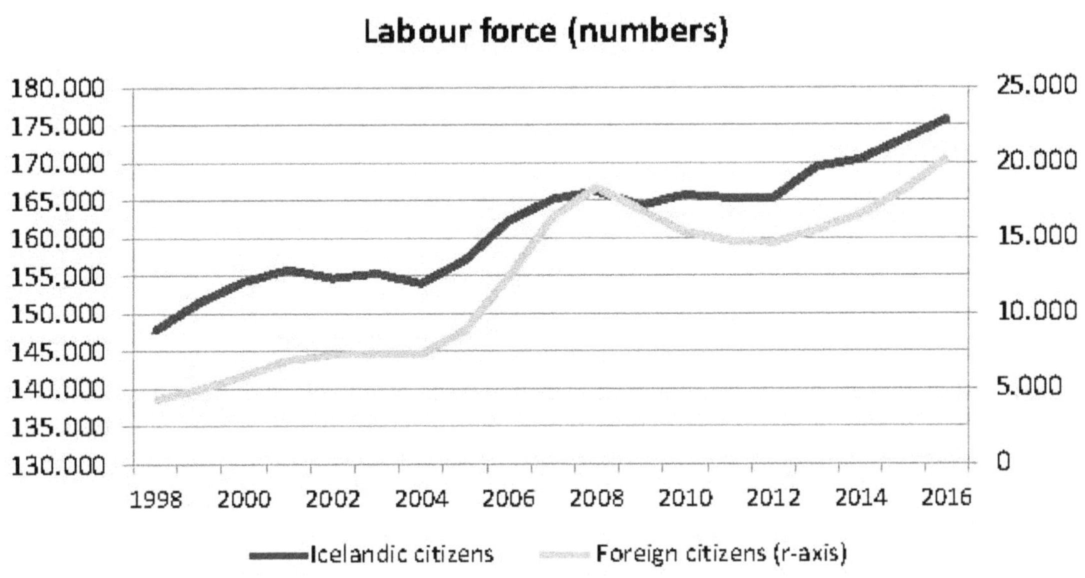

GINI COEFFICIENT IN SELECTED OECD COUNTRIES

The Gini coefficient is based on the comparison of cumulative proportions of the population against cumulative proportions of income they receive, and it ranges between 0 in the case of perfect equality and 1 in the case of perfect inequality. With a Gini coefficient of 0.24, Iceland's income inequality after government taxes and transfers is the lowest among OECD countries.

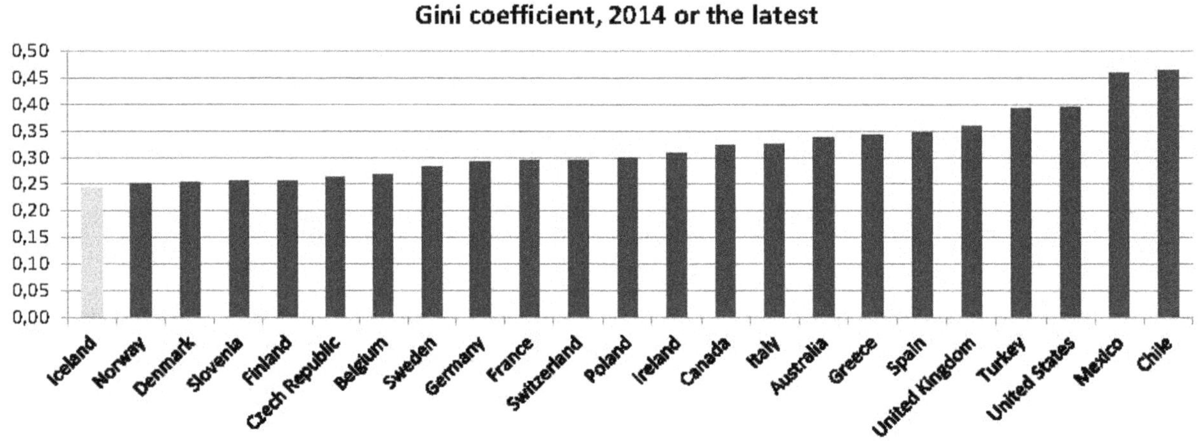

TOURISM

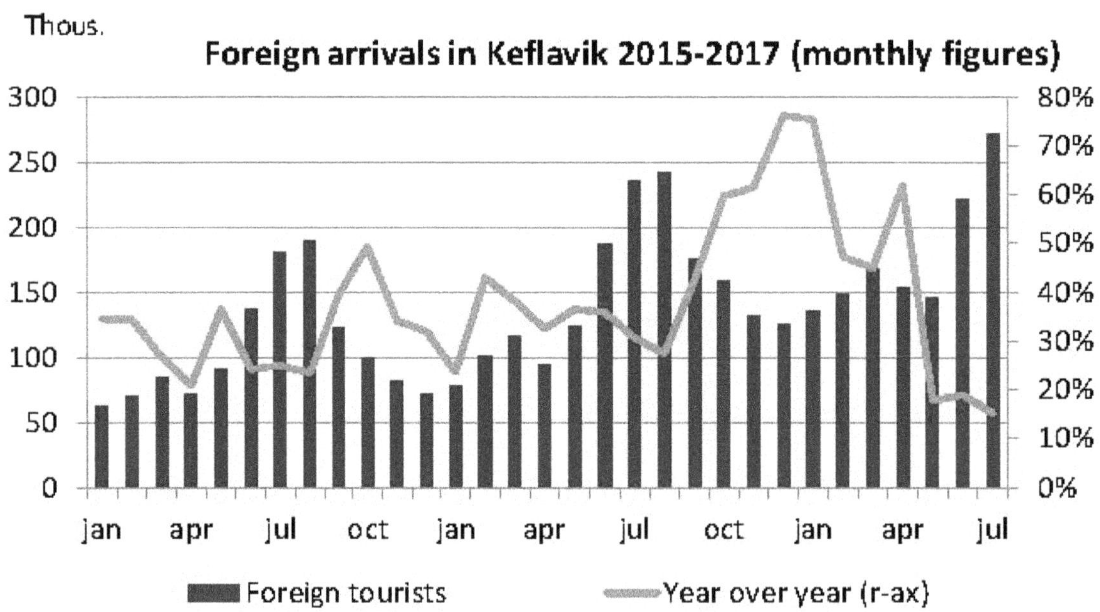

Source: Icelandic Tourist Board

•The total number of foreign visitors to Icelands was around 1,8 million in 2016

•That is a 39% increase from 2015

•In the first 5 months of 2017 the increase is 46,5%

•Higher growth in the winter months than summer

•The appreciation of Krona might shorten the dwelling time and cause less spending

Source: Icelandic Tourist Board

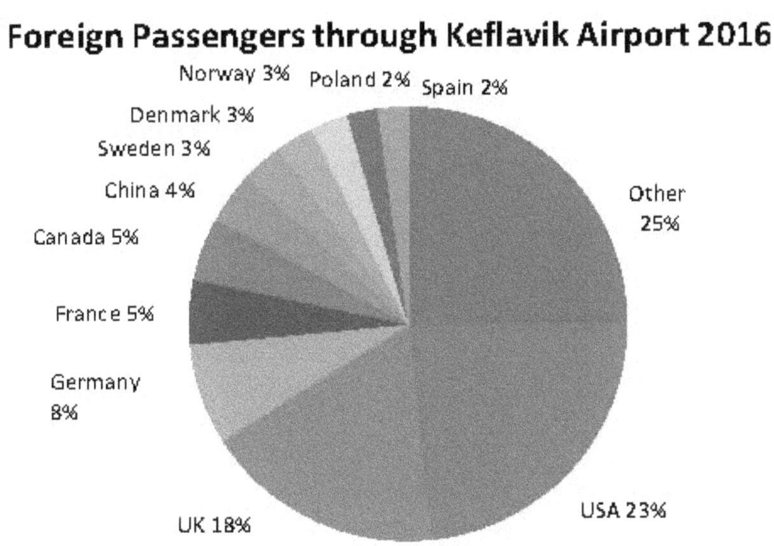

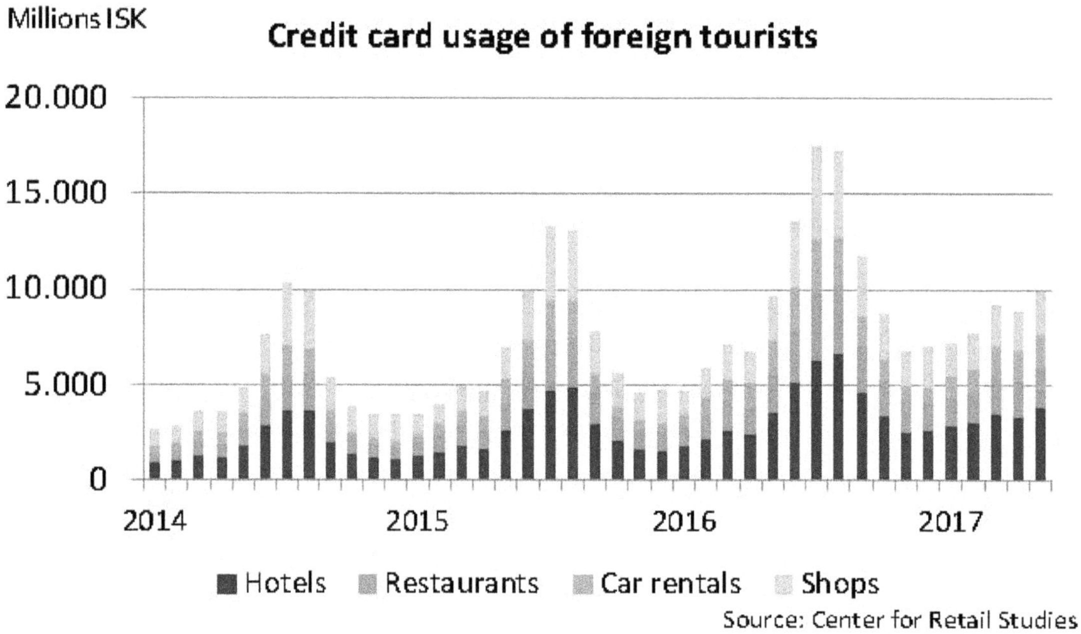

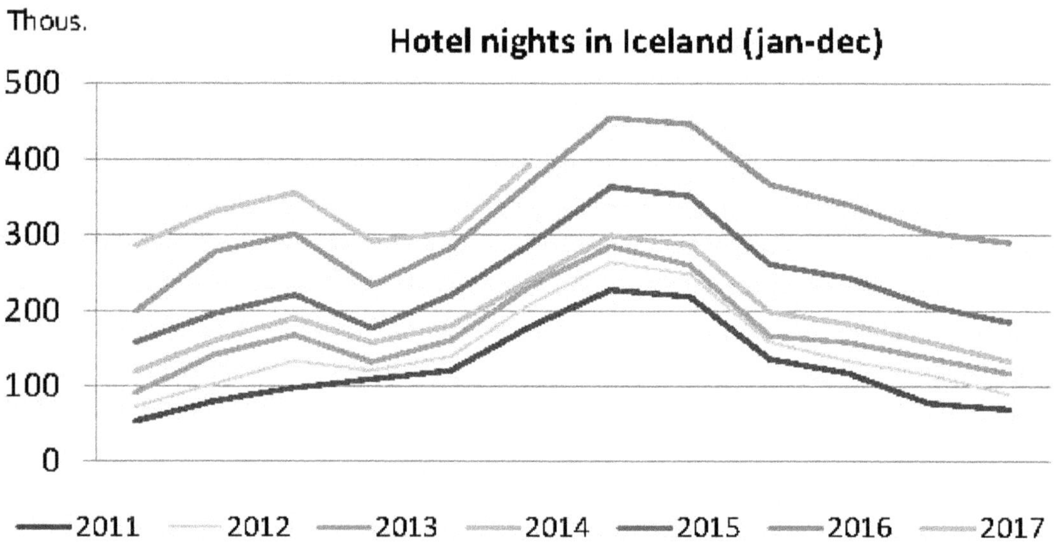

•Overnight stays in hotels increased by 6% in June, year on year.

•In the first six months of 2017 the overnight stays increased by 18%

•The occupancy rate stays high, especially in the capital area

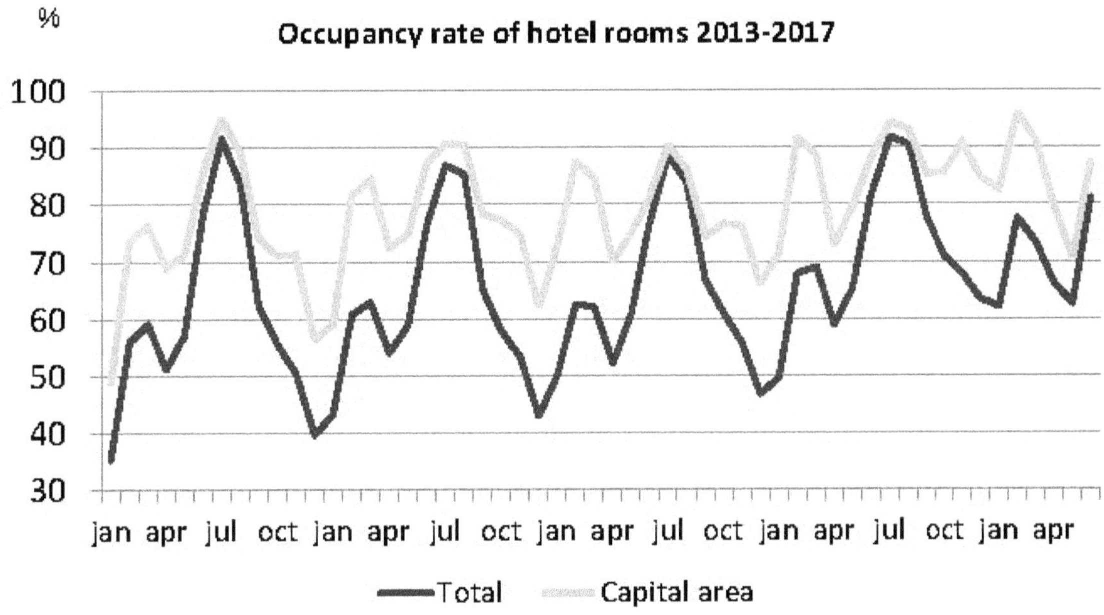

FISHING SECTOR

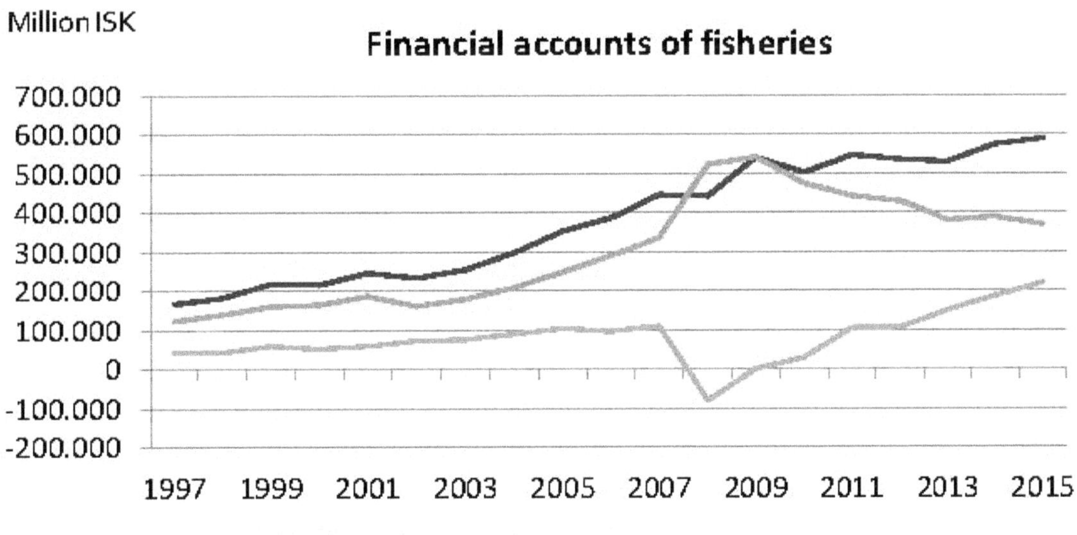

Source: Statistic Iceland

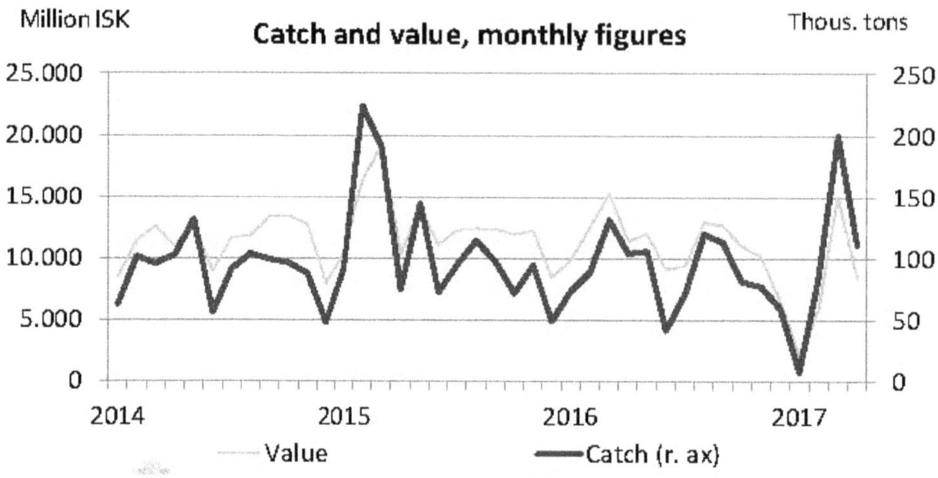

•Marine products have historically been the country´s leading export items.

•The fishing industry is one of the main pillars of the Icelandic economy.

•Iceland maintains a 200 nautical miles exclusive fishing zone, 7 times the area of Iceland itself

•A catch limitation system is the cornerstone of the Icelandic fisheries management system. The system is intended to limit the total catch and to prevent more fishing from the fish stocks than the authorities allow at any given time.

Source: Statistic Iceland

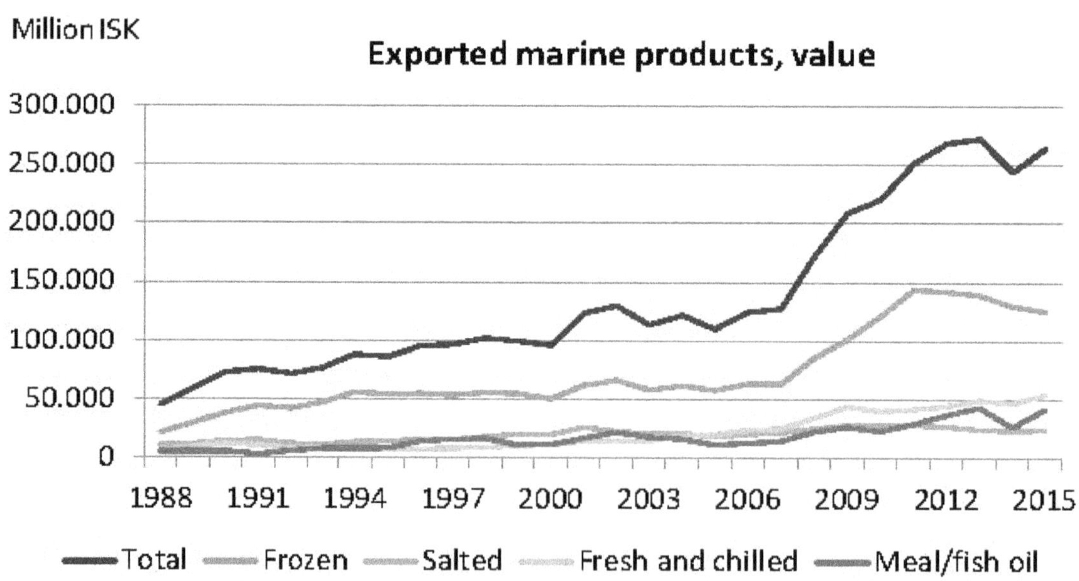

ALUMINIUM SECTOR

•Aluminium exports account for 20% of total exports of goods and services

•There are three aluminium smelters in Iceland, Alcoa (East Iceland), Century Aluminium (West Iceland) and Rio Tinto Alcan (South Coast Iceland)

•Production of aluminium started in Iceland in 1969 in Straumsvík (South Coast). During the first year, the production capacity was 33 thousand tonnes

•The capacity today for all three smelter is around 850 thousand tonnes per year

Source: Statistic Iceland

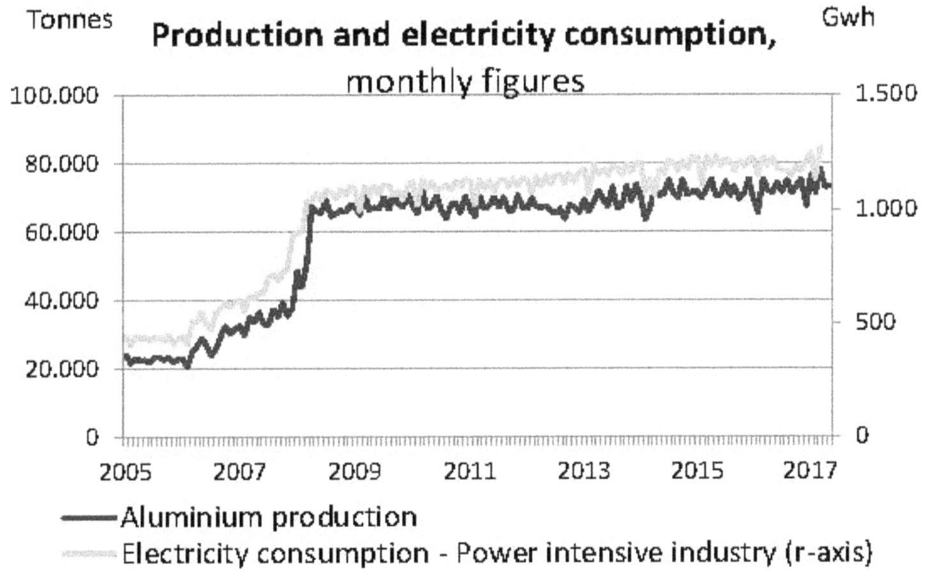

1

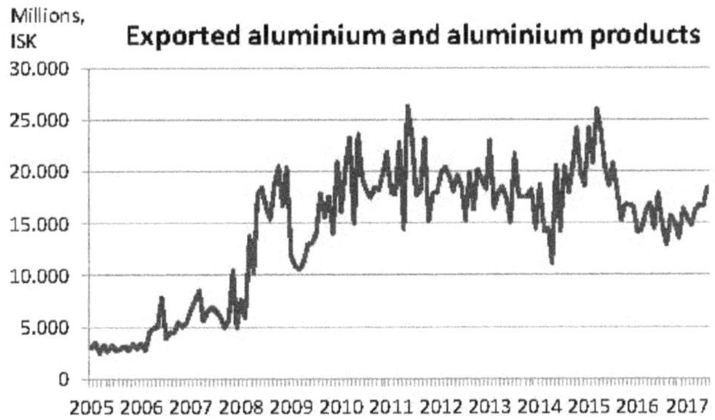

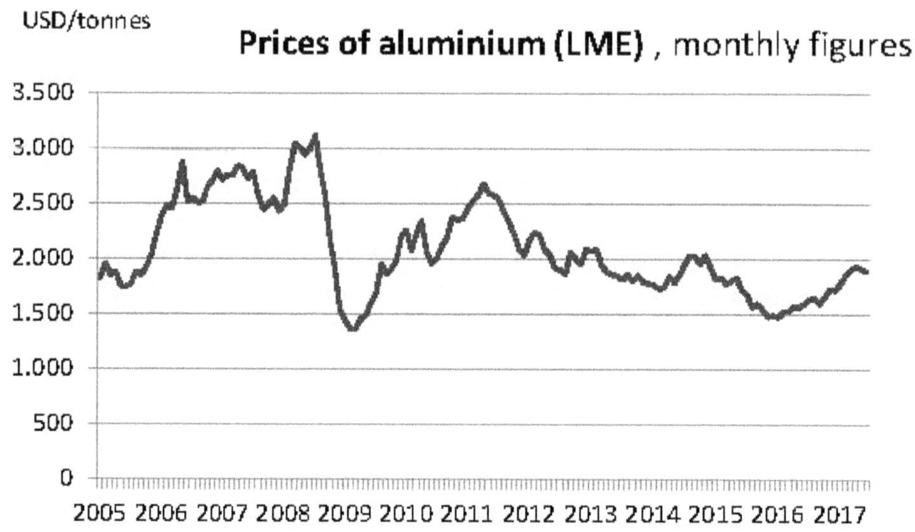

ENERGY CONSUMPTION – 80% RENEWABLE

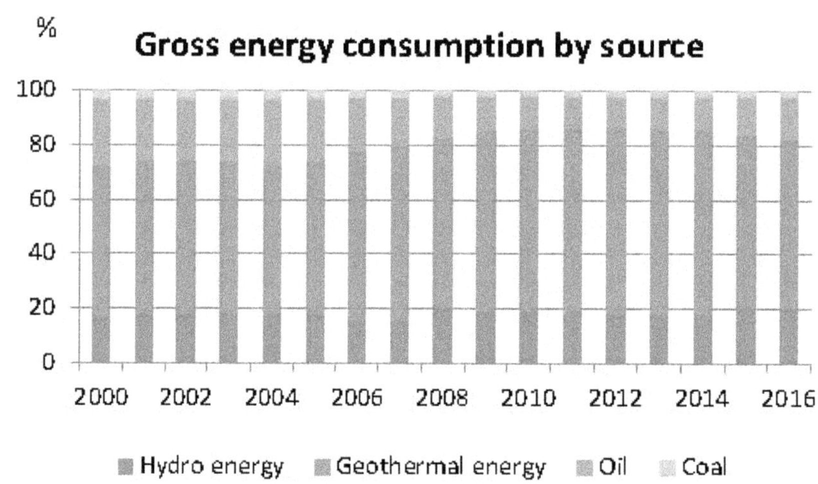

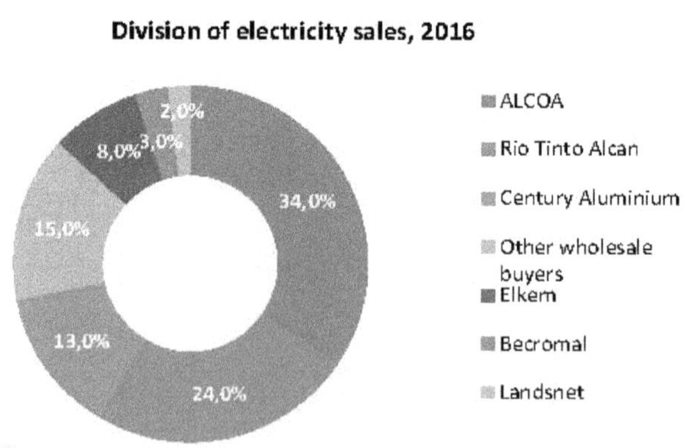

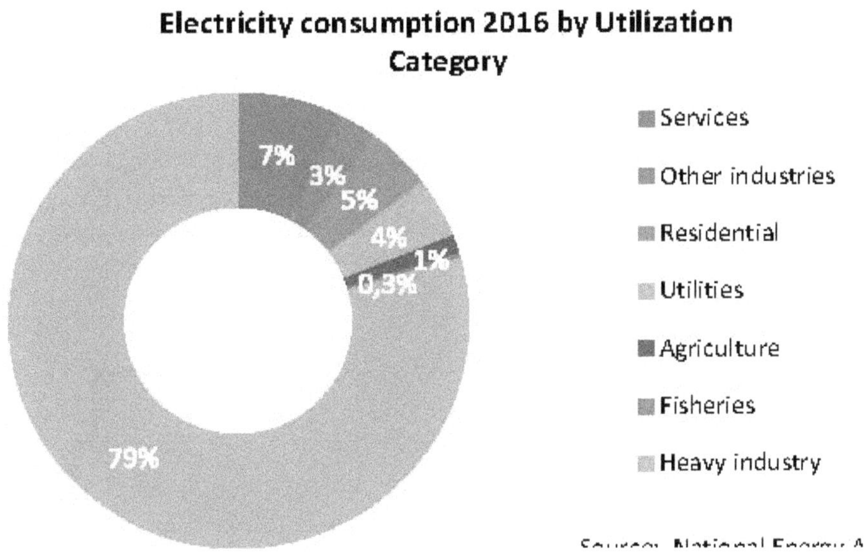

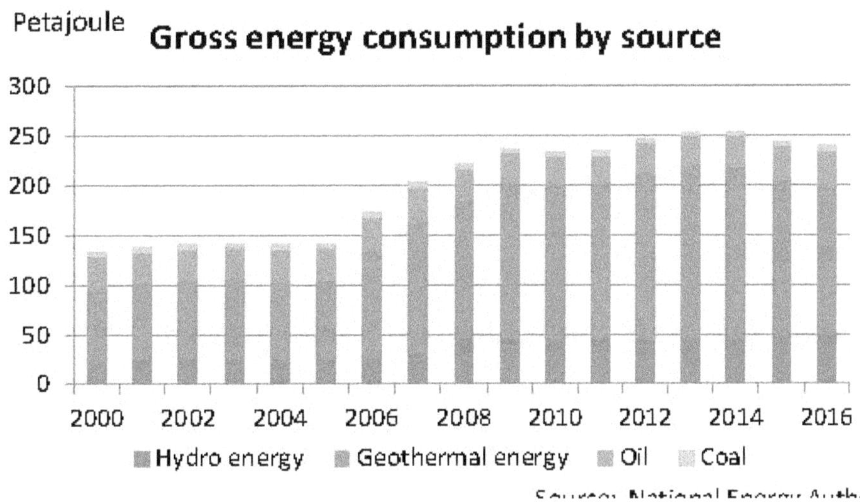

MONETARY POLICY

•The Monetary Policy Committee of the Central Bank of Iceland lowered the Bank's interest rates by 0.25 percentage points in June.

•The Bank's key interest rate – the rate on seven-day term deposits, are now 4,5%.

•The Central Bank has scaled down its intervention in the foreign exchange market in view of its strong foreign exchange reserves, as the appreciation of the króna is considered to reflect economic fundamentals. As before, the Bank will intervene in the market in order to mitigate volatility when it considers such intervention warranted.

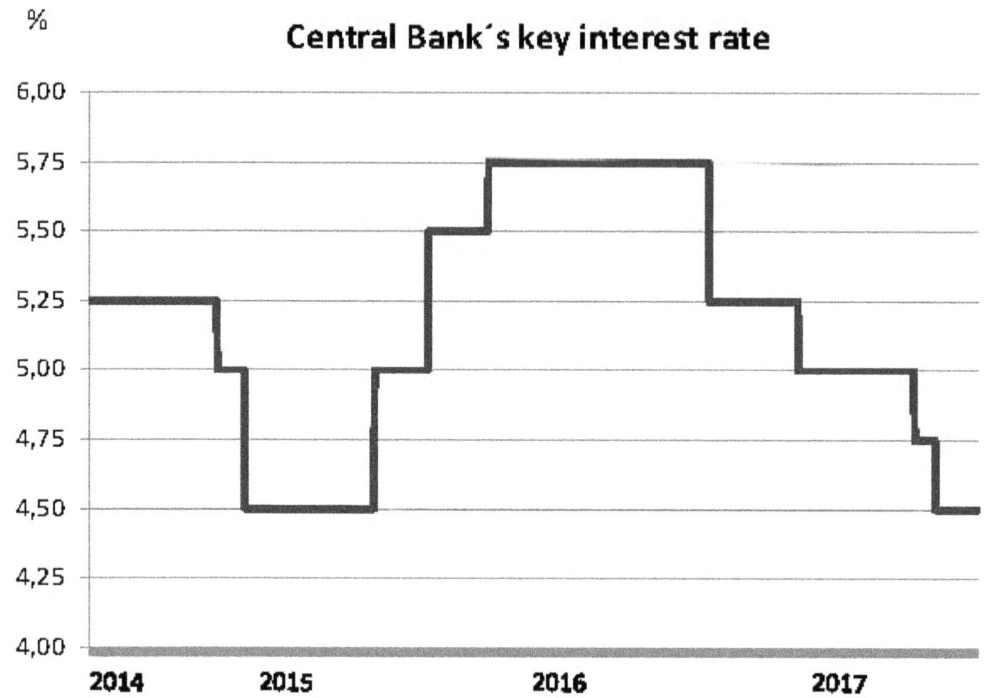

Source: Central Bank

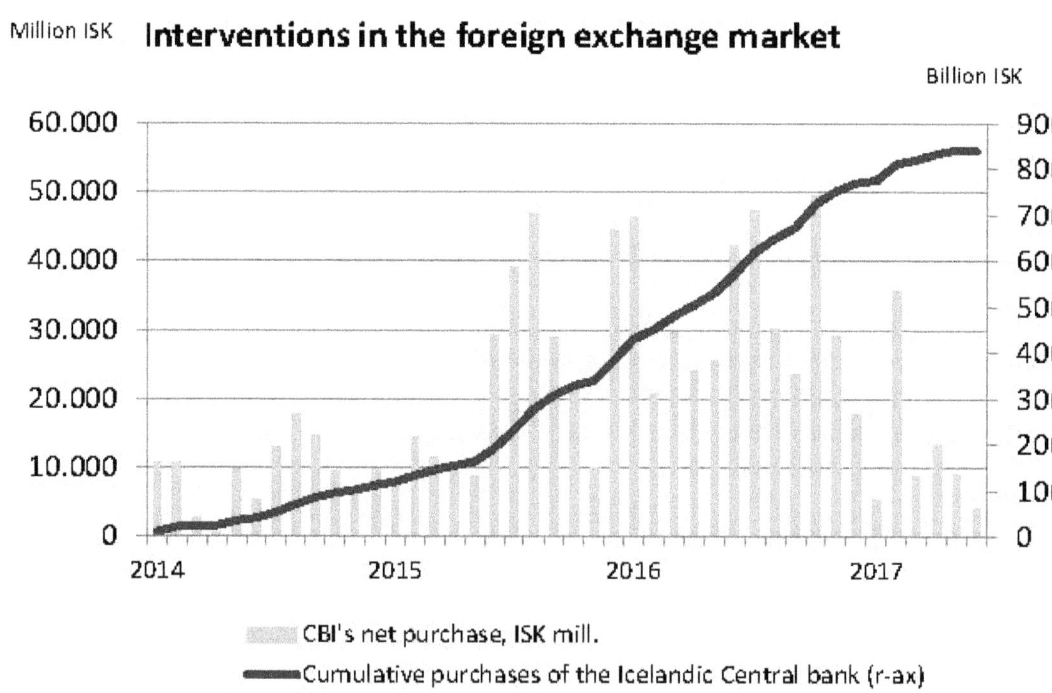

Million ISK

EXCHANGE RATE

•The króna appreciated 18% in 2016

•The króna continued to appreciate in the first quarter of 2017 but the strengthening of the króna has reversed and the exchange rate index in August is now similar as it was in the beginning of 2017

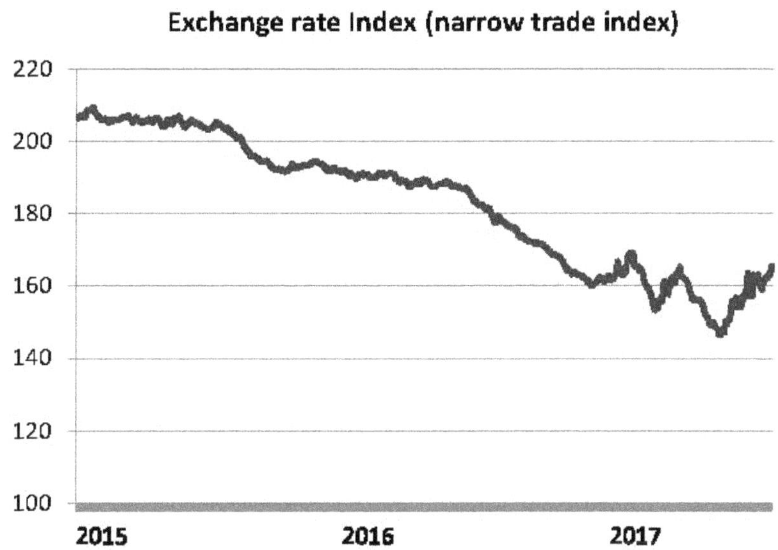

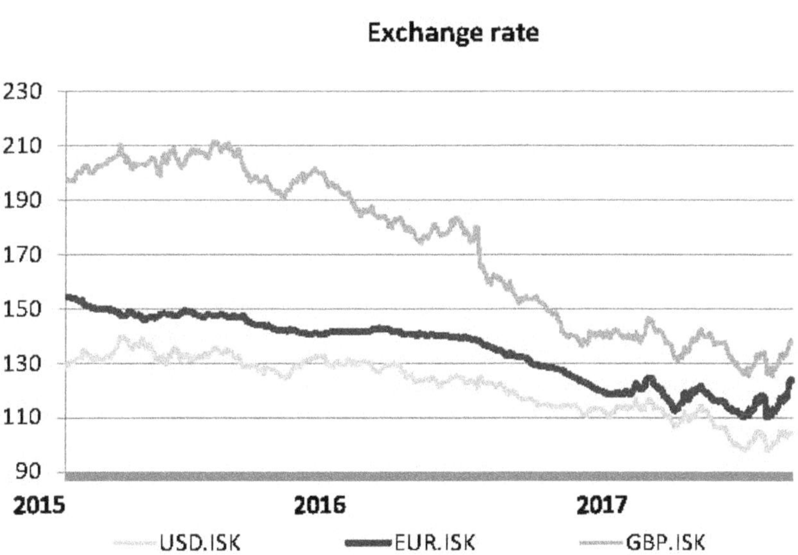

INTEREST RATES

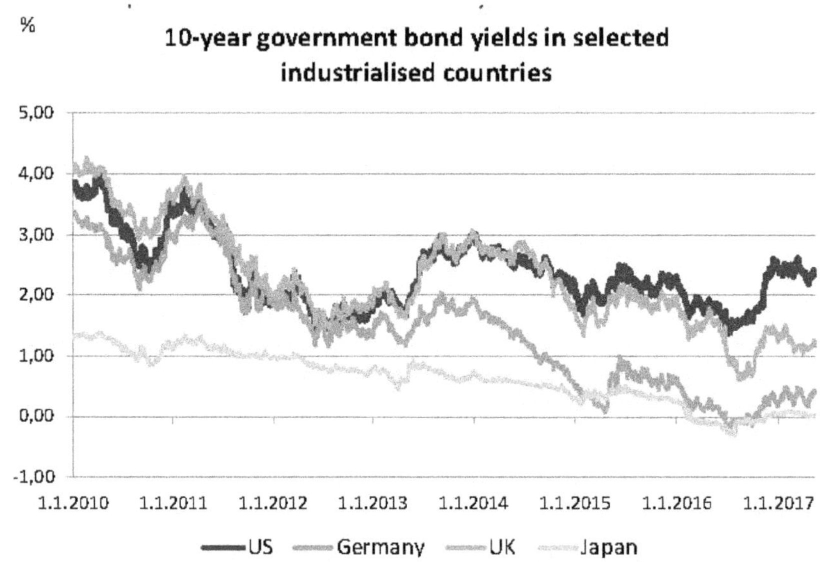

Source: Central Bank

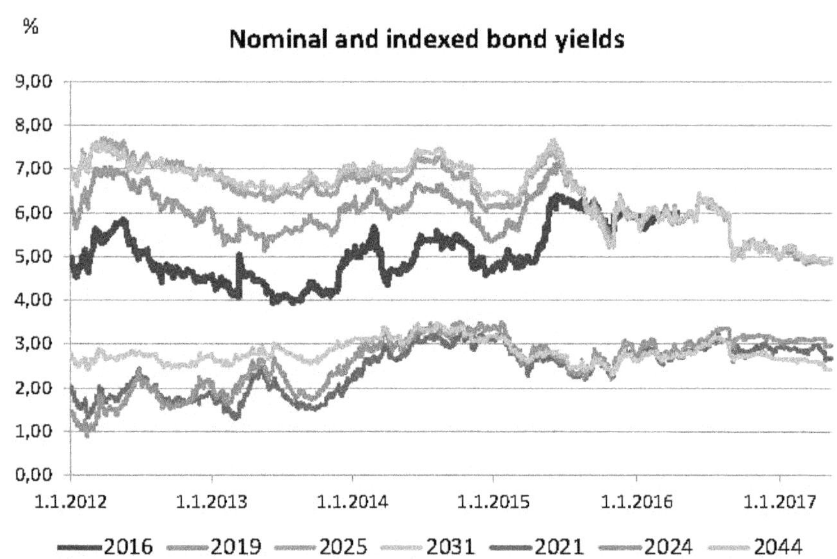

•The spread between long-term interest rates in the US and the UK has grown wider

•The yields on indexed and nominal bonds have fallen

•The decline in bond yields appear to reflect market agents' reduced inflation expectations and their expectations of a lower key rate

COMMERCIAL BANKS

Source: Central Bank

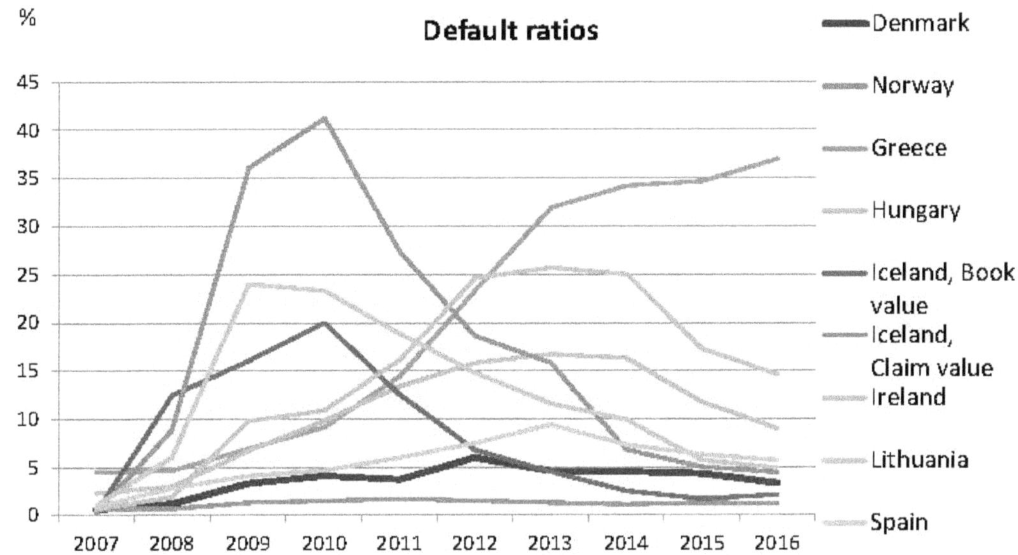

Source: Central Bank

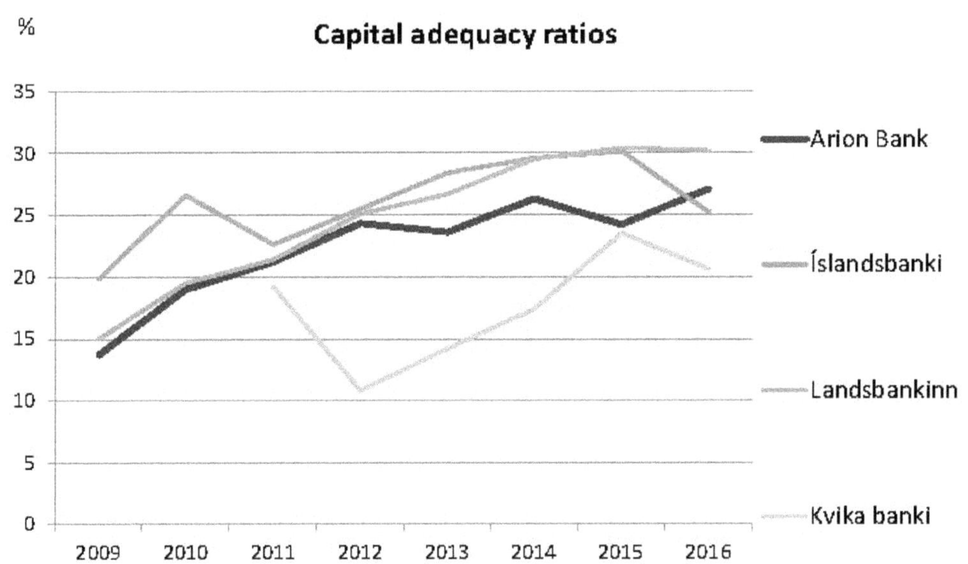

•Default ratios for households and business in Iceland have declined

•Capital position is strong and both capital and leverage ratios are high for the commercial banks in Iceland

DEBT MANAGEMENT 2017-2022

Ministry of Finance and Economic Affairs

•Proceeds from stability contributions used to pay down debt

oThe budget 2017 assumes that 105 bn. ISK will be used to pay down debt

oPlans are subject to the sale of 87% share in Arion bank takes place this

•Treasury ISK deposits in Central bank reduced

oDeposit levels reduced to 40 bn. ISK last fall when active liquidity managment implemented

•Irregular revenues – dividends, proceeds from asset disposal

oDuring the period, irregular income of 140 bn. ISK is assumed to be used to retire debt

•Central Bank bond fully repaid in 2017

•Outstanding amounts of RIKH 18 og RIKB 19 reduced by switch auctions and buy-backs

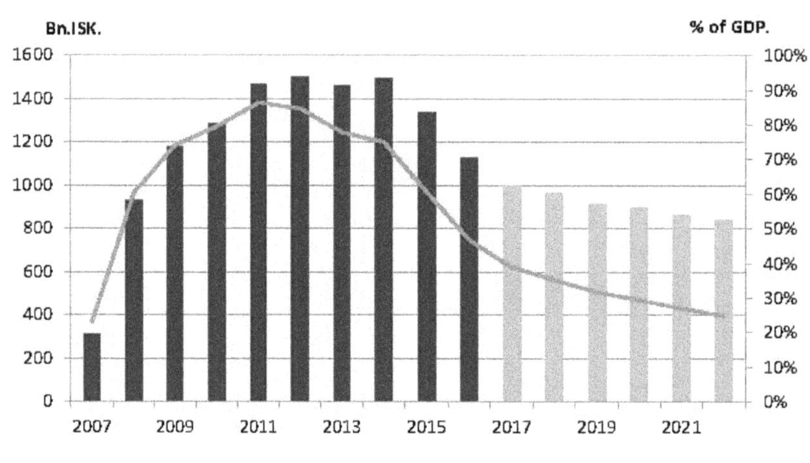

•Gross central government debt ratio peaked in 86% of GDP in2011, the ratio was down to 47% at end of 2016

•GDP growth and debt repayments are the contributing factors in lowered debt levels

•At the end of forecast period 2022 total debt is expected at 838 bn. ISK – 25% af VLF

Source: Ministry of Finance and economic affairs

ACT ON PUBLIC FINANCES - STRENGHTENS THE FISCAL FRAMEWORK

Ministry of Finance and Economic Affairs

•New Act on Public Finances came into force 1. January 2016. The architecture involves i.a. three main documents:

•Five-year Fiscal Policy Statement, a parliamentary resolution submitted every five years. When new Government takes office, it has to publish a new policy statement and strategy for the next 5 years, as soon as possible

•Fiscal Strategy for the next five years, a parliamentary resolution submitted every year.

•Budget Bill (submitted every year)

•The Policy Statement and the Strategy reflects the Government's objectives and emphasis concerning the economic policy effect of public finances, tax policy, and prioritization of spending.

•The five year Fiscal Policy Statement for this Government was approved in April 2016.

•The Fiscal Strategy was approved in May 2016.

TOTAL OUTCOME – GENERAL GOVERNMENT

•Stability contributions and other irregular income included

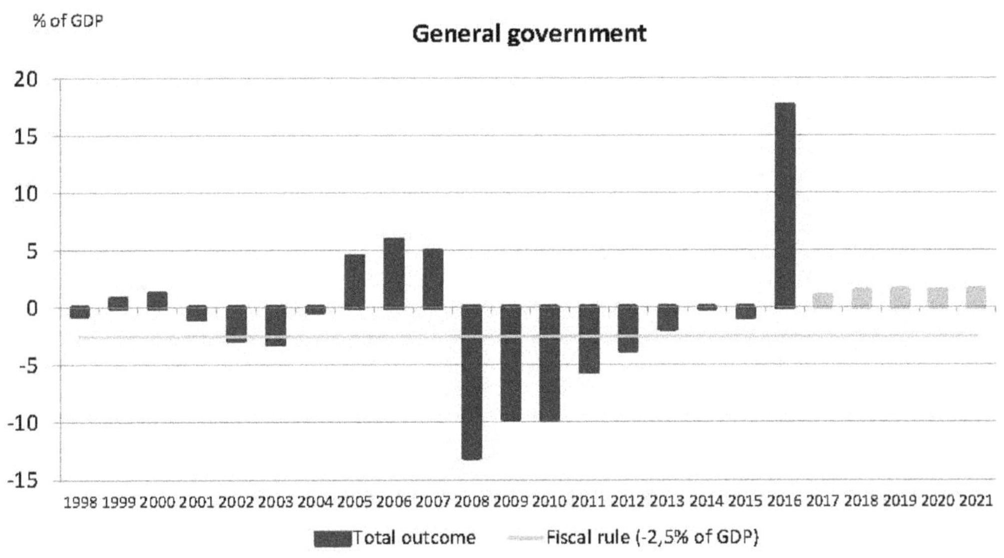

FISCAL STRATEGY PLAN 2017-2022 CENTRAL GOVERNMENT BALANCE

•Excluding irregular items such as revenues from stability contributions

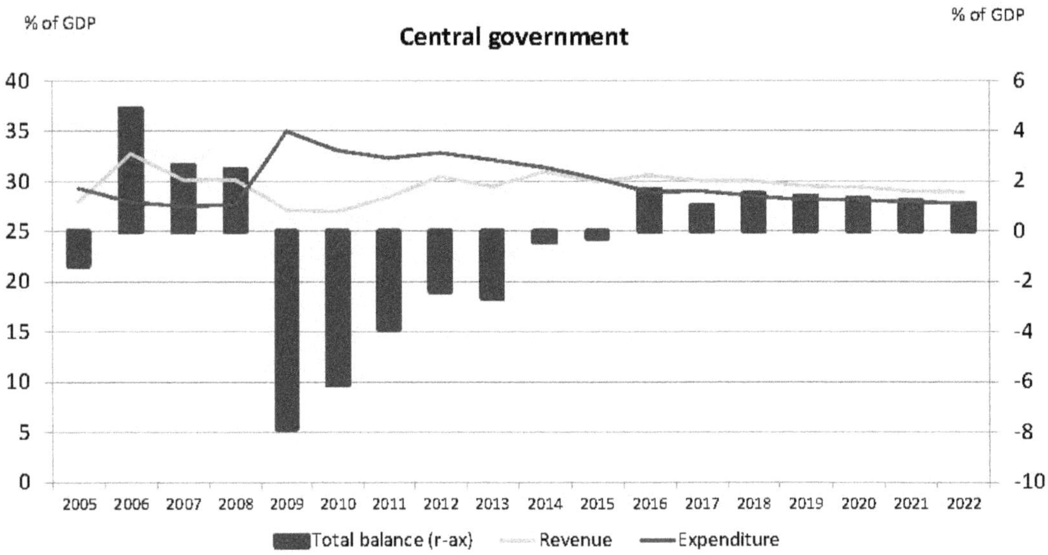

STRATEGIC ECONOMIC INFORMATION

AGREEMENT ON AGRICULTURE

Article 10 and 18.2; ES:1, ES:2	Export subsidy commitments	G/AG/N/ISL/39 G/AG/N/ISL/35	18/05/2017 16/09/2014
Article 18.2; DS:1	Domestic support	G/AG/N/ISL/40 G/AG/N/ISL/33	22/05/2017 10/09/2014
Article 18.2; MA:2	Tariff quotas	G/AG/N/ISL/37 G/AG/N/ISL/36 G/AG/N/ISL/32 G/AG/N/ISL/31	13/12/2016 26/09/2014 21/07/2014 19/11/2012
Articles 5.7 and 18.2; MA:5	Special safeguard	G/AG/N/ISL/38 G/AG/N/ISL/34	18/05/2017 16/09/2014

AGREEMENT ON THE IMPLEMENTATION OF ARTICLE VI OF THE GATT 1994 (ANTI-DUMPING)

Article 16.4 – semi annual	Anti-dumping actions (taken within the preceding six months)	G/ADP/N/216/Add.1/Rev.1	25/07/2012

GATT 1994 AND/OR GATS

Article XXIV:7(a) of GATT 1994	Notification of regional trade agreements or	WT/REG360/N/1 WT/REG323/N/1 WT/REG232/N/1/Add.2	08/01/2015 25/10/2012 27/06/2013

	changes: Bosnia and Herzegovina and EFTA States; Montenegro and the EFTA States; the Arab Republic of Egypt and the EFTA States; EFTA States and Croatia; EFTA States and Jordan; EFTA States and Morocco	WT/REG232/N/1/Add.3 WT/REG232/N/1/Add.4 WT/REG132/N/1/Add.5 WT/REG133/N/1/Add.1 WT/REG133/N/1/Add.2 WT/REG133/N/1/Add.3 WT/REG91/N/1/Add.2/Rev.1 WT/REG91/N/1/Add.3/Rev.1	27/06/2013 25/03/2015 26/11/2013 11/09/2013 11/09/2013 11/09/2013 25/03/2013 25/03/2013
Article XXIV:7(a) of GATT 1994 and Article V:7(a) of GATS	Notification of regional trade agreements: Chile and EFTA States; the Central American States and the EFTA States; Iceland and China; Hong Kong, China and the EFTA States; Colombia and the EFTA States; Mexico and EFTA States	WT/REG179/N/1/Add.4 WT/REG357/N/1 , S/C/N/774 WT/REG355/N/1 , S/C/N/771 WT/REG322/N/1 , S/C/N/654 WT/REG299/N/2 , S/C/N/600/Add.1 WT/REG126/N/1/Add.2 WT/REG126/N/1/Add.3 WT/REG126/N/1/Add.4 WT/REG126/N/1/Add.5 WT/REG126/N/1/Add.6	08/05/2017 21/11/2014 13/10/2014 01/10/2012 09/01/2015 18/09/2013 18/09/2013 18/09/2013 18/09/2013 18/09/2013
Article XXIV:7(c) of GATT 1994	Notification of regional trade agreements: EFTA States and the Republic of Lebanon	WT/REG224/N/1/Add.1	25/04/2013

GATT 1994 ARTICLE XVII AND THE UNDERSTANDING ON THE INTERPRETATION OF ARTICLE XVII

GATT 1994 Art. XVII:4(a) and Para. 1 of the Understanding on the Interpretation of Article XVII	New and full notification of state-trading enterprises	G/STR/N/15/ISL	07/06/2017

GENERAL AGREEMENT ON TRADE IN SERVICES

Services LDC Waiver	Preferential treatment to services and service suppliers of least developed countries	S/C/N/835	13/10/2015

AGREEMENT ON RULES OF ORIGIN

Paragraph 4 of Annex II	Preferential rules of origin	G/RO/N/82	31/08/2012

AGREEMENT ON SANITARY AND PHYTOSANITARY MEASURES

Article 7 Annex B	Sanitary and phytosanitary regulations	G/SPS/N/ISL/9	15/11/2012

		G/SPS/N/ISL/8	15/11/2012

AGREEMENT ON GOVERNMENT PROCUREMENT

Article XVI:4	Statistics reported under Article XVI:4 of the revised GPA	GPA/142/Add.2 GPA/137/Add.6	25/04/2017 25/04/2017
Article XXIV:5(b) and XXII:5	Notification of national implementing legislation	GPA/144	28/04/2017
Appendix I	Thresholds in national currency	GPA/W/336/Add.11 GPA/W/325/Add.9 GPA/W/314/Add.9	21/11/2016 22/07/2014 10/09/2012

Source: WTO Secretariat.

TABLE A2.2 ICELAND'S FREE TRADE AGREEMENTS, 2017

Free trade agreement	Date of entry into force	Coverage
EFTA – Bosnia and Herzegovina	1-Jan-15	Goods
EFTA – Central America (Costa Rica and Panama)	19-Aug-14	Goods & Services
EFTA – Gulf Cooperation Council	1-Jul-14	Goods & Services
Iceland – China	1-Jul-14	Goods & Services
EFTA – Hong Kong, China	1-Oct-12	Goods & Services
EFTA – Montenegro	1-Sep-12	Goods
EFTA – Ukraine	1-Jun-12	Goods & Services
EFTA – Colombia	1-Jul-11	Goods & Services
EFTA – Peru	1-Jul-11	Goods
EFTA – Albania	1-Nov-10	Goods
EFTA – Serbia	1-Oct-10	Goods
EFTA – Canada	1-Jul-09	Goods
EFTA – SACU	1-May-08	Goods
EFTA – Egypt	1-Aug-07	Goods
EFTA – Lebanon	1-Jan-07	Goods
Iceland – Faroe Islands	1-Nov-06	Goods & Services
EFTA – Republic of Korea	1-Sep-06	Goods & Services
EFTA – Tunisia	1-Jun-05	Goods
EFTA – Chile	1-Dec-04	Goods & Services
EFTA – Singapore	1-Jan-03	Goods & Services
EFTA – Jordan	1-Sep-02	Goods
EFTA – The former Yugoslav Republic of Macedonia	1-May-02	Goods
EFTA – Mexico	1-Jul-01	Goods & Services
EFTA – Morocco	1-Dec-99	Goods

EFTA – Palestinian Authority	1-Jul-99	Goods
European Economic Area (EEA)	1-Jan-94	Goods & Services
EFTA – Israel	1-Jan-93	Goods
EFTA – Turkey	1-Apr-92	Goods
Iceland – European Union (EU)	1-Apr-73	Goods
EFTA – Accession of Iceland	1-Mar-70	Goods
Iceland – European Free Trade Association (EFTA)	3-May-60 1-Jun-02	Goods Services
Iceland – Greenland	1-Feb-85	Goods

Source: Compiled by the WTO Secretariat.

GOVERNMENT CONTACTS

Office of the Prime Minister		
Postal Address: 150 Reykjavik, Iceland www.stjr.is/for	Prime Minister: Mr. Davíð Oddsson	Tel: +354 560-9400 Fax: +354 562-4014 postur@for.stjr.is
Ministry for Foreign Affairs	www.mfa.is	external@utn.stjr.is
Postal Address: 150 Reykjavik, Iceland	Minister: Mr. Halldór Ásgrímsson	Tel: +354 560-9900 Fax: +354 562-2386
Ministry of Finance		
Postal Address: 150 Reykjavik, Iceland www.stjr.is/fjr	Minister: Mr. Geir H. Haarde	Tel: +354 560-9200 Fax: +354 562-8280 postur@fjr.stjr.is
Ministry of Agriculture		
Postal Address: 150 Reykjavik, Iceland www.stjr.is/lan	Minister: Mr. Guðni Ágústsson	Tel: +354 560-9750 Fax: +354 552-1160 postur@lan.stjr.is
Ministry of Education, Science and Culture		
Postal Address: 150 Reykjavik, Iceland www.stjr.is/mrn	Minister: Mr. Björn Bjarnason	Tel: +354 560-9504 Fax: +354 562-3068 postur@mrn.stjr.is
Ministry for the Environment		
Postal Address: 150 Reykjavik, Iceland www.stjr.is/umh	Minister: Ms. Siv Friðleifsdóttir	Tel: +354 560-9600 Fax: +354 562 4566 postur@umh.stjr.is
Ministry of Fisheries		
Postal Address: 150 Reykjavik, Iceland www.stjr.is/sjr	Minister: Mr. Árni M. Matthiesen	Tel: +354 560-9670 Fax: +354 562-1853 sjavar@hafro.is
Ministry for Health and Social Security		
Postal Address: 150 Reykjavik, Iceland www.stjr.is/htr	Minister: Mr. Jón Kristjánsson	Tel: +354 560-9700 Fax: +354 551-9165 postur@htr.stjr.is
Ministeries of Industry and Commerce		

Postal Address: 150 Reykjavik, Iceland www.stjr.is/ivr	Minister: Ms. Valgerður Sverrisdóttir	Tel: +354 560-9070 Fax: +354 562-1289 postur@ivr.stjr.is
Ministry of Justice and Ecclesiastical Affairs		
Postal Address: 150 Reykjavik, Iceland www.stjr.is/dkm	Minister: Ms. Sólveig Pétursdóttir	Tel: +354 560-9010 Fax: +354 552-7340 postur@dkm.stjr.is
Ministry for Social Affairs		
Postal Address: 150 Reykjavik, Iceland www.stjr.is/fel	Minister: Mr. Páll Pétursson	Tel: +354 560-9010 Fax: +354 552-7340 postur@fel.stjr.is
Statistics Iceland		
Postal Address: 150 Reykjavik, Iceland www.stjr.is/for	Minister: Mr. Davíð Oddsson	Tel: +354 560-9800 Fax: +354 562-8865 postur@for.stjr.is
Ministry of Telecommunication and Transport		
Postal Address: 150 Reykjavik, Iceland www.stjr.is/sam	Minister: Mr. Sturla Böðvarsson	Tel: +354 560-9630 Fax: +354 562-1702 postur@sam.stjr.is

BUSINESS CONTACTS

USEFUL ADDRESSES AND TELEPHONE NUMBERS

All Icelandic telephone numbers are 7-digit, with no regional codes. The international code for Iceland is 354.

INVEST IN ICELAND AGENCY

Invest in Iceland Agency
– General Investments
(Fjárfestingarstofan)
Hallveigarstígur 1
101 Reykjavík
Tel.: 511 4000
Fax: 511 4040
e-mail: invest@icetrade.is
Website: www.invest.is

Invest in Iceland Agency
– Energy Marketing
Háaleitisbraut 68
103 Reykjavík
Tel.: 515 9000
Fax: 515 9003
e-mail: mil@lv.is
Website: www.invest.is

TRADE

EuroInfo Centre
(Information Centre of the EU)
Hallveigarstígur 1
101 Reykjavík
Tel.: 511 4000
Fax: 511 4040
e-mail: euroinfo@icetrade.is
Website: www.icetrade.is

Federation of Icelandic Industries
(Samtök iðnaðarins)
Hallveigarstígur 1
101 Reykjavík
Tel.: 511 5555
Fax: 511 5566
e-mail: mottaka@si.is
Website: www.si.is

Iceland Chamber of Commerce
(Verzlunarráð Íslands)
Hús verslunarinnar
Kringlan 7
103 Reykjavík
Tel.: 588 6666
Fax: 568 6564
e-mail: mottaka@chamber.is
Website: www.chamber.is

New Business Venture Fund
(Nýsköpunarsjóður)
Sudurlandsbraut 4
108 Reykjavík
Tel.: 510 1800
Fax: 510 1809
e-mail: nsa@nsa.is
Website: www.nsa.is

Trade Council of Iceland
(Útflutningsráð Íslands)
Hallveigarstígur 1
101 Reykjavík
Tel.: 511 4000
Fax: 511 4040
e-mail: tradecouncil@icetrade.is
Website: www.icetrade.is

EMPLOYERS & LABOUR

Confederation of Icelandic Employers
(Vinnuveitendasamband Íslands)
Gardastræti 41
101 Reykjavík
Tel.: 511 5000
Fax: 511 5050
e-mail: skrifstofa@vsi.is
Website: www.vsi.is

Federation of Icelandic Labour
(Alþýðusamband Íslands)
Grensásvegur 16a
108 Reykjavík
Tel.: 581 3044
Fax: 568 0093
e-mail: asi@asi.is
Website: www.asi.is

GOVERNMENT & MINISTRIES

Ministry of Industry and Commerce
(Iðnaðar- og viðskiptaráðuneyti)
Arnarhvoll
150 Reykjavík
Tel.: 560 9070
Fax: 562 1289
e-mail: postur@ivr.stjr.is
Website: www.stjr.is/ivr

Ministry for Foreign Affairs
(Utanríkisráðuneyti)
Raudarárstígur 25
150 Reykjavík
Tel.: 560 9900
Fax: 560 9925
e-mail: postur@utn.stjr.is
Website: www.stjr.is/utn

Ministry for the Environment
(Umhverfisráðuneyti)
Vonarstræti 4
150 Reykjavík
Tel.: 560 9600
Fax: 562 4566
e-mail: postur@umh.stjr.is
Website: www.stjr.is/umh

Ministry of Finance
(Fjármálaráðuneyti)
Arnahvoll
150 Reykjavík
Tel.: 560 9200
Fax: 562 8280
e-mail: postur@fjr.stjr.is
Website: www.stjr.is/fjr

Ministry of Justice Arnarhvoll
(Dómsmálaráðuneyti)
150 Reykjavík
Tel.: 560 9010

Fax: 552 7340
e-mail: postur@dkm.stjr.is
Website: www.stjr.is/dkm

STOCK EXCHANGE

Iceland Stock Exchange
(Verðbréfaþing Íslands)
Engjateigur 9
105 Reykjavík
Tel.: 569 9776
Fax: 569 9777
e-mail: vi@vi.is
Website: www.vi.is

TOURIST INFORMATION

Icelandic Tourist Board
(Ferðamálaráð Íslands)
Gimli
Lækjargata 3
101 Reykjavík
Tel.: 552 7488
Fax: 5624749
e-mail: info@icetourist.is
Website: www.icetourist.is

ACCOUNTANTS

The Association of Chartered
Public Accountants in Iceland
(Félag löggiltra endurskoðenda)
Suðurlandsbraut 6
108 Reykjavík

Tel.: 568 8118 Fax: 568 8139
e-mail: fle@islandia.is
Website: www.ncd.is/fle

CONSULTANCY

Association of Consulting Engineers
(Félag ráðgjafarverkfræðinga)
Engjateigur 9
105 Reykjavík
Tel.: 553 4200
Fax: 568 9703
e-mail: frv@frv.is
Website: www.frv.is

PUBLIC INSTITUTIONS

The Central Bank of Iceland
(Seðlabanki Íslands)
Kalkofnsvegur 1
150 Reykjavík
Tel.: 569 9600
Fax: 569 9605
e-mail: sedlabanki@sedlabanki.is
Website: www.sedlabanki.is

Competition and Fair Trading Authority
(Samkeppnisstofnun)
Raudarárstígur 10
105 Reykjavík
Tel.: 552 7422
Fax: 562 7422
e-mail: samkepp@samkeppnisstofnun.is
Website: www.samkeppnisstofnun.is

Directorate of Customs
(Tollstjóraembætti)
Tollhúsid, Tryggvagata 19
101 Reykjavík
Tel.: 560 0500
Fax: 552 5826
e-mail: rikistollstjori@tollur.is
Website: www.tollur.is

Icelandic International Development Agency
(Þróunarsamvinnustofnun Íslands)
Raudarárstígur 25
150 Reykjavík
Tel.: 560 9980 Fax: 560 9982
e-mail: iceida@utn.stjr.is
Website: (Ministry for Foreign Affairs)

The Icelandic Patent Office
(Einkaleyfastofan)
Lindargata 9
101 Reykjavík
Tel.: 560 9450
Fax: 562 9434
e-mail: postur@els.stjr.is
Website: www.els.stjr.is

Inland Revenue
(Ríkisskattstjóri)
Laugavegur 166
150 Reykjavík
Tel.: 563 1100
Fax: 562 44440
e-mail: rsk@skattur.is
Website: www.rsk.is

National Economic Institute
(Þjóðhagsstofnun)

Kalkofnsvegur 1
150 Reykjavík
Tel.: 569 9500
Fax: 562 6540
e-mail: ths@centbk.is
Website: www.ths.is

Regional Development Institute
(Byggðastofnun)
Engjateigur 3
105 Reykjavík
Tel.: 560 5400
Fax: 560 5499
e-mail: bygg@bygg.is
Website: www.bygg.is

Register of Limited Companies
(Hlutafélagaskrá)
Website: www.statice.is

ASSOCIATION OF ICELANDIC IMPORTERS, EXPORTERS AND WHOLESALE MERCHANTS

Hús verslunarinnar,
103 Reykjavík
Tel. +(354) 588 8910
Fax +(354) 568 8441

ICELAND CHAMBER OF COMMERCE
Kringlan 7
103 Reykjavík
Tel. +(354) 588 6666
Fax +(354) 568 6564

INVEST IN ICELAND BUREAU
Hallveigarstígur 1
101 Reykjavík
Tel. +(354) 511 4000
Fax +(354) 511 4040

LAW SOCIETY (legal services)
Álftamýri 9
104 Reykjavík
Tel. +(354) 568 5620
Fax +(354) 568 7057

Research Council
(Rannsóknarráð Íslands)
Laugavegur 15
101 Reykjavík
Tel.: 5621320
Fax: 5529814
e-mail: rannis@rannis.is
Website: www.rannis.is

Statistics Iceland
(Hagstofa Íslands)
Skuggasund 3
150 Reykjavík
Tel.: 560 9800
Fax: 562 8865
e-mail: statice@statice.is
Website: www.statice.is

MINISTRY OF FOREIGN AFFAIRS
Trade Department
Rauðarárstígur 25
150 Reykjavík
Tel. +(354) 560 9930
Fax +(354) 562 4878

MINISTRY OF INDUSTRY AND COMMERCE
Arnarhvoll
150 Reykjavík
Tel. +(354) 560 9070
Fax +(354) 562 1289

The Icelandic Tourist Board
Lækjargata 3 · Gimli
101 Reykjavík
Tel. +(354) 5527488
Fax +(354) 562 4749

Trade Council of Iceland
Hallveigarstígur 1
101 Reykjavík
Tel. +(354) 511 4000
Fax +(354) 511 4040

EMBASSIES

Denmark
Hverfisgata 29
101 Reykjavík
tel. 562 1230
fax 562 3316
telex 2008 ambdan is

Finland
Túngata 30

101 Reykjavík
tel. 510 0100
fax 562 3880

France
Túngata 22
101 Reykjavík
tel. 551 7621/2
fax 562 8177
telex 2063 ambfra is

Germany
Laufásvegur 31
101 Reykjavík
tel. 551 9535/6
fax 552 5699
telex 2002 aa rvk is

Norway
Fjólugata 17
101 Reykjavík
tel. 551 3065
fax 552 9553
telex 2163 noramb is

People's Republic of China
Víðimelur 29
107 Reykjavík
tel. 552 6751
fax 562 6110
telex 2148 kinemb is

Russian Federation
Garðastræti 33
101 Reykjavík
tel. 562 0455
fax 562 0633
telex 2200 soverm is

Sweden
Lágmúli 7
108 Reykjavík
tel. 520 1230
fax 520 1235
telex 2087 svensk is

United Kingdom
Laufásvegur 31
101 Reykjavík
tel. 550 5100
fax 550 5105
telex 2037 ukreyk is

United States of America
Laufásvegur 21
101 Reykjavík
tel. 562 9100
fax 562 9110

For information on consuls contact:
The Ministry of Foreign Affairs, Rauðarárstígur 25, 150 Reykjavík, Tel. 560 9900

BANKS

BÚNAÐARBANKI ÍSLANDS

Austurstræti 5 101 Reykjavík
Tel. 525 6500 - Fax 525 6349
e-mail: intdiv@bi.is
http://www.list.is/

LANDSBANKI ÍSLANDS - NATIONAL BANK

Austurstræti 11 REY
Tel. 560 6600 - Fax 552 9882

WWW: **www.lais.is**
e-mail: info@lais.is

MARKETING

TRADE COUNCIL OF ICELAND

Hallveigarstígur 1 REY
Tel. 511 4000 - Fax 511 4040

Marketing Consulting and Research, Marketing Consulting and Research, Information

REAL ESTATE

FOLD - REAL ESTATE

Laugavegur 170 105 Reykjavík
Tel. 552 1400 - Fax 552 1405

WWW: **www.fold.is**
e-mail: fold@fold.is

EXPORT-IMPORT

HRAÐFLUTNINGAR EHF - FEDERAL EXPRESS

Skútuvogur 16 104 Reykjavík
Tel. 535 8170 - Fax 535 8190

WWW: **www.hradi.is**
e-mail: fedex@hradi.is

Export Information, Importers, Customs Clearance, Express and Freight Delivery, Parcels, Information, Airline Contractors, Cargo Transportation, Courier Service

MINSTRY FOR FOREIGN AFFAIRS AND EXTERNAL TRADE

Rauðarárstígur 25 105 Reykjavík
Tel. 560 9900 - Fax 562 4878

WWW: **www.utn.stjr.is**
e-mail: postur@utn.stjr.is
Export Information, Importers

BASIC TITLES FOR ICELAND

IMPORTANT!
All publications are updated annually!
Please contact IBP, Inc. at ibpusa3@gmail.com for the latest ISBNs and additional information

TITLE
Iceland A "Spy" Guide - Strategic Information and Developments
Iceland A Spy" Guide"
Iceland Banking & Financial Market Handbook
Iceland Banking & Financial Market Handbook
Iceland Business and Investment Opportunities Yearbook
Iceland Business and Investment Opportunities Yearbook
Iceland Business and Investment Opportunities Yearbook Volume 1 Strategic Information and Opportunities
Iceland Business and Investment Opportunities Yearbook Volume 2 Leading Export-Import, Business, Investment Opportunities and Projects
Iceland Business Intelligence Report - Practical Information, Opportunities, Contacts
Iceland Business Intelligence Report - Practical Information, Opportunities, Contacts
Iceland Business Law Handbook - Strategic Information and Basic Laws
Iceland Business Law Handbook - Strategic Information and Basic Laws
Iceland Business Law Handbook - Strategic Information and Basic Laws
Iceland Business Law Handbook - Strategic Information and Basic Laws
Iceland Business Law Handbook Volume 2 Investment and Trade Laws Volume 2 Investment and Trade Laws
Iceland Business Success Guide - Basic Practical Information and Contacts
Iceland Company Laws and Regulations Handbook
Iceland Company Laws and Regulations Handbook - Strategic Information and Basic Laws
Iceland Constitution and Citizenship Laws Handbook - Strategic Information and Basic Laws
Iceland Country Study Guide - Strategic Information and Developments
Iceland Country Study Guide - Strategic Information and Developments
Iceland Country Study Guide - Strategic Information and Developments Volume 1 Strategic Information and Developments
Iceland Criminal Laws, Regulations and Procedures Handbook - Strategic Information, Regulations, Procedures
Iceland Customs, Trade Regulations and Procedures Handbook
Iceland Customs, Trade Regulations and Procedures Handbook
Iceland Diplomatic Handbook - Strategic Information and Developments
Iceland Diplomatic Handbook - Strategic Information and Developments
Iceland Ecology & Nature Protection Handbook
Iceland Ecology & Nature Protection Handbook
Iceland Ecology & Nature Protection Laws and Regulation Handbook
Iceland Economic & Development Strategy Handbook
Iceland Economic & Development Strategy Handbook
Iceland Electoral, Political Parties Laws and Regulations Handbook - Strategic Information, Regulations, Procedures
Iceland Energy Policy, Laws and Regulation Handbook
Iceland Export-Import Trade and Business Directory
Iceland Export-Import Trade and Business Directory
Iceland Fishing and Aquaculture Industry Handbook - Strategic Information, Regulations, Opportunities
Iceland Foreign Policy and Government Guide
Iceland Foreign Policy and Government Guide
Iceland Immigration Laws and Regulations Handbook - Strategic Information and Basic Laws
Iceland Industrial and Business Directory
Iceland Industrial and Business Directory
Iceland Insolvency (Bankruptcy) Laws and Regulations Handbook - Strategic Information and Basic Laws
Iceland Internet and E-Commerce Investment and Business Guide - Strategic and Practical Information: Regulations and Opportunities

TITLE
Iceland Internet and E-Commerce Investment and Business Guide - Strategic and Practical Information: Regulations and Opportunities
Iceland Investment and Business Guide - Strategic and Practical Information
Iceland Investment and Business Guide - Strategic and Practical Information
Iceland Investment and Business Guide - Strategic and Practical Information
Iceland Investment and Business Guide - Strategic and Practical Information
Iceland Investment and Business Guide Volume 2 Business, Investment Opportunities and Incentives
Iceland Investment and Business Profile - Basic Information and Contacts for Succesful investment and Business Activity
Iceland Investment and Trade Laws and Regulations Handbook
Iceland Investment, Trade Strategy and Agreements Handbook - Strategic Information and Basic Agreements
Iceland Labor Laws and Regulations Handbook - Strategic Information and Basic Laws
Iceland Land Ownership and Agriculture Laws Handbook
Iceland Mineral & Mining Sector Investment and Business Guide - Strategic and Practical Information
Iceland Mineral & Mining Sector Investment and Business Guide - Strategic and Practical Information
Iceland Mining Laws and Regulations Handbook
Iceland Recent Economic and Political Developments Yearbook
Iceland Recent Economic and Political Developments Yearbook
Iceland Recent Economic and Political Developments Yearbook
Iceland Starting Business (Incorporating) in Iceland Guide
Iceland Starting Business (Incorporating) in....Guide
Iceland Tax Guide
Iceland Tax Guide
Iceland Tax Guide Volume 1 Strategic Information and Basic Regulations
Iceland Taxation Laws and Regulations Handbook
Iceland Telecom Laws and Regulations Handbook
Iceland Telecommunication Industry Business Opportunities Handbook
Iceland Telecommunication Industry Business Opportunities Handbook
Iceland Transportation Policy and Regulations Handbook
Iceland: How to Invest, Start and Run Profitable Business in Iceland Guide - Practical Information, Opportunities, Contacts

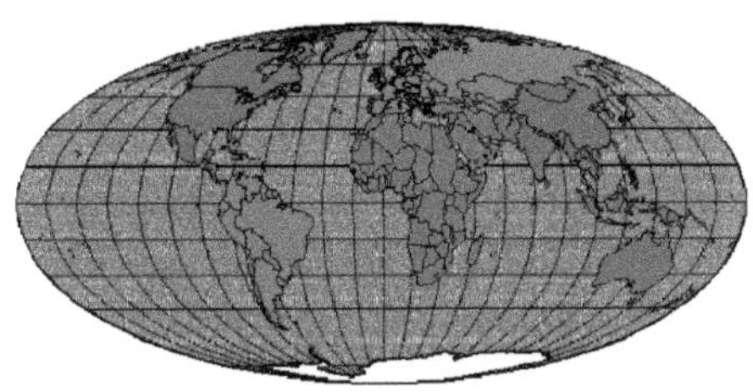

TITLE
Belgium Business and Investment Opportunities Yearbook Volume 1 Strategic, Practical Information and Opportunities
Belize Business and Investment Opportunities Yearbook Volume 1 Strategic, Practical Information and Opportunities
Benin Business and Investment Opportunities Yearbook Volume 1 Strategic, Practical Information and Opportunities
Bermuda Business and Investment Opportunities Yearbook Volume 1 Strategic, Practical Information and Opportunities
Bhutan Business and Investment Opportunities Yearbook Volume 1 Strategic, Practical Information and Opportunities
Bolivia Business and Investment Opportunities Yearbook Volume 1 Strategic, Practical Information and Opportunities
Bosnia and Herzegovina Business and Investment Opportunities Yearbook Volume 1 Strategic, Practical Information and Opportunities
Botswana Business and Investment Opportunities Yearbook Volume 1 Strategic, Practical Information and Opportunities
Brazil Business and Investment Opportunities Yearbook Volume 1 Strategic, Practical Information and Opportunities
Brunei Business and Investment Opportunities Yearbook Volume 1 Strategic, Practical Information and Opportunities
Bulgaria Business and Investment Opportunities Yearbook Volume 1 Strategic, Practical Information and Opportunities
Burkina Faso Business and Investment Opportunities Yearbook Volume 1 Strategic, Practical Information and Opportunities
Burundi Business and Investment Opportunities Yearbook Volume 1 Strategic, Practical Information and Opportunities
Cambodia Business and Investment Opportunities Yearbook Volume 1 Strategic, Practical Information and Opportunities
Cameroon Business and Investment Opportunities Yearbook Volume 1 Strategic, Practical Information and Opportunities
Canada Business and Investment Opportunities Yearbook Volume 1 Strategic, Practical Information and Opportunities
Cape Verde Business and Investment Opportunities Yearbook Volume 1 Strategic, Practical Information and Opportunities
Cayman Islands Business and Investment Opportunities Yearbook Volume 1 Strategic, Practical Information and Opportunities
Central African Republic Business and Investment Opportunities Yearbook Volume 1 Strategic, Practical Information and Opportunities
Chad Business and Investment Opportunities Yearbook Volume 1 Strategic, Practical Information and Opportunities
Chile Business and Investment Opportunities Yearbook Volume 1 Strategic, Practical Information and Opportunities
China Business and Investment Opportunities Yearbook Volume 1 Strategic, Practical Information and Opportunities
Colombia Business and Investment Opportunities Yearbook Volume 1 Strategic, Practical Information and Opportunities
Comoros Business and Investment Opportunities Yearbook Volume 1 Strategic, Practical Information and Opportunities
Congo Business and Investment Opportunities Yearbook Volume 1 Strategic, Practical Information and Opportunities
Congo, Democratic Republic Business and Investment Opportunities Yearbook Volume 1 Strategic, Practical Information and Opportunities
Cook Islands Business and Investment Opportunities Yearbook Volume 1 Strategic, Practical Information and Opportunities
Costa Rica Business and Investment Opportunities Yearbook Volume 1 Strategic, Practical Information and Opportunities

TITLE
Cote d'Ivoire Business and Investment Opportunities Yearbook Volume 1 Strategic, Practical Information and Opportunities
Croatia Business and Investment Opportunities Yearbook Volume 1 Strategic, Practical Information and Opportunities
Cuba Business and Investment Opportunities Yearbook Volume 1 Strategic, Practical Information and Opportunities
Cyprus Business and Investment Opportunities Yearbook Volume 1 Strategic, Practical Information and Opportunities
Czech Republic Business and Investment Opportunities Yearbook Volume 1 Strategic, Practical Information and Opportunities
Denmark Business and Investment Opportunities Yearbook Volume 1 Strategic, Practical Information and Opportunities
Djibouti Business and Investment Opportunities Yearbook Volume 1 Strategic, Practical Information and Opportunities
Dominica Business and Investment Opportunities Yearbook Volume 1 Strategic, Practical Information and Opportunities
Dominican Republic Business and Investment Opportunities Yearbook Volume 1 Strategic, Practical Information and Opportunities
Ecuador Business and Investment Opportunities Yearbook Volume 1 Strategic, Practical Information and Opportunities
Egypt Business and Investment Opportunities Yearbook Volume 1 Strategic, Practical Information and Opportunities
El Salvador Business and Investment Opportunities Yearbook Volume 1 Strategic, Practical Information and Opportunities
Equatorial Guinea Business and Investment Opportunities Yearbook Volume 1 Strategic, Practical Information and Opportunities
Eritrea Business and Investment Opportunities Yearbook Volume 1 Strategic, Practical Information and Opportunities
Estonia Business and Investment Opportunities Yearbook Volume 1 Strategic, Practical Information and Opportunities
Ethiopia Business and Investment Opportunities Yearbook Volume 1 Strategic, Practical Information and Opportunities
Falkland Islands Business and Investment Opportunities Yearbook Volume 1 Strategic, Practical Information and Opportunities
Faroes Islands Business and Investment Opportunities Yearbook Volume 1 Strategic, Practical Information and Opportunities
Fiji Business and Investment Opportunities Yearbook Volume 1 Strategic, Practical Information and Opportunities
Finland Business and Investment Opportunities Yearbook Volume 1 Strategic, Practical Information and Opportunities
France Business and Investment Opportunities Yearbook Volume 1 Strategic, Practical Information and Opportunities
Gabon Business and Investment Opportunities Yearbook Volume 1 Strategic, Practical Information and Opportunities
Gambia Business and Investment Opportunities Yearbook Volume 1 Strategic, Practical Information and Opportunities
Georgia Business and Investment Opportunities Yearbook Volume 1 Strategic, Practical Information and Opportunities
Germany Business and Investment Opportunities Yearbook Volume 1 Strategic, Practical Information and Opportunities
Ghana Business and Investment Opportunities Yearbook Volume 1 Strategic, Practical Information and Opportunities
Gibraltar Business and Investment Opportunities Yearbook Volume 1 Strategic, Practical Information and Opportunities
Greece Business and Investment Opportunities Yearbook Volume 1 Strategic, Practical Information and Opportunities

TITLE
Greenland Business and Investment Opportunities Yearbook Volume 1 Strategic, Practical Information and Opportunities
Grenada Business and Investment Opportunities Yearbook Volume 1 Strategic, Practical Information and Opportunities
Guam Business and Investment Opportunities Yearbook Volume 1 Strategic, Practical Information and Opportunities
Guatemala Business and Investment Opportunities Yearbook Volume 1 Strategic, Practical Information and Opportunities
Guernsey Business and Investment Opportunities Yearbook Volume 1 Strategic, Practical Information and Opportunities
Guinea Business and Investment Opportunities Yearbook Volume 1 Strategic, Practical Information and Opportunities
Guinea-Bissau Business and Investment Opportunities Yearbook Volume 1 Strategic, Practical Information and Opportunities
Guyana Business and Investment Opportunities Yearbook Volume 1 Strategic, Practical Information and Opportunities
Haiti Business and Investment Opportunities Yearbook Volume 1 Strategic, Practical Information and Opportunities
Honduras Business and Investment Opportunities Yearbook Volume 1 Strategic, Practical Information and Opportunities
Hungary Business and Investment Opportunities Yearbook Volume 1 Strategic, Practical Information and Opportunities
Iceland Business and Investment Opportunities Yearbook Volume 1 Strategic, Practical Information and Opportunities
India Business and Investment Opportunities Yearbook Volume 1 Strategic, Practical Information and Opportunities
Indonesia Business and Investment Opportunities Yearbook Volume 1 Strategic, Practical Information and Opportunities
Iran Business and Investment Opportunities Yearbook Volume 1 Strategic, Practical Information and Opportunities
Iraq Business and Investment Opportunities Yearbook Volume 1 Strategic, Practical Information and Opportunities
Ireland Business and Investment Opportunities Yearbook Volume 1 Strategic, Practical Information and Opportunities
Israel Business and Investment Opportunities Yearbook Volume 1 Strategic, Practical Information and Opportunities
Italy Business and Investment Opportunities Yearbook Volume 1 Strategic, Practical Information and Opportunities
Jamaica Business and Investment Opportunities Yearbook Volume 1 Strategic, Practical Information and Opportunities
Japan Business and Investment Opportunities Yearbook Volume 1 Strategic, Practical Information and Opportunities
Jersey Business and Investment Opportunities Yearbook Volume 1 Strategic, Practical Information and Opportunities
Jordan Business and Investment Opportunities Yearbook Volume 1 Strategic, Practical Information and Opportunities
Kazakhstan Business and Investment Opportunities Yearbook Volume 1 Strategic, Practical Information and Opportunities
Kenya Business and Investment Opportunities Yearbook Volume 1 Strategic, Practical Information and Opportunities
Kiribati Business and Investment Opportunities Yearbook Volume 1 Strategic, Practical Information and Opportunities
Korea, North Business and Investment Opportunities Yearbook Volume 1 Strategic, Practical Information and Opportunities
Korea, South Business and Investment Opportunities Yearbook Volume 1 Strategic, Practical Information and Opportunities

TITLE
Kosovo Business and Investment Opportunities Yearbook Volume 1 Strategic, Practical Information and Opportunities
Kurdistan Business and Investment Opportunities Yearbook Volume 1 Strategic, Practical Information and Opportunities
Kuwait Business and Investment Opportunities Yearbook Volume 1 Strategic, Practical Information and Opportunities
Kyrgyzstan Business and Investment Opportunities Yearbook Volume 1 Strategic, Practical Information and Opportunities
Laos Business and Investment Opportunities Yearbook Volume 1 Strategic, Practical Information and Opportunities
Latvia Business and Investment Opportunities Yearbook Volume 1 Strategic, Practical Information and Opportunities
Lebanon Business and Investment Opportunities Yearbook Volume 1 Strategic, Practical Information and Opportunities
Lesotho Business and Investment Opportunities Yearbook Volume 1 Strategic, Practical Information and Opportunities
Liberia Business and Investment Opportunities Yearbook Volume 1 Strategic, Practical Information and Opportunities
Libya Business and Investment Opportunities Yearbook Volume 1 Strategic, Practical Information and Opportunities
Liechtenstein Business and Investment Opportunities Yearbook Volume 1 Strategic, Practical Information and Opportunities
Lithuania Business and Investment Opportunities Yearbook Volume 1 Strategic, Practical Information and Opportunities
Luxembourg Business and Investment Opportunities Yearbook Volume 1 Strategic, Practical Information and Opportunities
Macao Business and Investment Opportunities Yearbook Volume 1 Strategic, Practical Information and Opportunities
Macedonia Business and Investment Opportunities Yearbook Volume 1 Strategic, Practical Information and Opportunities
Madagascar Business and Investment Opportunities Yearbook Volume 1 Strategic, Practical Information and Opportunities
Madeira Business and Investment Opportunities Yearbook Volume 1 Strategic, Practical Information and Opportunities
Malawi Business and Investment Opportunities Yearbook Volume 1 Strategic, Practical Information and Opportunities
Malaysia Business and Investment Opportunities Yearbook Volume 1 Strategic, Practical Information and Opportunities
Maldives Business and Investment Opportunities Yearbook Volume 1 Strategic, Practical Information and Opportunities
Mali Business and Investment Opportunities Yearbook Volume 1 Strategic, Practical Information and Opportunities
Malta Business and Investment Opportunities Yearbook Volume 1 Strategic, Practical Information and Opportunities
Man Business and Investment Opportunities Yearbook Volume 1 Strategic, Practical Information and Opportunities
Marshall Islands Business and Investment Opportunities Yearbook Volume 1 Strategic, Practical Information and Opportunities
Mauritania Business and Investment Opportunities Yearbook Volume 1 Strategic, Practical Information and Opportunities
Mauritius Business and Investment Opportunities Yearbook Volume 1 Strategic, Practical Information and Opportunities
Mayotte Business and Investment Opportunities Yearbook Volume 1 Strategic, Practical Information and Opportunities
Mexico Business and Investment Opportunities Yearbook Volume 1 Strategic, Practical Information and Opportunities

TITLE
Micronesia Business and Investment Opportunities Yearbook Volume 1 Strategic, Practical Information and Opportunities
Moldova Business and Investment Opportunities Yearbook Volume 1 Strategic, Practical Information and Opportunities
Monaco Business and Investment Opportunities Yearbook Volume 1 Strategic, Practical Information and Opportunities
Mongolia Business and Investment Opportunities Yearbook Volume 1 Strategic, Practical Information and Opportunities
Montserrat Business and Investment Opportunities Yearbook Volume 1 Strategic, Practical Information and Opportunities
Montenegro Business and Investment Opportunities Yearbook Volume 1 Strategic, Practical Information and Opportunities
Morocco Business and Investment Opportunities Yearbook Volume 1 Strategic, Practical Information and Opportunities
Mozambique Business and Investment Opportunities Yearbook Volume 1 Strategic, Practical Information and Opportunities
Myanmar Business and Investment Opportunities Yearbook Volume 1 Strategic, Practical Information and Opportunities
Nagorno-Karabakh Republic Business and Investment Opportunities Yearbook Volume 1 Strategic, Practical Information and Opportunities
Namibia Business and Investment Opportunities Yearbook Volume 1 Strategic, Practical Information and Opportunities
Nauru Business and Investment Opportunities Yearbook Volume 1 Strategic, Practical Information and Opportunities
Nepal Business and Investment Opportunities Yearbook Volume 1 Strategic, Practical Information and Opportunities
Netherlands Business and Investment Opportunities Yearbook Volume 1 Strategic, Practical Information and Opportunities
New Caledonia Business and Investment Opportunities Yearbook Volume 1 Strategic, Practical Information and Opportunities
New Zealand Business and Investment Opportunities Yearbook Volume 1 Strategic, Practical Information and Opportunities
Nicaragua Business and Investment Opportunities Yearbook Volume 1 Strategic, Practical Information and Opportunities
Niger Business and Investment Opportunities Yearbook Volume 1 Strategic, Practical Information and Opportunities
Nigeria Business and Investment Opportunities Yearbook Volume 1 Strategic, Practical Information and Opportunities
Niue Business and Investment Opportunities Yearbook Volume 1 Strategic, Practical Information and Opportunities
Northern Cyprus (Turkish Republic of Northern Cyprus) Business and Investment Opportunities Yearbook Volume 1 Strategic, Practical Information and Opportunities
Northern Mariana Islands Business and Investment Opportunities Yearbook Volume 1 Strategic, Practical Information and Opportunities
Norway Business and Investment Opportunities Yearbook Volume 1 Strategic, Practical Information and Opportunities
Oman Business and Investment Opportunities Yearbook Volume 1 Strategic, Practical Information and Opportunities
Pakistan Business and Investment Opportunities Yearbook Volume 1 Strategic, Practical Information and Opportunities
Palau Business and Investment Opportunities Yearbook Volume 1 Strategic, Practical Information and Opportunities
Palestine (West Bank & Gaza) Business and Investment Opportunities Yearbook Volume 1 Strategic, Practical Information and Opportunities
Panama Business and Investment Opportunities Yearbook Volume 1 Strategic, Practical Information and Opportunities

TITLE
Papua New Guinea Business and Investment Opportunities Yearbook Volume 1 Strategic, Practical Information and Opportunities
Paraguay Business and Investment Opportunities Yearbook Volume 1 Strategic, Practical Information and Opportunities
Peru Business and Investment Opportunities Yearbook Volume 1 Strategic, Practical Information and Opportunities
Philippines Business and Investment Opportunities Yearbook Volume 1 Strategic, Practical Information and Opportunities
Pitcairn Islands Business and Investment Opportunities Yearbook Volume 1 Strategic, Practical Information and Opportunities
Poland Business and Investment Opportunities Yearbook Volume 1 Strategic, Practical Information and Opportunities
Polynesia French Business and Investment Opportunities Yearbook Volume 1 Strategic, Practical Information and Opportunities
Portugal Business and Investment Opportunities Yearbook Volume 1 Strategic, Practical Information and Opportunities
Qatar Business and Investment Opportunities Yearbook Volume 1 Strategic, Practical Information and Opportunities
Romania Business and Investment Opportunities Yearbook Volume 1 Strategic, Practical Information and Opportunities
Russia Business and Investment Opportunities Yearbook Volume 1 Strategic, Practical Information and Opportunities
Rwanda Business and Investment Opportunities Yearbook Volume 1 Strategic, Practical Information and Opportunities
Sahrawi Arab Democratic Republic Volume 1 Strategic Information and Developments
Saint Kitts and Nevis Business and Investment Opportunities Yearbook Volume 1 Strategic, Practical Information and Opportunities
Saint Lucia Business and Investment Opportunities Yearbook Volume 1 Strategic, Practical Information and Opportunities
Saint Vincent and The Grenadines Business and Investment Opportunities Yearbook Volume 1 Strategic, Practical Information and Opportunities
Samoa (American) A Business and Investment Opportunities Yearbook Volume 1 Strategic, Practical Information and Opportunities
Samoa (Western) Business and Investment Opportunities Yearbook Volume 1 Strategic, Practical Information and Opportunities
San Marino Business and Investment Opportunities Yearbook Volume 1 Strategic, Practical Information and Opportunities
Sao Tome and Principe Business and Investment Opportunities Yearbook Volume 1 Strategic, Practical Information and Opportunities
Saudi Arabia Business and Investment Opportunities Yearbook Volume 1 Strategic, Practical Information and Opportunities
Scotland Business and Investment Opportunities Yearbook Volume 1 Strategic, Practical Information and Opportunities
Senegal Business and Investment Opportunities Yearbook Volume 1 Strategic, Practical Information and Opportunities
Serbia Business and Investment Opportunities Yearbook Volume 1 Strategic, Practical Information and Opportunities
Seychelles Business and Investment Opportunities Yearbook Volume 1 Strategic, Practical Information and Opportunities
Sierra Leone Business and Investment Opportunities Yearbook Volume 1 Strategic, Practical Information and Opportunities
Singapore Business and Investment Opportunities Yearbook Volume 1 Strategic, Practical Information and Opportunities
Slovakia Business and Investment Opportunities Yearbook Volume 1 Strategic, Practical Information and Opportunities

TITLE
Slovenia Business and Investment Opportunities Yearbook Volume 1 Strategic, Practical Information and Opportunities
Solomon Islands Business and Investment Opportunities Yearbook Volume 1 Strategic, Practical Information and Opportunities
Somalia Business and Investment Opportunities Yearbook Volume 1 Strategic, Practical Information and Opportunities
South Africa Business and Investment Opportunities Yearbook Volume 1 Strategic, Practical Information and Opportunities
Spain Business and Investment Opportunities Yearbook Volume 1 Strategic, Practical Information and Opportunities
Sri Lanka Business and Investment Opportunities Yearbook Volume 1 Strategic, Practical Information and Opportunities
St. Helena Business and Investment Opportunities Yearbook Volume 1 Strategic, Practical Information and Opportunities
St. Pierre & Miquelon Business and Investment Opportunities Yearbook Volume 1 Strategic, Practical Information and Opportunities
Sudan (Republic of the Sudan) Business and Investment Opportunities Yearbook Volume 1 Strategic, Practical Information and Opportunities
Sudan South Business and Investment Opportunities Yearbook Volume 1 Strategic, Practical Information and Opportunities
Suriname Business and Investment Opportunities Yearbook Volume 1 Strategic, Practical Information and Opportunities
Swaziland Business and Investment Opportunities Yearbook Volume 1 Strategic, Practical Information and Opportunities
Sweden Business and Investment Opportunities Yearbook Volume 1 Strategic, Practical Information and Opportunities
Switzerland Business and Investment Opportunities Yearbook Volume 1 Strategic, Practical Information and Opportunities
Syria Business and Investment Opportunities Yearbook Volume 1 Strategic, Practical Information and Opportunities
Taiwan Business and Investment Opportunities Yearbook Volume 1 Strategic, Practical Information and Opportunities
Tajikistan Business and Investment Opportunities Yearbook Volume 1 Strategic, Practical Information and Opportunities
Tanzania Business and Investment Opportunities Yearbook Volume 1 Strategic, Practical Information and Opportunities
Thailand Business and Investment Opportunities Yearbook Volume 1 Strategic, Practical Information and Opportunities
Timor Leste (Democratic Republic of Timor-Leste) Business and Investment Opportunities Yearbook Volume 1 Strategic, Practical Information and Opportunities
Togo Business and Investment Opportunities Yearbook Volume 1 Strategic, Practical Information and Opportunities
Tonga Business and Investment Opportunities Yearbook Volume 1 Strategic, Practical Information and Opportunities
Trinidad and Tobago Business and Investment Opportunities Yearbook Volume 1 Strategic, Practical Information and Opportunities
Tunisia Business and Investment Opportunities Yearbook Volume 1 Strategic, Practical Information and Opportunities
Turkey Business and Investment Opportunities Yearbook Volume 1 Strategic, Practical Information and Opportunities
Turkmenistan Business and Investment Opportunities Yearbook Volume 1 Strategic, Practical Information and Opportunities
Turks & Caicos Business and Investment Opportunities Yearbook Volume 1 Strategic, Practical Information and Opportunities
Tuvalu Business and Investment Opportunities Yearbook Volume 1 Strategic, Practical Information and Opportunities

TITLE
Uganda Business and Investment Opportunities Yearbook Volume 1 Strategic, Practical Information and Opportunities
Ukraine Business and Investment Opportunities Yearbook Volume 1 Strategic, Practical Information and Opportunities
United Arab Emirates Business and Investment Opportunities Yearbook Volume 1 Strategic, Practical Information and Opportunities
United Kingdom Business and Investment Opportunities Yearbook Volume 1 Strategic, Practical Information and Opportunities
United States Business and Investment Opportunities Yearbook Volume 1 Strategic, Practical Information and Opportunities
Uruguay Business and Investment Opportunities Yearbook Volume 1 Strategic, Practical Information and Opportunities
Uzbekistan Business and Investment Opportunities Yearbook Volume 1 Strategic, Practical Information and Opportunities
Vanuatu Business and Investment Opportunities Yearbook Volume 1 Strategic, Practical Information and Opportunities
Vatican City (Holy See) Business and Investment Opportunities Yearbook Volume 1 Strategic, Practical Information and Opportunities
Venezuela Business and Investment Opportunities Yearbook Volume 1 Strategic, Practical Information and Opportunities
Vietnam Business and Investment Opportunities Yearbook Volume 1 Strategic, Practical Information and Opportunities
Virgin Islands, British Business and Investment Opportunities Yearbook Volume 1 Strategic, Practical Information and Opportunities
Wake Atoll Business and Investment Opportunities Yearbook Volume 1 Strategic, Practical Information and Opportunities
Wallis & Futuna Business and Investment Opportunities Yearbook Volume 1 Strategic, Practical Information and Opportunities
Western Sahara Business and Investment Opportunities Yearbook Volume 1 Strategic, Practical Information and Opportunities
Yemen Business and Investment Opportunities Yearbook Volume 1 Strategic, Practical Information and Opportunities
Zambia Business and Investment Opportunities Yearbook Volume 1 Strategic, Practical Information and Opportunities
Zimbabwe Business and Investment Opportunities Yearbook Volume 1 Strategic, Practical Information and Opportunities

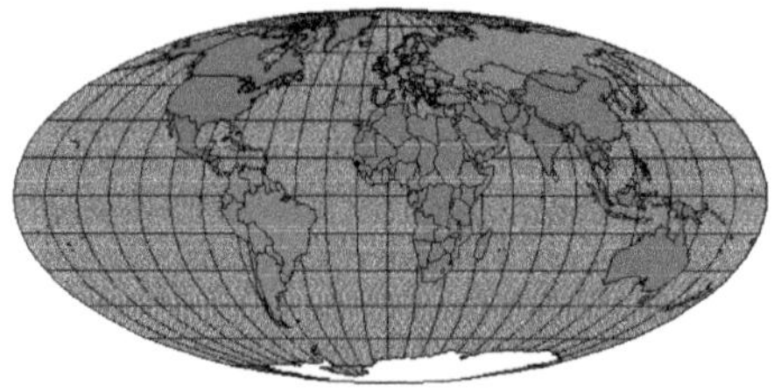

WORLD RECENT ECONOMIC AND POLITICAL DEVELOPMENT YEARBOOK LIBRARY

Price: $99.95 Each

TITLE
Afghanistan Recent Economic and Political Developments Yearbook
Aland Recent Economic and Political Developments Yearbook
Albania Recent Economic and Political Developments Yearbook
Algeria Recent Economic and Political Developments Yearbook
Andorra Recent Economic and Political Developments Yearbook
Angola Recent Economic and Political Developments Yearbook
Anguilla Recent Economic and Political Developments Yearbook
Antigua and Barbuda Recent Economic and Political Developments Yearbook
Antilles (Netherlands) Recent Economic and Political Developments Yearbook
Argentina Recent Economic and Political Developments Yearbook
Armenia Recent Economic and Political Developments Yearbook
Aruba Recent Economic and Political Developments Yearbook
Australia Recent Economic and Political Developments Yearbook
Austria Recent Economic and Political Developments Yearbook
Azerbaijan Recent Economic and Political Developments Yearbook
Bahamas Recent Economic and Political Developments Yearbook
Bahrain Recent Economic and Political Developments Yearbook
Bangladesh Recent Economic and Political Developments Yearbook
Barbados Recent Economic and Political Developments Yearbook
Belarus Recent Economic and Political Developments Yearbook
Belgium Recent Economic and Political Developments Yearbook
Belize Recent Economic and Political Developments Yearbook
Benin Recent Economic and Political Developments Yearbook
Bermuda Recent Economic and Political Developments Yearbook
Bhutan Recent Economic and Political Developments Yearbook
Bolivia Recent Economic and Political Developments Yearbook
Bosnia and Herzegovina Recent Economic and Political Developments Yearbook
Botswana Recent Economic and Political Developments Yearbook
Brazil Recent Economic and Political Developments Yearbook
Brunei Recent Economic and Political Developments Yearbook
Bulgaria Recent Economic and Political Developments Yearbook
Burkina Faso Recent Economic and Political Developments Yearbook
Burundi Recent Economic and Political Developments Yearbook
Cambodia Recent Economic and Political Developments Yearbook
Cameroon Recent Economic and Political Developments Yearbook
Canada Recent Economic and Political Developments Yearbook
Cape Verde Recent Economic and Political Developments Yearbook
Cayman Islands Recent Economic and Political Developments Yearbook
Central African Republic Recent Economic and Political Developments Yearbook
Chad Recent Economic and Political Developments Yearbook

TITLE
Chile Recent Economic and Political Developments Yearbook
China Recent Economic and Political Developments Yearbook
Colombia Recent Economic and Political Developments Yearbook
Comoros Recent Economic and Political Developments Yearbook
Congo Recent Economic and Political Developments Yearbook
Congo, Democratic Republic Recent Economic and Political Developments Yearbook
Cook Islands Recent Economic and Political Developments Yearbook
Costa Rica Recent Economic and Political Developments Yearbook
Cote d'Ivoire Recent Economic and Political Developments Yearbook
Croatia Recent Economic and Political Developments Yearbook
Cuba Recent Economic and Political Developments Yearbook
Cyprus Recent Economic and Political Developments Yearbook
Czech Republic Recent Economic and Political Developments Yearbook
Denmark Recent Economic and Political Developments Yearbook
Djibouti Recent Economic and Political Developments Yearbook
Dominica Recent Economic and Political Developments Yearbook
Dominican Republic Recent Economic and Political Developments Yearbook
Ecuador Recent Economic and Political Developments Yearbook
Egypt Recent Economic and Political Developments Yearbook
El Salvador Recent Economic and Political Developments Yearbook
Equatorial Guinea Recent Economic and Political Developments Yearbook
Eritrea Recent Economic and Political Developments Yearbook
Estonia Recent Economic and Political Developments Yearbook
Ethiopia Recent Economic and Political Developments Yearbook
Falkland Islands Recent Economic and Political Developments Yearbook
Faroes IslandsRecent Economic and Political Developments Yearbook
Fiji Recent Economic and Political Developments Yearbook
Finland Recent Economic and Political Developments Yearbook
France Recent Economic and Political Developments Yearbook
Gabon Recent Economic and Political Developments Yearbook
Gambia Recent Economic and Political Developments Yearbook
Georgia Recent Economic and Political Developments Yearbook
Germany Recent Economic and Political Developments Yearbook
Ghana Recent Economic and Political Developments Yearbook
Gibraltar Recent Economic and Political Developments Yearbook
GlobalRecent Economic and Political Developments Yearbook
Greece Recent Economic and Political Developments Yearbook
Greenland Recent Economic and Political Developments Yearbook
Grenada Recent Economic and Political Developments Yearbook
Guam Recent Economic and Political Developments Yearbook
Guatemala Recent Economic and Political Developments Yearbook
Guernsey Recent Economic and Political Developments Yearbook
Guinea Recent Economic and Political Developments Yearbook
Guinea-Bissau Recent Economic and Political Developments Yearbook
Guyana Recent Economic and Political Developments Yearbook
Haiti Recent Economic and Political Developments Yearbook
Honduras Recent Economic and Political Developments Yearbook
Hungary Recent Economic and Political Developments Yearbook
Iceland Recent Economic and Political Developments Yearbook
India Recent Economic and Political Developments Yearbook

TITLE
Indonesia Recent Economic and Political Developments Yearbook
InternationalRecent Economic and Political Developments Yearbook
Iran Recent Economic and Political Developments Yearbook
Iraq Recent Economic and Political Developments Yearbook
Ireland Recent Economic and Political Developments Yearbook
Israel Recent Economic and Political Developments Yearbook
Italy Recent Economic and Political Developments Yearbook
Jamaica Recent Economic and Political Developments Yearbook
Japan Recent Economic and Political Developments Yearbook
Jersey Recent Economic and Political Developments Yearbook
Jordan Recent Economic and Political Developments Yearbook
Kazakhstan Recent Economic and Political Developments Yearbook
Kenya Recent Economic and Political Developments Yearbook
Kiribati Recent Economic and Political Developments Yearbook
Korea, North Recent Economic and Political Developments Yearbook
Korea, South Recent Economic and Political Developments Yearbook
KosovoRecent Economic and Political Developments Yearbook
KurdistanRecent Economic and Political Developments Yearbook
Kuwait Recent Economic and Political Developments Yearbook
Kyrgyzstan Recent Economic and Political Developments Yearbook
Laos Recent Economic and Political Developments Yearbook
Latvia Recent Economic and Political Developments Yearbook
Lebanon Recent Economic and Political Developments Yearbook
Lesotho Recent Economic and Political Developments Yearbook
Liberia Recent Economic and Political Developments Yearbook
Libya Recent Economic and Political Developments Yearbook
Liechtenstein Recent Economic and Political Developments Yearbook
Lithuania Recent Economic and Political Developments Yearbook
Luxembourg Recent Economic and Political Developments Yearbook
Macao Recent Economic and Political Developments Yearbook
Macedonia,Recent Economic and Political Developments Yearbook
Madagascar Recent Economic and Political Developments Yearbook
MadeiraRecent Economic and Political Developments Yearbook
Malawi Recent Economic and Political Developments Yearbook
Malaysia Recent Economic and Political Developments Yearbook
Maldives Recent Economic and Political Developments Yearbook
Mali Recent Economic and Political Developments Yearbook
Malta Recent Economic and Political Developments Yearbook
Man Recent Economic and Political Developments Yearbook
Marshall Islands Recent Economic and Political Developments Yearbook
Mauritania Recent Economic and Political Developments Yearbook
Mauritius Recent Economic and Political Developments Yearbook
Mayotte Recent Economic and Political Developments Yearbook
Mexico Recent Economic and Political Developments Yearbook
Micronesia Recent Economic and Political Developments Yearbook
Moldova Recent Economic and Political Developments Yearbook
Monaco Recent Economic and Political Developments Yearbook
Mongolia Recent Economic and Political Developments Yearbook
Monserrat Recent Economic and Political Developments Yearbook
Morocco Recent Economic and Political Developments Yearbook

TITLE
Mozambique Recent Economic and Political Developments Yearbook
Myanmar Recent Economic and Political Developments Yearbook
Namibia Recent Economic and Political Developments Yearbook
Nauru Recent Economic and Political Developments Yearbook
Nepal Recent Economic and Political Developments Yearbook
Netherlands Recent Economic and Political Developments Yearbook
New Caledonia Recent Economic and Political Developments Yearbook
New Zealand Recent Economic and Political Developments Yearbook
Nicaragua Recent Economic and Political Developments Yearbook
Niger Recent Economic and Political Developments Yearbook
Nigeria Recent Economic and Political Developments Yearbook
Niue Recent Economic and Political Developments Yearbook
Northern Mariana Islands Recent Economic and Political Developments Yearbook
Norway Recent Economic and Political Developments Yearbook
OffshoreRecent Economic and Political Developments Yearbook
Oman Recent Economic and Political Developments Yearbook
Pakistan Recent Economic and Political Developments Yearbook
Palau Recent Economic and Political Developments Yearbook
Palestine Recent Economic and Political Developments Yearbook
Panama Recent Economic and Political Developments Yearbook
Papua New Guinea Recent Economic and Political Developments Yearbook
Paraguay Recent Economic and Political Developments Yearbook
Peru Recent Economic and Political Developments Yearbook
Philippines Recent Economic and Political Developments Yearbook
Pitcairn Islands Recent Economic and Political Developments Yearbook
Poland Recent Economic and Political Developments Yearbook
Polynesia French Recent Economic and Political Developments Yearbook
Portugal Recent Economic and Political Developments Yearbook
Qatar Recent Economic and Political Developments Yearbook
Romania Recent Economic and Political Developments Yearbook
Russia Recent Economic and Political Developments Yearbook
Rwanda Recent Economic and Political Developments Yearbook
Saint Kitts and Nevis Recent Economic and Political Developments Yearbook
Saint Lucia Recent Economic and Political Developments Yearbook
Saint Vincent and The Grenadines Recent Economic and Political Developments Yearbook
Samoa (American) A Recent Economic and Political Developments Yearbook
Samoa (Western) Recent Economic and Political Developments Yearbook
San Marino Recent Economic and Political Developments Yearbook
Sao Tome and Principe Recent Economic and Political Developments Yearbook
Saudi Arabia Recent Economic and Political Developments Yearbook
Scotland Recent Economic and Political Developments Yearbook
Senegal Recent Economic and Political Developments Yearbook
SerbiaRecent Economic and Political Developments Yearbook
Seychelles Recent Economic and Political Developments Yearbook
Sierra Leone Recent Economic and Political Developments Yearbook
Singapore Recent Economic and Political Developments Yearbook
Slovakia Recent Economic and Political Developments Yearbook
Slovenia Recent Economic and Political Developments Yearbook
Solomon Islands Recent Economic and Political Developments Yearbook
Somalia Recent Economic and Political Developments Yearbook

TITLE
South Africa Recent Economic and Political Developments Yearbook
Spain Recent Economic and Political Developments Yearbook
Sri Lanka Recent Economic and Political Developments Yearbook
St. Helena Recent Economic and Political Developments Yearbook
St. Pierre & Miquelon Recent Economic and Political Developments Yearbook
Sudan Recent Economic and Political Developments Yearbook
Suriname Recent Economic and Political Developments Yearbook
Swaziland Recent Economic and Political Developments Yearbook
Sweden Recent Economic and Political Developments Yearbook
Switzerland Recent Economic and Political Developments Yearbook
Syria Recent Economic and Political Developments Yearbook
Taiwan Recent Economic and Political Developments Yearbook
Tajikistan Recent Economic and Political Developments Yearbook
Tanzania Recent Economic and Political Developments Yearbook
Thailand Recent Economic and Political Developments Yearbook
Togo Recent Economic and Political Developments Yearbook
Tonga Recent Economic and Political Developments Yearbook
Trinidad and Tobago Recent Economic and Political Developments Yearbook
Tunisia Recent Economic and Political Developments Yearbook
Turkey Recent Economic and Political Developments Yearbook
Turkmenistan Recent Economic and Political Developments Yearbook
Turks & Caicos Recent Economic and Political Developments Yearbook
Tuvalu Recent Economic and Political Developments Yearbook
Uganda Recent Economic and Political Developments Yearbook
Ukraine Recent Economic and Political Developments Yearbook
United Arab Emirates Recent Economic and Political Developments Yearbook
United Kingdom Recent Economic and Political Developments Yearbook
United States Recent Economic and Political Developments Yearbook
Uruguay Recent Economic and Political Developments Yearbook
Uzbekistan Recent Economic and Political Developments Yearbook
Vanuatu Recent Economic and Political Developments Yearbook
Vatican City Recent Economic and Political Developments Yearbook
Venezuela Recent Economic and Political Developments Yearbook
Vietnam Recent Economic and Political Developments Yearbook
Virgin Islands, British Recent Economic and Political Developments Yearbook
Wake Atoll Recent Economic and Political Developments Yearbook
Wallis & Futuna Recent Economic and Political Developments Yearbook
Western Sahara Recent Economic and Political Developments Yearbook
Yemen Recent Economic and Political Developments Yearbook
Zambia Recent Economic and Political Developments Yearbook
Zimbabwe Recent Economic and Political Developments Yearbook

www.ingramcontent.com/pod-product-compliance
Ingram Content Group UK Ltd.
Pitfield, Milton Keynes, MK11 3LW, UK
UKHW051509290926
15471UKWH00008B/1517

9 781433 063633